Shelf COOKING 101

Your How-to Guide to Frugal Meal Planning, Shopping Your Pantry, and Getting Creative with Leftovers

JORDAN PAGE

WHY DOES SHELF COOKING MATTER?

It's kinder to your wallet. You'll be amazed at the money you save.

It reduces waste. Forget about the carbon footprint for a minute and consider all the leftover-sludge footprints. That's good money you're just throwing away.

It teaches you how to cook from scratch, as well as, some other nifty skills.

It's healthier and delicious. You decide what goes into your food.

It helps teach your kids good habits—not only about what they eat but about how to make it happen without breaking the bank.

And, maybe best of all, it keeps things creative and exciting in the kitchen—and who doesn't want that?

Designed by Melanie Burk.

FIRST EDITION

ISBN 978-0-578-69482-5
shelfcooking.com

To Bubba, our 8 crazy-cute kids (and our two dogs, of course), and each and every Freeb. Thank you for joining me on this wild ride.

CONTENTS

CONTENTS

Brilliant Tips

Look for these quick, time-saving tips throughout the book.
They will leave you saying, "Ah ha!"

CONTENTS

Freeze it!

Look for this icon on our recipes. It will let you know that you can freeze for later, saving time and money!

A NOTE FROM THE AUTHOR

Truth: I don't like cooking. Now, before you drive me to the hills with pitchforks declaring me a fraud for writing a cookbook, here's the reality of the situation: whether we like it or not, COOKING and MEAL PLANNING are important. In fact, they're some of the most important things we will do in any given week. And yet we just...don't.

It's too complicated. It's too expensive. It takes too much time. There's too much waste. We're too busy. Our kids are too picky. It doesn't taste as good as takeout. It's too overwhelming. So, we don't cook. We eat out, order meal subscription boxes, buy pre-made meals from the freezer section, or pour it out of cans. When we do cook, it's an expensive, giant mess that ends in a lot of waste because no one will eat the leftovers.

It's no wonder so many people are in debt and struggle to afford the lifestyle they want. Could it possibly be that we've been cooking wrong all along? Could it be that the way most of us feed our families is costing a whole lot more than it should? Yes, that's exactly what it means.

Before my dear Grandma Mary died, she left me with a recipe binder of favorite family recipes. Her recipes are different than the recipes I find on the web. They are chicken-scratch notes that include "use this, or whatever you have..." and "add such and such until you get the flavor you like..." and "cook until the consistency is how you want it." She cooked with her taste buds, not with properly written recipes. She tweaked and improved with her eyes, not with perfectly crafted Pinterest photos. She cooked first and foremost using what she had on her shelf at home...not from the shelf at the store.

After a decade of working with hundreds of thousands of families across the globe, I quickly realized that the way we cook and think about meals is backward. We rely on conveniences, recipes, and catchy cooking videos on Instagram to tell us what to make for our families, overspending by thousands of dollars per month.

I am on a mission to bring cooking back to what it should be. Shelf Cooking is a smarter, faster, cheaper way of preparing delicious food and bringing your family back to the dinner table—together. And you won't believe how easy it is. Let's do this!

Jordan

THE SIMPLE STEPS

Shelf cooking is fun and easy! Let's break it down into simple steps!

1

INVENTORY

Take inventory of what you have, starting with the fridge, then freezer, then pantry. Keep the list handy for quick reference.

2

USE WHAT YOU HAVE

Find and adapt recipes that use ingredients you already have on hand, in order of what you need to use up first.

3

SUPPLEMENT

Go to the store only for supplemental ingredients and on-sale items to keep on your shelf. Shop no more than 1x a week.

let's do this!

4

STOCK UP

Double the recipe and freeze as you cook. As you shop, buy one for now, two for later to slowly develop a stockpile.

5

FAVORITE RECIPES

Keep a recipe binder of recipes you tried and liked. Write down the date and how you adapted them for future reference.

6

GET SOCIAL

Join the revolution online! Join us @shelfcooking and use #shelfcooking to show off your creative cooking!

Brilliant Tip

Don't have room to stockpile food? It just takes a little creativity! See page 12 for creative food storage tips!

simply
Campbell's
chicken noodle
Campbell's
CONDENSED
GREAT FOR COOKING
Cream of Mushroom
SOUP
KIRKLAND
CUT
GREEN BEANS
WITH SEA SALT
KIRKLAND
CUT
GREEN BEANS
WITH SEA SALT
BUSH'S BEST
Black Beans
Frijoles Negros
Del Monte
Quality
MADE WITH
Fresh Cut
100% NATURAL
Borden
EAGLE BRAND
AMERICA'S MOST TRUSTED
Sweetened
Condensed
Milk
Leche Condensada Endulzada
NO ARTIFICIAL INGREDIENTS
JUST MILK & SUGAR

getting started:

INVENTORY & MEAL PLANNING

INVENTORY & MEAL PLAN

Before you run to the store, start by focusing on the food already in your house to build a less expensive meal plan.

FOOD STORAGE & INVENTORY

Figure out how to store food in your home and how to keep track of what you have on hand.

PAGE 12

MEAL PLANNING

Make a plan for the week based on your inventory and what's on sale at the store.

PAGE 20

DINNER DILEMMA

This section offers tips for how to solve common meal-planning problems.

PAGE 24

DINNER IDEAS

Check out this list with dozens of meal ideas to get your creative juices flowing.

PAGE 28

creative and easy

FOOD STORAGE SOLUTIONS

If I had a nickel for every person who's told me they just don't have enough room to store food for shelf cooking, I'd be a nickel-aire! Lucky for you, there are so many creative ways to keep your food organized, hidden, and ready to use—and we're gonna show you how to do it, room by room. But first...

HOW you store your food is as important as WHERE you store it. Here are some tips for protecting the nutrient value of your food (and the food itself):

- Keep food away from baseboards, sunlight, and other heat sources.
- Keep food away from moisture, animals, bugs, and outdoor weather conditions.
- Store food somewhere cool and dry. A cement basement at a constant 50-60°F is ideal.
- If you don't have a basement, keep food stored at a constant temperature of about 70°F.
- If you live in a hot and humid area, consider a dehumidifier.

Be real about your food storage. If filling your living room ottoman with bags of rice isn't helping you live your best life, don't do it. If stuffing your medicine cabinet with Beanee Weenee cans makes you sad every time you open the mirrored door, it's not worth it. An occasional nuisance here and there isn't going to kill you, but on the whole, storing your food shouldn't make you miserable. With that in mind, let's dig into the creative ways to have fun storing your food!

CREATIVE FOOD STORAGE PLACES

- THE KITCHEN
- THE PANTRY
- THE LIVING ROOM
- THE OFFICE
- THE BEDROOM
- CLOSETS
- OTHER SPACES
- GARAGE & CARPORTS

WHERE TO STORE YOUR FOOD

So, where do you store packages and packages of pinto beans, canned peaches, pasta, and rice, especially when you're limited on space? Here are some clever ways to create mini pantries throughout your home to keep your food safe and accessible.

THE KITCHEN

- Use wire baskets above cabinets for lighter items (mixes, dry ingredients, and cereals).
- Add pull-out drawers to deep cabinets.
- Label the tops of cans stored upright in drawers with permanent marker.
- Use lazy Susans in corner cabinets and other hard-to-reach areas.
- Place stackable shelves under the sink and inside cabinets.
- Add a pull-out pantry to an empty space between cabinets.
- Used tiered organizers and stagger cans to see what's in the back.
- Add under-shelf baskets to cabinets.
- Move spices to cupboard door racks or shallow ledges to free up space.
- Add free-standing shelves to take advantage of vertical storage.

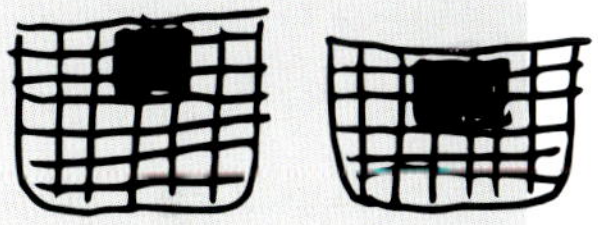

Brilliant Tip Don't store food on top of the refrigerator or above the stove due to heat. Instead, store small kitchen appliances above the fridge, and use that cabinet space to store food.

THE PANTRY

- Hang can-depth metal shelves on the inside of the door for more storage.
- Flip a wire shelf upside down and on an angle to create a gravity-fed can dispenser.
- Use under-shelf or stackable baskets in between shelves.
- Repurpose empty soda can boxes for clever canned food storage.
- Install corner lazy Susans to access stored items that get lost in the back.
- Use back wall storage by adding DVD shelves (they're perfect!) to house cans.
- Install extra shelves in between shelves to maximize vertical space.

Brilliant Tip Tape a list of everything you're storing on buckets, boxes, the inside of the door, wall, or shelf. Keep an ongoing inventory to track food storage (and amounts).

WHERE TO STORE YOUR FOOD

THE LIVING ROOM

- Keep food secure in storage ottomans.
- Hide food in bins and cover with a tablecloth to use as an end table or TV stand.
- Store food in electronics storage consoles.
- Stack buckets or boxes behind the couch.
- Fill empty decorative wicker baskets and oversized vases with food.
- Fill an empty toy box or blanket chest with canned and bagged food.

Brilliant Tip When hiding food under or behind furniture, keep packages away from heat registers, air conditioning vents, and anything that can damage the longevity of food (or that blocks your vents).

THE OFFICE

- Use sturdy filing cabinets to store canned and dry goods, especially in lower drawers.
- Add bins to bookcases for food storage.
- Store food in empty photograph boxes and shoe boxes.
- Use wide magazine holders to store cans on their sides.
- Use plastic tubs to keep items away from humidity and light.

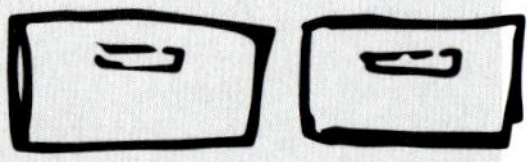

Brilliant Tip Keep short-term items where you can see them and get to them on a regular basis. Store the "longest term" food away from easy reach. They don't need to be readily accessible.

THE BEDROOM

- Add bed risers for more storage height. Cinder blocks are cheap and easy to find.
- Use under-bed rolling drawers and crates.
- Cut cardboard boxes to fit under beds.
- Place food in reinforced lower dresser drawers and/or in nightstands.
- Stack buckets of bulk foods behind the headboard.
- Stack boxes of food, cover with a pretty tablecloth and use as nightstands.
- Look for a used armoire or dresser and fill it with food.

Brilliant Tip To rotate your food supply, add new cans of food under one side of the bed and pull from the other side of the bed.

WHERE TO STORE YOUR FOOD

CLOSETS

- Rearrange or donate unused items to create space.
- Add shelves.
- Install shelf racks on door backs.
- Place long-term food on high shelves.
- Stack boxes and large cans of food at the ends of the closet.
- Fill empty suitcases and luggage with non-perishables.

Brilliant Tip Enhance your closet space and boost your storage with a one- or two-tiered lazy Susan.

OTHER SPACES

- In the laundry room, store non-food items between the washer and dryer, in/on cabinets, and in under-appliance drawers.
- Under stairs, create shelving or store buckets under the stairs.
- In the attic, store non-food items: toilet paper, sanitation needs, paper towels, toothbrushes, etc...
- In the basement, use a covered, insulated window well to store items in mild weather.

Brilliant Tip Consider swapping out your coffee table and getting yourself a cool trunk or an ottoman with built-in storage.

GARAGE, CARPORT, COVERED PORCH

- Add insulated walls to control the temperature.
- Install floor-to-ceiling shelves.
- Add free-standing shelf units.
- Suspend storage from the ceiling.
- Build a loft.
- Stack empty wooden crates on their sides for makeshift food storage shelves.

Brilliant Tip If you've already maximized space inside your home, consider an outside shed. Though keeping your food outside isn't ideal, it's better than nothing.

let's get started

KEEP AN INVENTORY

Now that you know WHERE you can store extra food, let's keep TRACK of all that food, glorious food! Having a stockpile of food won't do you much good if you don't know exactly what you have or when it expires. This is where keeping a detailed inventory comes in!

Listen, save the eye rolls. and hear me out! Sure, it takes some work to do it the first time. And it does take a bit of commitment to keep it going. But it's absolutely critical to your success as a shelf-cooker, and is easier than you might think!

There are three basic things you need to inventory regularly: your freezer, your fridge, and your pantry. Okay and you will need something to write with. But that's obvious, so it doesn't count. There are several ways to keep an inventory. Whether it is in print or digital, you can choose what works best for you. Here are just a few examples:

WHERE TO KEEP YOUR INVENTORY

- **PLASTIC PROTECTOR ON THE FRIDGE**
  Use a paper checklist/inventory and put it in a plastic page protector; then hang it on the fridge, freezer, or pantry door. Mark off quantities with a wet-erase marker as food gets used. My mom used to do this, and it worked great for her.

- **PAPER CHECKLIST IN THE PANTRY**
  Use a paper checklist/inventory on a clipboard in the pantry with a pen nearby. It's always at your fingertips.

- **DIGITAL SPREADSHEET**
  If you're more adept with a screen, use a digital spreadsheet in a program like Google Sheets. A digital inventory is quick and easy to update.

- **FREE INVENTORY SHEETS**
  There are all kinds of inventory sheets available online, some you can use digitally, and others you can print. I have some great printable ones on ShelfCooking.com/kitchen-inventory.

STEP-BY-STEP INVENTORY

Since the process is basically the same for the freezer, fridge, and pantry, I'm going to give you a blow-by-blow account on how to inventory what's in your FREEZER. Then you can wash, rinse, and repeat for the fridge and the pantry.

Aside from learning how to buy extra food items while they're on sale so you can build your freezer stockpile, the real trick is to inventory your freezer. So you know what's in there. That way, you can rotate the food regularly. Ready? Here's how to do it:

1. PULL EVERYTHING OUT

Warning: Things are about to get cray. Remember *If You Give a Mouse a Cookie?* Well, this is like that—on steroids! But it's fun, I promise. (Okay, maybe "fun" is a strong word. "Really super-duper helpful" is probably more like it.) Choose one side or area of your freezer, and completely empty all the contents onto the floor. You can keep all the stuff you pull out of the freezer in a pile on the floor or counter—it won't thaw out fast enough to do any harm. If you're the super cautious type and you're worried about it, pile it into a cooler and keep it in there. Keep a garbage bag close by, and toss anything that is super old, funky-looking, or funky-smelling.

2. CLEAN OUT THE CREEPY GUNK

Ewww. We all have it. I hope no one ever judges me by the toxic crud in the bottom of my freezer. Why is that ice cream container still in there, you wonder? Because it was basically glued down by some unknown sticky substance that makes even Oscar the Grouch's toes curl. But this isn't just for the freezer! Fridge drawers, pantry shelves and baskets, all can collect germs, residue, and crud that needs to be tackled.

Use a vacuum to suck out any crusty stuff you can, then use some heavy elbow grease and cleaning spray to wipe out the rest. Not a fan of chemicals? A homemade solution of one part distilled vinegar and five parts water put in a spray bottle should do the trick.

Ahhh . . . that looks (and smells) a lot better.

Brilliant Tip

Don't have room for extra food? Don't have an extra freezer? Turn back to page 12 and get creative!

3. ORGANIZE IT!

Now that your space is sparkling clean and de-cluttered, it's time to put it all back! Here's the important inventory part: Write down every item as you go. That may sound daunting, but it's not as bad as it sounds. Here's how I do it:

- Start with the least-used, bulkiest stuff. Put those things at the bottom/back of the freezer. For the pantry, put your most used items on the shelves you can reach best.
- Group like-minded items together. "A place for everything, and everything in its place" will keep things tidy and regularly rotated through. For example, here's how I organized my kitchen pull-out freezer:

  LEFT SIDE: Frozen meals/soup, meat, purees, salsa, and similar items.

  RIGHT SIDE: Veggies, fruit, dairy, baking goods, and similar items.

  TOP MINI DRAWER: Small, random items and regularly used items, like butter, cream cheese, string cheese, bagged shredded cheese, yogurt, breads, frozen sandwiches, and ice cream.

4. USE YOUR INVENTORY

Ladies and gentlemen, now for the star of the show...the inventory! (*the crowd goes wild*) Keep up with your newly organized freezer, pantry, and fridge by crossing off the things you use as you use them. When you buy new items, write them on the inventory list and put them where they belong. Regardless of whether you're using print or digital, keep your inventory list current as you buy and use things. The result? At any given time, you'll know exactly what you have on-hand.

5. DO THE SAME FOR THE FRIDGE AND PANTRY

The steps you just went through to clean, organize, and inventory your freezer? Do the same thing for your fridge and pantry!

FRIDGE INVENTORY TIPS:

Aside from condiments and things that have a several-month shelf-life, most of what is in your fridge has a short shelf-life. As a result, keeping a long-term inventory isn't necessary. Make a short-term inventory each week as you go grocery shopping. Toss out what's gone bad, jot down what you have left that needs to be used up, then delete or toss the list and start over the next week.

PANTRY INVENTORY TIPS:

Items in your pantry tend to have the longest shelf-life, especially items in jars and cans. To ensure you are rotating the old items with the new, organize your pantry with the nearest expiration date placed at the front of the shelf. To keep items like pasta and crackers fresher longer, consider transferring them into airtight containers. Not only do they stack well, but they look real purdy too.

EVERYBODY (SPENDING) FREEZE!!!!!!

Now that you have all this newly discovered food in your life and a way to keep it organized and inventoried. **Let's put an extra $500+ in your pocket!** How? Do a one-week spending freeze! Here's how it works:

- For one week—a full 7 days—you spend nothing on food, groceries, coffee runs, eating out, fast food...$0. Not a single cent. During that time, you live entirely on the food you have in your pantry, fridge, and freezer. (Time to dust off the ol' coffee maker!) Want to take it one step further? Spend NO MONEY AT ALL. Not just food, but leave your wallet home for a week!

- At the end of the freeze, take every dollar you WOULD have spent on food or anything else and physically withdraw it from your bank account. Take that money and put it first, toward pressing debt like credit cards. If credit cards are paid off, put it into savings or toward other debts, and enjoy how quickly you were able to save $500 or more in just a few days!

Q & A TIPS FOR SUCCESS

HOW DO I PREPARE? Simple: DON'T! It's only 7 days, people! I can guarantee that almost everyone has enough food lying around to live off of for 7 days! Sure, it might be boxed mac n cheese or soup from the can. But you have what you NEED for 7 little days! The only preparations you should allow would be to buy a gallon of milk, baby formula, or one or two small imperative items that you can't live without. No, those chocolates you've been craving don't count.

DO I BUY 2X THE GROCERIES WHEN THE FREEZE IS OVER? Heck no! That defeats the whole purpose! Once the freeze is done, go about shopping AS USUAL, staying strictly within your weekly budget. Simply pretend the freeze didn't exist.

A spending freeze will not only force you to use what you have, but it's a great way to save a LOT of money in a short amount of time. It's liberating, motivating, and empowering—a lot like a juice cleanse for your body. Just think: In one week you could save enough money to completely pay for Christmas. I don't know about you, but that sure seems worth 7 short days to me!

easy peasy

MEAL PLANNING

Now you have all this great food, and it's all stored and inventoried, what do you do with it? You plan your meals! Most people plan meals backward. The most cost-effective way to meal-plan — and the basis for shelf-cooking—involves three simple steps:

1. **MAKE A LIST OF INGREDIENTS YOU NEED TO USE UP**
2. **FIND MEALS THAT INCLUDE THOSE INGREDIENTS**
3. **REPURPOSE, REUSE, DON'T WASTE ANYTHING**

Told you it's easy! Now, that being said, the specific way in which you plan your meals ultimately depends upon your individual situation. Let's look at common dinner dilemmas and some possible solutions. Ready?

1. MAKE A LIST OF INGREDIENTS YOU NEED TO USE UP

The first step in meal planning is to take a full inventory of all the food in your kitchen. Go through your fridge, freezer, and pantry and make a physical list of everything (except for staple items you always keep on hand) and how much you have.

RUMMAGE THROUGH THE REFRIGERATOR

Start with your fridge because those items are perishable and tend to go bad the fastest. Look at your inventory. What items need to be used up first? Inventory in this order:

- Produce Drawer - It's the healthiest food in the refrigerator, and it's also the first food to go bad. Make a list of the things in there that need to be used first.
- Leftovers - Don't waste those leftovers. Repurpose them! Whether it's shredded taco chicken, a container of corn, or roasted veggies, you can use them (yes!) yet again!
- Foods You Don't Replenish Often - Dairy, condiments nearing expiration, or sour cream. How can you creatively use these up?

FORAGE THE FREEZER

While food in the freezer lasts longer than it does in the refrigerator, it doesn't last forever. Here are some good rules of thumb for shelf cooking:

- Look for Food That Needs to Be Used - Foods close to their expiration dates or foods on the verge of freezer burn are the perfect candidates.
- Grab Food That's in the Way - Have a huge turkey that keeps threatening to fall out and land on your foot every time you open the freezer door? Use it, and you'll free up a ton of space for future meals.
- Look for Half-Empty Containers - Things like half-eaten ice cream containers take up a lot of space.

PILLAGE THE PANTRY

Your pantry inventory list will probably be the shortest. It's shelf-stable so a lot of it doesn't have to be used up as quickly. Start with:

- Items Without a Home - Do you have hamburger buns just sitting out from your last cookout? Make a plan to use them.
- Foods Close to Their Expiration Dates - Stuff that'll go bad such as breads, almost-empty containers of food that take up a lot of space, vegetables, etc.
- Half-Empty Containers - If you have a large snack container with only a few mini pretzels left, plan to either use a smaller container or repurpose those bite-sized beauties.

2. FIND MEALS THAT USE THOSE INGREDIENTS

You've got items that need to be used up–let's find recipes that use those ingredients! Make sure you use up items in your meal plan before it goes bad. There are a few ways to do this:

- Glance through your inventory list. What jumps out at you?
- Start with the proteins.
- Pull out your cookbooks and search the indexes by ingredient.
- Use technology to search sites like AllRecipes.com or ShelfCooking.com. Or use an app like Favoreats to find recipes that include the ingredients you have.
- Screenshot or print the recipe, so you have it on hand. When you have a winning recipe, add notes and the dates you made it and save it to your favorite recipes binder.
- Search for meals that use up the most ingredients the fastest for the start of the week.
- Save meals like barbecue for the end of the week to use up anything left in the fridge.

SET THEMED NIGHTS

Is it Meatless Mondays? Taco Tuesdays? Pizza Fridays? When you're struggling to come up with new meal ideas, themes days help simplify meal planning. Just remember to allow for some flexibility.

- Set a Daily Theme - This will narrow down your search! Not only does it make the recipe search easier, it makes the meals more fun and helps get the kids excited!
- Plan for What Needs to Go - Keep your theme night secondary to using up the ingredients you have on hand.
- Keep it Simple - Don't forget to keep your themes basic and broad so that they can incorporate a variety of meals.

KEEP A RECIPE BINDER

Once you find a recipe that your family likes, print it, photocopy it, hand-write it on a recipe card, and keep all your favorites in one binder. Organize the recipes by protein, so you can quickly find those that match up with the ingredients you need to use that week. No more spending 30 minutes hunting for "that one recipe." Now they are in one place for quick and easy access!

SEARCH BY INGREDIENT

The best way to find delicious recipes to use up what you've got, is to search by ingredient - NOT by recipe! For example, if you have chicken and spinach in your fridge, head to the index of this book! Look up "spinach" or "chicken," and see what your options are. Alternatively, head to Google, Pinterest, or your favorite recipe site and type "chicken + spinach recipes." You'll be amazed at how quickly you will find a delicious recipe that your family will love!

DOUBLE AND FREEZE

"Do the work once, benefit twice!" If you're cooking, why not double and freeze?! Make a double batch of whatever you're cooking, put one batch in a freezer-safe disposable baking dish, cover tightly, label (recipe name, instructions, and date), and bam! Homemade dinner on a busy night.

3. REPURPOSE, REUSE, DON'T WASTE ANYTHING

Set yourself up for meal planning success: repurpose, reuse, and don't waste food! Follow these smart meal planning tips to get the most bang for your grocery budget!

DON'T MAKE MEALS YOU WON'T REHEAT

If there's a meal with leftovers you just don't like, save it for those times when you're going to have family or friends over. Make sure enough people come to help eat it the same night you make it.

REPURPOSE YOUR LEFTOVERS

Truth: I don't love eating the same thing more than one or two days in a row. Further truth: you don't have to either! Turn that leftover white rice into a beautiful fried rice. Turn that leftover Sunday roast into a delicious pan of shredded beef enchiladas. Turn that baked potato into fried breakfast hash. Deconstruct your meal and find ways to make those ingredients brand new again! (Psst... don't worry, this book will show you how.)

USE THOSE KITCHEN APPLIANCES

If you have a hard time cooking meals, enlist the help of your slow cooker, air fryer, or Instant Pot! They will save you time and make mealtime a breeze!

BE PICKY ABOUT WHAT YOU BUY IN BULK

We love that Costco (or Sam's Club) membership as much as the next frugalista, but if you're not careful, you might just end up wasting ingredients (and money). Here's how to save:

- Ask "Can I Store This for A While?" - Avoid buying bulk unless it's something you can freeze or that will last a long time in the pantry.
- Choose Air-Tight Containers - Help your food last as long as possible! We recommend airtight containers for storing any perishables in the pantry.
- Buy What's on Sale - For those items that you would normally buy in bulk, stick with sale items at smaller stores. We all love Costco, but you'll probably end up wasting more than you save on some of those products.
- Buy with Purpose - Make sure any food you buy for the week can be used in multiple meals you have planned!

PLAN FOR EATING AWAY FROM THE HOUSE

When there's a night you don't eat at home, plan for it, whether it's date night, getting together with friends, or a work event. This prevents planning for seven meals at home when it's unnecessary.

TEACH THE KIDS HOW TO MEAL PLAN

There is no better way to meal plan with kids than to get them involved in the process. No matter the age, sit down with your kids and let them help choose meals for the week. You'll be glad you did!

DINNER DILEMMA

SINGLE, STUDENT, OR WORKING PROFESSIONAL

DINNER BUDGET DILEMMA:

"I have no time to cook between working and social life, so I tend to eat out/buy food on the go, which really adds up."

SOLUTIONS:

Slow-cooker, meal prep, slow cooker, meal trades. Did I mention slow cooker?!

- Every week choose two or three meals to prepare and focus on the slow-cooker as your main tool. Toss the food in the slow-cooker before work or class, set it on low, and eight hours later, you have a hot meal ready and waiting for you when you come home. You can prep and freeze these meals in advance, then dump the frozen bag of goodies in the slow cooker before running out the door!
- Prep! Prep it reeeeeal good! Typically, preparing food is what takes the longest. Brown, sautee, chop, roast, or blend anything and everything for your recipes over the weekend. Then, when it's time to cook dinner after a long day at work, all you have to do is dump. You could take it one step further and actually cook 2-3 meals on Sunday, divide them up, and have pre-cooked grab-and-go meals all week long!
- Buddy-up with a roommate or friend and rotate days where you cook for everyone in the house. That way you have a home-cooked meal every night, but you only have to cook once or twice a week. This will help reduce your grocery bill as well.
- Schedule time to eat out into your week. Let's be realistic here, people! By scheduling lunches or dinners out, you are more intentional and aware of eating out and cuts down on impulsive drive-through runs.

DINNER IDEA:

Toss chicken breasts in the slow-cooker. Dump BBQ sauce over it (no need to measure!), cook eight hours on low, and shred and eat on buns or eat whole with rice or veggies. You'll have BBQ chicken thirty seconds after you get home! Other ideas for the slow-cooker include baked potatoes, salsa chicken, or taco soup.

Brilliant Tip

For shared spaces with minimal storage, get creative! Consider keeping canned goods and other non-perishables in unusual places, like a dresser drawer or bins under your bed, so you can stick with one trip to the store per week.

PARENT OF YOUNG CHILDREN

DINNER BUDGET DILEMMA:

"By the end of the day, I'm so exhausted, and my young kids are so cranky, I just don't have the energy to cook, or I look at the clock and it's already five, and we need dinner right now. At that point, we go for expensive frozen meals or order pizza."

SOLUTIONS:

Build-your-own meals, freezer meals, one-pan/dump meals

- Kids love options! (...and mommy hates whining!) That being said, PARENTS: you are NOT a short-order cook! Kids tend to have picky palettes, but that doesn't mean you need to cater to their picky tastes. In order to create good eaters, don't focus your meals around "kid food" (e.g., chicken nuggets, quesadillas, and the mac and cheese they love oh so much). Give them grownup food, but give it to them in options. Build-your-own meals such as a taco bar are great for kids. Require them to pick one meat and two veggies to put on their taco. They get to choose, but in the end, you're the one that wins.
- If you're doing the work anyway, double and freeze! There are very few meals that can't be frozen (just keep reading! I'll prove it to you.), so do the work once and enjoy a freezer stocked with slow cooker or oven-ready meals.
- The last thing a busy (read: EXHAUSTED) parent needs is more to clean up at the end of the night! Focus your meal planning around hearty meals that only dirty one dish - casseroles, sheet pan dinners, instant pot/slow cooker (with a disposable liner! They are amazing!), one-pot meals, etc. These types of meals also make it easy to chop up and sneak in healthy veggies that your kids will never even notice!

DINNER IDEA:

Anything that can be baked in a 9 x 13 pan (such as casseroles, lasagna, baked pastas, chicken and rice). I particularly love the disposable aluminum pans you can find at most grocery stores and even the dollar store! Pan meals can typically be prepped as early as the night before, and 9 x 13 pans are easy to freeze: just stick the lid on, freeze, then pop in the oven—still frozen when you need a quick meal.

HOUSE FULL OF TEENAGERS

DINNER BUDGET DILEMMA:

"These teenagers eat me out of house and home! My meal budget has tripled, especially when they invite their friends over!"

SOLUTIONS:

Focus on sales, "stretch meals," and intentional snacking

- Each week, plan your meals around what's on sale that week. You can look at store ads, focus on the front and back pages as the middle pages aren't usually that great. If beef, corn on the cob, zucchini, or WHATEVER goes on sale, stock up and center your meals around that!
- Focus on what I like to call "stretch meals." What that means is, make the protein the sidekick, not the hero! Sure, a steak or grilled chicken breast tastes great. But that will cost you a small fortune if you've got a house full of teens! Instead of serving everyone an entire chicken breast, cook up 2 or 3 chicken breasts, shred or chop them small them, and turn it into burritos, soup, fried rice, or pasta. Make the star of the meal an inexpensive ingredient that "stretches" the meal such as rice, lettuce, bread, pasta, veggies, or potatoes.
- If you aren't careful, your teens can eat you out of house and home BETWEEN meals! Help your teens be intentional about snacking. One rule I suggest is, "if it's in a wrapper, you don't eat it at home." Save the granola bars and expensive packaged snacks for when you're on the go. Make a big batch of protein balls, homemade granola bars, trail mix, big bowls of fruit salad, and individual containers of leftovers handy for quick-to-grab snacks that are far more affordable.

DINNER IDEA:

Potatoes are the king of stretch meals! They are not only hearty and versatile, but they are inexpensive and last a long time when stored properly. See our "Naked Potatoes" section for tons of ideas on how to turn plain potatoes into an incredible meal!

Brilliant Tip!

Get your teenagers involved in cooking and shopping. Show them your budget and challenge them to stick with it.

EMPTY NESTERS

DINNER BUDGET DILEMMA:

"Now that I'm cooking for just one or two again, I find myself wasting so much food because we just can't seem to eat it all! We get sick of eating the same leftovers day after day, and we end up throwing them away. I'm still in the habit of cooking for a big family!"

SOLUTIONS:

Reinvent leftovers, half-and-freeze, adjust quantities, and shop differently.

- Plan your meals one week in advance, and use your leftovers to go toward the next meal. That way you'll use every drop of the food you cook, but you won't notice you're "repurposing" it. Keep reading for tons of ideas on how to do this!
- When you cook, instead of the "double and freeze" method, use the "half and freeze" method! Stick half your meal in the freezer, either in its entirety or in individual portion sizes, so you have a future meal ready and keep serving sizes smaller.
- Adjust a recipe quantity to adjust the serving size. Most meals feed 4-6. So do the math and cut the recipe down, to reduce the amount of leftovers. See our "CONVERSIONS" section where we do the math for you!
- Ok Costco lovers, listen up! Now might be the time to stop buying in bulk. (I know, I can't believe I said it!) For food, anyway. Stick with food items at your local grocery stores, and if you must buy bulk, do so for non-food items that have a much longer shelf-life.

DINNER IDEA:

Monday night: Rotisserie chicken and potatoes. Tuesday: Use the same chicken but serve it over rice and pour a creamy sauce over it. Wednesday: Use the same rotisserie leftovers, but chop it up and make chicken enchiladas and add taco seasoning to the rice to make Mexican rice.

Brilliant Tip!

If you still want to buy bulk to get the best price per ounce or price per unit, split the bulk items with a friend!

here are some go-to

DINNER IDEAS

If you're anything like me, coming up with what to make for dinner is the dreaded chore of the week! To help "cooker's block" as my son calls it, I keep a big LIST of dinner ideas by my fridge. This is SUPER-DUPER helpful in coming up with a variety of meals that can be made with things I typically have on hand. I also can't live without my "recipe binder" -- a place where I keep copies of my favorite recipes so they are all in one place. That way I never have to say, "Now, where was that awesome chicken recipe?"

Brilliant Tip!

Make your own recipe binder! It's a great way to keep your favorite recipes on hand, rather than digging through screenshots on your phone or rifling through stacks of cookbooks to find it. Head to ShelfCooking.com/RecipeBinder for tips and info on how to make yours!

LIST OF 75+ DINNER IDEAS

Here's a list of dinner ideas that you can adapt or find a recipe for in a pinch!
Copy this page and keep it on your fridge for easy meal planning.

PASTA DINNER IDEAS

- Homemade mac and cheese
- Lasagna/lasagna rolls
- Baked pasta (ziti, rotini, baked chicken spaghetti)
- Fettuccine alfredo (chicken or shrimp)
- Spaghetti (with or without meatballs)
- Stuffed pasta (shells, manicotti, tortellini, ravioli)
- Pesto pasta
- Chicken Parmesan or eggplant Parmesan
- Stroganoff (chicken or beef)
- Bowtie pasta with chicken & veggies
- Pad thai
- Low mein noodles

SALADS OR SANDWICHES FOR DINNER

- Paninis
- Shredded meat on rolls
- Grilled cheese (can add lunch meat)
- BLTs
- Taco salad
- Chef salad
- Asian or mediterranean salad (with chicken)

SOUP DINNER IDEAS

- Taco/tortilla soup
- Minestrone soup
- Chicken noodle soup
- Potato soup
- Chili/white chili
- Chowder (clam, corn, ham, etc)
- Bisque
- Tortellini soup
- French onion soup
- Stew

GRILLED DINNER IDEAS

- Grilled meat (season/marinade and grill!)
- Kabobs
- Burgers & dogs
- Grilled pizza
- Grilled veggies

BREAKFAST FOR DINNER

- French toast (stuffed/regular)
- Waffles/pancakes
- Crepes
- Omelets
- Eggs (fried, scrambled, hard boiled, etc) with side (hash browns, bacon, sausage, veggies)
- Breakfast Cabin Casserole*
- Hash/breakfast bowls
- Frittata/quiche

SLOW-COOKER DINNER IDEAS

- Meat and rice (chicken, pork, beef)
- Shredded meat (for tacos, sandwiches, enchiladas, casseroles)
- Pot roast, pork loin
- Pasta
- Soup
- Lasagna
- Curry
- Fajitias, burrito bowls

BAKED DINNER IDEAS

- Homemade pizza/calzones
- Potatoes (check out page 187 for ideas!)
- Dinner pie (chicken pot pie, shepherd's pie)
- Enchiladas/chimichangas/taquitos
- Egg rolls
- Stuffed green peppers
- Sheet pan dinner (chicken/beef/fish/pork/shrimp with veggies)
- Casserole
- Chicken cordon bleu
- Baked "fried" chicken
- Homemade chicken nuggets/wings/fingers
- Meatloaf
- Baked sandwiches
- Baked meat (ham, roast, pork tenderloin, whole chicken, steak, etc.)
- Fish sticks/crab cakes
- Lasagna (Mexican, traditional, veggie)
- Baked pasta dish

*Find the recipe for Cabin Casserole on page 222 in our book!

let's get going:

BUDGETING, SHOPPING, & ORGANIZATION

BUDGETING, SHOPPING, & ORGANIZATION

Now that you have an inventory, meal plan, and know how to shelf cook...
let's set a budget, hit the store, and get cooking!

SET A BUDGET

Don't know how much to spend? We walk you step-by-step through setting a reasonable budget for your family!

PAGE 34

STAY ON BUDGET

A budget serves no purpose unless you actually stick to it! We show you the SIMPLE way to never go over-budget again.

PAGE 36

GO SHOPPING

Budget is set, let's head to the store! This section gives you some fantastic tips to maximize savings.

PAGE 38

ORGANIZE ALL THE THINGS

Save money and time by organizing your kitchen and pantry into helpful zones. A place for everything, and everything in its place!

PAGE 42

money money money!

MAKING A BUDGET

Let's start with the million-dollar question: how much money should you spend on groceries?

THE BUDGET

Here's the short answer, a suggested grocery budget is $100 per person per month, starting at $300. (You households with only two people just drew a get-out-of-jail-free card!) Here's what that means: each person in your house—newborn baby, grade-schooler, teenager, or adult—gets $100 per month.

This is for groceries (food & drinks), as well as consumables (things you use up and replace regularly: cleaning supplies, paper products, diapers and wipes, dog food, shampoo... you get the idea. Note: this budget should not include eating out (that should come from an "entertainment" budget), but it would include meal subscription plans.

GROCERY BUDGET

$100 per person per month
starting at $300 for two people

To some, that $100 per person may seem like plenty. Others may have just broken out in hives and a cold sweat. Before you run and grab your pitchforks and start shaking your fists at me, just know that I've been consulting families across the globe, blogging, teaching, and doing national television segments about this for years.

When people legitimately take my advice into consideration and do the work it takes to grocery shop and meal plan the frugal way, $100 per person is not only doable, it's reasonable. And yes, even Rachael Ray agrees with this! (She told me herself one of the times I was on her show!)

Savings Tip For more budgeting tips and info head to ShelfCooking.com/grocery-budget

HOW TO BUDGET

I recommend breaking down your family budget into three categories: grocery, other, and family.

TRACKING

The real secret sauce, however, is to take the total budget amount (let's say $500/month for a family of 5) and divide it out per week. Using our example, $500 divided by 4 weeks in a month = $125 per week for groceries. Now you have a reasonable-but-tight budget that you only have to track for 7 little days! Why track weekly? Ask yourself this question, why don't you count your calories one month at a time? Easy, for starters, the numbers get too hard to track, it involves a hefty amount of math, and it's challenging to pace yourself. Budgets are the same way! If you break your budgets down, so you're only tracking them for seven days at a time, you'll be able to stay on budget 1078 percent more effectively! (Okay ... I made that up—but you get the point!)

ADAPTATIONS

All that being said, a budget doesn't do you any good if it's unreasonable. So, some adaptations may be necessary! Try the $100pp budget for 3 full months. If that budget is absolutely impossible for you, for example, if you live in midtown Manhattan, have very particular health issues, dietary restrictions in your family, or live out in the boonies and have only one very expensive store within fifty miles), that's okay! Add $25 per person, per month. Try it for a time, and see how that does. But again, only do this after you have tried for at least 3 months! You will likely be surprised at how much you can do with $100!

STAY ON BUDGET

The number-one way to stay within an established grocery budget is to become an expert at shelf cooking. One of the primary benefits of shelf cooking is the impact it has on what you're spending on groceries every month. Here are some other sure-fire ways to help you stay on budget.

MAKE FRUGAL MEALS

Save "fancy" meals that include expensive meats and finer ingredients for Sundays, rather than making them throughout the week. Remember, make the protein the sidekick, not the hero!

DIGITAL GROCERY SHOPPING

Order your groceries online! You see your cart total as you're shopping and clearly see what is on sale and what's in stock without driving anywhere. Grocery pick-up is typically free, saves time, and cuts down on impulse buys.

DON'T WASTE A THING

Don't throw away your money! Use, use again! Don't let anything go to waste. There are millions of ways to repurpose leftovers into new meals if you're sick of eating the same thing day in and day out. See the leftovers section for some great ideas.

MAKE EXTRA & FREEZE IT

If you're cooking something, double and freeze it, so you have an inexpensive freezer meal for a crazy day when take-out looks appealing. Check out the Freezing and Thawing sections for great info on how to make it work.

PICK AND CHOOSE

You might have a favorite store, but it might not have the best prices. Or perhaps you prefer to eat organic. Pick and choose! What are the few things your favorite store provides that no one else does? What are your top 10 "must-buy" organic foods? Bend on the rest, and you'll save hundreds!

BUY EXTRAS ON SALE

Buy extra when items are on sale and freeze the extras for later! If something is on sale, don't buy just one—buy several and store them in the pantry or freezer. Keep these sale items on hand, so you aren't paying full price when you need something.

SPECIAL DIETARY NEEDS AND THE 70% RULE

If someone in your family has special dietary needs, or if you choose to eat clean/organic, you already know the impact that can have on your food budget. You may not believe it, but we have thousands of shelf cooking pros with special dietary restrictions that easily stay within a tight grocery budget each month! Here are some tips to help you keep your specialty food budget in check:

- Buy the things that are on sale and stock up.
- Pick your battles. You most likely don't need to buy EVERYTHING from a specialty store.
- Even organic things can be bought at a discount from places like Costco.
- Grow your own organic veggies, and you will significantly save on your grocery bill. Gardens can be BIG—and once you've invested a little seed money (literally), they are virtually free!
- Cook from scratch. Instead of buying expensive loaves of gluten-free bread, buy the ingredients (in bulk if possible to save on cost), and bake it yourself!
- Don't cook the specialty food for those who don't need it. This might add a little work on your part, but it's worth the cost savings! My son, McEwan, can't have dairy of any kind. Instead of using expensive lactose-free milk or cheese in meals, I cook the meal as usual but will make a small, dairy-free portion for him. We save so much money with the other 9 of us eating non-specialty food that I can afford to get a few specialty items for him from time to time. It might be tough for him to eat differently than everyone else at first, but he will be faced with that the rest of his life, so learning to adapt will eventually serve him well.

THE 70% RULE

Your budget is YOUR BUDGET. At the end of the day, YOU get to choose how much you want to spend! And that is fantastic! Some people vacation often. Some buy high-end shoes. Some have an expensive cable bill. If you choose to spend more on groceries than my suggested budget, that is your choice, and that is okay! Just choose other areas in your life where you can sacrifice and be disciplined in so it all balances out. My 70% rule of budgeting can help you with this:

RULE: You should only spend 70% or less of your take-home income.
70% - spending (bills, groceries, entertainment, travel, anything you spend money on)
20% - savings (divided between 10% to emergency savings and 10% to regular family savings)
10% - something philanthropic or proactive (tithe to your church, donate to charity, investments, retirement fund, or put it toward extra debt payments)

So long as all your spending—on food and everything else—fits within 70% or less of your monthly take-home income, you're fine!

Quick Tip

For more info on this 70% rule head to Shelfcooking.com/70percent *time to go*

GROCERY SHOPPING

Honey, I don't know how to break this to you but...

...you're grocery shopping all wrong.

Well, you're PROBABLY grocery shopping wrong, at least partially. If you go to the store more than once per week, wander the aisles, buy only the ingredients you need for the meal you plan to cook that day, don't check the ads first, or toss whatever sounds good into your cart, you're most likely doing yourself and your family a disservice. It's certainly better than ordering takeout, and I'm proud of you for shopping and cooking! But chances are you're paying way too much for groceries—and the only one who wins is the grocery store.

News flash, you could save as much as HALF on your grocery bill by changing a few simple things!

Best Shopping Tips

BRING YOUR OWN SHOPPING BAGS

They're more environmentally friendly, and many stores offer discounts for every reusable bag you bring yourself.

CHECK THE COST PER OUNCE

Don't rely on sales signage for the lowest pricing. Discounted items aren't always the best deals.

ADD DAIRY AND MEAT ITEMS TO YOUR CART LAST

This keeps those foods fresh and less likely to spoil.

GROCERY SHOPPING TIPS

ONLY GO ONCE

This is my number-one single most important trick on the entire grocery planet: only go to the store 1x per week, no matter what! Why? Because that one gallon of milk will cost you $50 in things you suddenly "need to have." Six days is not that long; you can do it! Plan your meals, stay up on your inventory, then choose one day to go shopping. Run out of milk? Eat toast instead of cereal. Run out of eggs? Use substitutions! (psst we have dozens of them starting on page 82.)

LOOK AT THE ADS

Check the store's website, app, or "junk mail" mailer before deciding where to shop. Pro tip: The front and back pages usually have the best deals!

SHOP SEASONALLY

Keep the season in mind! Focus your meals around produce and ingredients that are in season, or popular to the season, as they will likely be cheaper.

REMEMBER SHELF COOKING

It's your new mantra: cook first with what you DO have; not with what you DON'T have.

ALWAYS SHOP WITH A LIST

It's pretty much guaranteed that shopping without a list will not only cost you more, but you're likely to forget something and be tempted to break the "one store per week" rule above. Pro-tip, Keep your shopping list on your phone, not on paper! You're bound to leave a paper list behind at some point, but let's be honest, most of us don't even go to the bathroom without our phones, let alone all the way to the store!

NEVER SHOP HUNGRY

You'll grab all kinds of things you don't need. Keep snacks in your purse or car just in case!

TAKE YOUR KIDS

Honestly, this is a surprising one for many people. Yes, it's more challenging. But it gets you out of the store more quickly and also provides an opportunity for you to teach them how to grocery shop while you're at it!

SHOP MID WEEK

Sales often switch over mid-week, and some stores will even honor both weeks' sales. Plus, crowds and lines tend to be much shorter during the week, which is a bonus! I like to plan my meals on Sunday and do grocery pick-up on Monday.

GROCERY SHOPPING TIPS

GENERIC BRAND VERSUS NAME BRAND

Prices for name brand foods almost always cost more than store brands—also called "off-brand" or "generic." The high price of name brands is rarely due to better quality. In fact, most of them are made in the same factories as generic brands! The price is higher because you're paying for product testing, commercials, advertising, overhead costs, etc. Again, Rachael Ray, who used to be a buyer for grocery stores, confirmed this! #RachKnowsBest

CHECK THE TAG

How do you know if it's a good deal or not? Don't just look at the overall price of the item; look at the unit price! Every tag on the shelf at the grocery store will show you a per unit price. Compare that price per unit among brands, so you can get the biggest bang for your buck.

BUY IN BULK

Most of the time, buying the larger package may cost a little bit more up front, but it will save you money in the long run. You can always re-package it yourself in smaller amounts and freeze it for later. But sometimes biggest isn't always cheapest--check the price per ounce before buying in bulk.

DO IT YOURSELF

While pre-packed and pre-chopped food is tempting, don't fall for it! Not only will chopping, dividing, and mixing yourself save money, but your food will be fresher and be less likely to have chemicals and preservatives.

AVOID EYE LEVEL

Companies pay a lot of money for their brands to be at eye level. Go up or down a couple of shelves, you can save so much money!

LOOK AT THE DATES

Check the dates! The oldest products are usually at the front of the shelf or refrigerator shelf. Reach to the back and grab the freshest product you can, especially in the dairy section! It'll last longer and will help you not have to throw food out that goes bad before you can finish it.

GROCERY SHOPPING TIPS

WATCH FOR SALE STICKERS

I find sales stickers tend to be most useful in the meat section. These stickers usually mean that the meat is getting close to its "sell by" date, so the store wants to move that product off its shelves. Don't worry, the meat still has plenty of life in it! It just means the store wants to rotate it out. Also, don't be blinded by sale stickers! Just because it says "special" or "sale" doesn't mean it's the best price. This is where my next tip comes in handy...

KEEP A "PRICE NOTEBOOK"

A price notebook can literally be a little notebook you keep in your purse, or you can just keep the notes in your phone. As you shop, write down the prices for the typical grocery items you buy, making note of good sale prices. Then when you're at the store, and you see something that's below your expected price, you know it's a good deal. Pro tip: remember to note the price per unit and not overall price!

STOCK UP

As you become more proficient in shelf cooking, you will find that only a portion of your budget will be needed for your menu plan that week. The rest of your budget should then be used to build a stockpile! My mantra is, "one, for now, two for later," especially on sale items. If you need frozen corn for a recipe, buy three and store the other two! That way, you're slowly building a stockpile, while staying within budget.

HIT THE FREEZER SECTION

All right, here is one of my favorite tips. Head to the freezer section—not to buy anything, but to learn what you can make and freeze at home! You will pay two to three times more for pre-made frozen meals at the store than what you would spend making those same meals at home. Plus, home-cooked is just plain healthier! Be sure to keep a good stock of disposable aluminum baking dishes on hand for this reason as well.

Brilliant Tip!

Before you throw everything in the fridge and pantry as-is, take a few minutes to cut it up, portion it out, and prep it for later. For example, instead of freezing two pounds of ground beef, maybe freeze four bags each with a half-pound portion. This will save you time later and lower the risk of food waste.

get in the zone

ORGANIZE YOUR KITCHEN

By now, you know shelf cooking is a way to dish up delicious home-cooked, budget-friendly meals. Now here's the catch: keeping a good stash of food at home can be a major benefit to your wallet—but if all that food is disorganized, messy, and cluttered, nobody wins.

A key to making it all work is organization. If you're like me, getting and staying organized is not your favorite activity. But trust me—it's worth the effort, and it will make a world of difference. And if you do it right to begin with, it's pretty painless to maintain. Honest.

How do you start right? It's simpler than you think, and I'm going to tell you how. We'll start with some kitchen basics and then move to the center of it all: the dreaded pantry.

ORGANIZE YOUR KITCHEN IN ZONES

- **THE COOKING ZONE**
  All the things that you use when you cook: spices, pots and pans, and most used appliances
- **THE BAKING AND PREP ZONE**
  All those yummy baking things: sugar, flour, vanilla, and of course chocolate chips. Throw your baking sheets in too!
- **THE EATING AND ENTERTAINMENT ZONE**
  This is the stuff you need for serving and eating: everyday dishes, glasses, tablecloths, etc.

- **THE CLEANING ZONE**
  Here's the stuff that makes it easy to clean: soap, scrub brushes, and stuff for leftovers too.

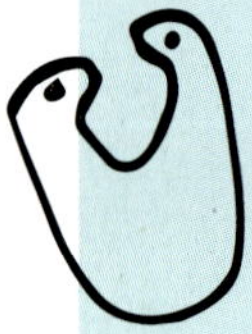

- **THE KIDS ZONE**
  All the things that the littles need: dishes, bowls, bibs, etc. and keep it at kid level!

GET IN THE ZONE

Here's a straightforward way to get and stay organized—and it's like the gift that keeps on giving. It makes a lot of sense and will make your kitchen work for you. Ready?

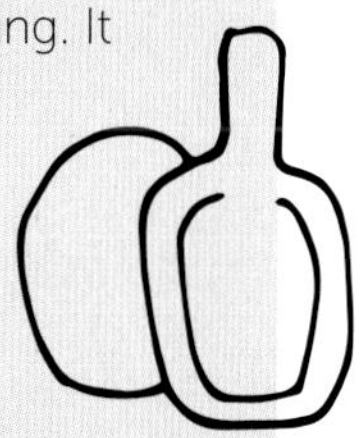

THE COOKING ZONE

In the "cooking zone" of your kitchen, dedicate your shelf, cupboard, and counter space for all the things you use when you cook: spices, seasoning, cooking oils, cutting boards, pots and pans, cooking utensils, hot pads, and the appliances you use regularly.

If you have a skinny drawer, throw your small spice bottles in there. And alphabetize them—it'll be a cinch to find exactly what you need. Keep large, oversize spices in a top cupboard in your cooking zone; put the ones you use most often in front. And use a drying rack to organize the lids for your pots and pans.

THE BAKING AND PREP ZONE

Here's where you keep all the stuff you use for baking—you know, stuff like flour, sugar, powdered sugar, vanilla, coconut, and chocolate chips. You'll also want to keep baking pans, sheets, rolling pins, and cookie cutters in this zone.

You may want to keep your favorite go-to cookbooks in this zone as well. I love to keep mine on a shelf in my kitchen—I organize them by rainbow color, which is a fun and easy way to brighten up a space. You could also organize your cookbooks on a pantry shelf or opt for a kitchen cabinet.

THE EATING AND ENTERTAINMENT ZONE

Here's where you keep all the stuff you need to put your meal on the table, like everyday dishes, glasses, flatware, placemats, tablecloths, napkins, and all that good paraphernalia.

As for entertaining, stash your fancy dishes, upscale serving platters and bowls, ritzy flatware, glasses or goblets, gorgeous tablecloths and matching napkins, candlesticks, vases, and decorations all in one place. Makes it a cinch to get ready for company.

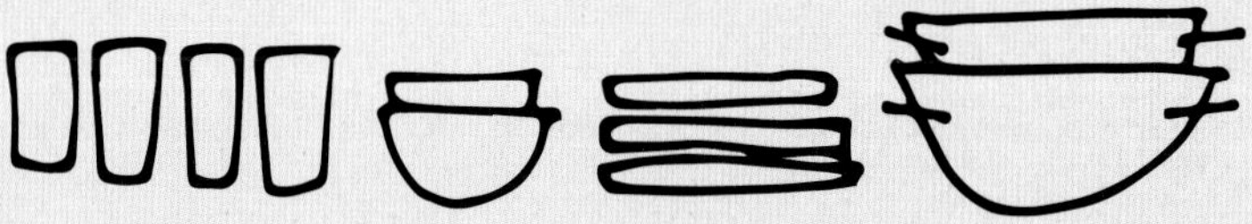

GET IN THE ZONE

THE CLEANING ZONE

For me, this area includes under the sink and a drawer next to it. Keep all the things you need when it's time to wash your hands, wash the dishes, or clean the kitchen. My oversized items like brooms and vacuums are together in a nearby closet.

Your cleaning zone should also contain the things you use to pack up and put away leftovers. Here's another great use for those skinny drawers: load one with things like zip-lock bags, aluminum foil, plastic wrap, and so on.

THE KIDS ZONE

If you have littles at your house, create a kids zone where you can stock all the things they need, such as kid cups, bowls, spoons, bibs, etc. Pro-tip, keep them in a drawer or cabinet at kid level! Makes life a whole lot easier for everyone when they can help themselves.

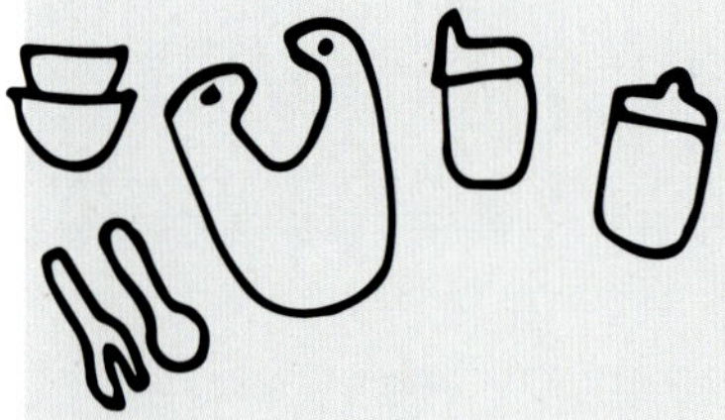

Brilliant Tip!

Hang a chalkboard or dry erase board near your kitchen table. Use it for spelling words and homework assignments, then multi-task while your family eats!

PANTRY ORGANIZATION

After many years of trial and error, I finally found a pantry organization system that works for me! Obviously, you'll want to tailor this for your specific needs, but I want to share my pantry organization ideas and tips, which will hopefully give you some inspiration for your space.

I'm very fortunate that my current pantry is gigantic. But I've spent a long time in kitchens with had itty, bitty, BITTY pantries that didn't offer much in the way of storage space. So I've been there. And I haven't forgotten. The tips and tricks I'm about to share can be adapted to any pantry/storage space, large or small.

LINE YOUR SHELVES

You'd be amazed at how messy, scratched, and dinged-up your pantry shelves can get when you use baskets and containers. To keep everything looking nice and new, try lining your pantry shelves with some shelf-liner paper. There are loads of cute prints and designs to choose from.

Along with the shelf liner, I also stuck little felt dot pads to the bottom corners of my wire baskets to keep the sharp corners from shredding and cutting the liner paper. And they slide out nice and smoothly.

ORGANIZE BY USE

When it comes to organizing a pantry the PRACTICAL way, do it by what makes the most sense based on USE—not by what LOOKS the prettiest. Don't be fooled by the amazing pantry pics on Pinterest—they're just for show and not very practical. As you figure out how to organize your own space, focus on use, use, use!

Keep the things you use most often on the most convenient shelf (which is typically the shelf that's at eye level). Keep things your kids use most often on the shelf that's at their eye level. It may not look as pretty as the magazine-worthy photos you see online, but this is all about productivity and efficiency. The things you use most often should be easily accessible. Looks come second, mama!

PANTRY ORGANIZATION

INVEST IN STORAGE BASKETS

Professional organizers may try to convince you that the best way to organize a pantry is to keep food perfectly lined up in small acrylic trays. That may work for some. For the other 99% of us, it just isn't practical! (Trust me, I tried for years!) Stacking food boxes and cans also isn't great either, as items inevitably get shoved to the back.

So what's my suggested solution? So glad you asked! The day I decided to keep everything in storage baskets, the skies parted, and my whole world changed!

Measure your pantry shelves (height, length, and width). Find sturdy baskets that fill as much of the space as possible, especially height-wise; that is typically very under-utilized space.) Simply sort your food by type, assign it a basket, toss the food in, and voila! Contained, looks great, and you don't have to worry every time your kid wants a granola bar that it will mess up your perfect little row of snacks.

Some example basket categories are canned vegetables, canned fruit, tomatoes and pasta sauce, grains, baking, pasta, crackers, cereal, kid snacks, treats, and so on. Smaller baskets are perfect for items that get tossed around and lost in the back of cupboards, such as some baking goods. They're also ideal for packets of seasonings, dressing mixes, sauce mixes, soup mixes, and other things that come in small packets.

You can use any kind of container that works for you—wire, mesh, plastic, sturdy cardboard, or even wicker (though, I find that wicker baskets look pretty, but tend to shed and break down in time). I got my baskets for around $8 to $15 each from TJ Maxx, Ross, Target, and Home Goods, but Amazon has various sizes as well. Airtight containers and cereal containers are great for opened bags of baking goods, grains, crackers, and treats. For additional ideas and a tour of my own pantry, head to ShelfCooking.com/organizedpantry.

CATEGORIZE AND LABEL

Containers are great, but they won't do you any good if no one knows what's in them or where anything goes! Give each container a label, so you know where everything goes. With wire and plastic baskets, sticky labels just don't stick. I opted for some gift tags that attached with a cute little string.

chop, dice, stir, and mix

FOOD PREP & COOKING

FOOD PREP & COOKING

Whether you're an established cook or beginner in the kitchen, follow these tips to practice your skills while saving time and money.

PANTRY STAPLES

Every good shelf cooker has an arsenal of pantry staples on hand at all times.

PAGE 52

FRUITS & VEGGIES

Save money by properly choosing and storing the tastiest, juiciest, and freshest produce.

PAGE 60

FOOD HACKS

Do you know how to tell if your eggs are fresh, or when to use dental floss? This is the section for you.

PAGE 72

SUBSTITUTIONS & CONVERSIONS

Learn what you can use as a substitution in a pinch and how to convert a recipe.

PAGE 80

some things you will need

ESSENTIALS IN EVERY KITCHEN

One thing you might not know about me is that I'm a self-proclaimed Maximalist. Yes, that is a term I made up (so, stick with me here, ha!) to describe the fact that I am about as opposite of a minimalist as one can be! I love having options. I love trying new things. I love having everything I need on hand. Yes, sometimes it can be a problem. But mostly, it's just FUN.

When it comes to the kitchen, however, I have a few essentials that I reach for EVERY. SINGLE. TIME. It's amazing how few items you need to produce amazing meals for your family! Here's a list of kitchen essentials that will provide endless cooking opportunities:

LESS IS MORE IN A KITCHEN

You don't need a "Master Chef" kitchen to make fabulous meals. Just a few key tools in the kitchen will help you do everything you need!

THE ESSENTIALS

KNIVES/CUTTING
- Paring knife
- Chef's knife
- Cutting board
- Long, serrated knife

POTS AND PANS
- 2-Quart saucepan with lid
- 9-Quart stockpot with lid
- 10-Inch frying pan with lid

BOWLS AND TOOLS
- Set of mixing bowls
- Can opener
- Wooden spoons
- Set of silicone spatulas
- Colander
- Tongs
- Peeler

STORAGE & HOUSEHOLD
- Aluminum foil
- Storage baggies
- Plastic wrap

APPLIANCES
- Hand mixer or stand mixer
- Slow cooker or Instant Pot
- Blender or food processor
- Air Fryer

BAKING
- 9X13 pan
- Bread pan
- Cookie sheet/sheet pan
- Round pie pan
- Rolling pin
- Set of baking dishes
- Disposable baking pans (for freezer meals!)

MEASURING CUPS & SPOONS
- 4-6 cup glass measuring cup for liquid
- Set of measuring cups for dry ingredients
- Set of measuring spoons

NICE TO HAVE ITEMS
- Silicone baking mat
- Food thermometer
- Tiny spatula
- Potato masher
- Cooling rack

PANTRY STAPLES

CANNED GOODS
- Applesauce
- Beef broth base
- Black beans
- Chicken broth base
- Chiles
- Cooked chicken
- Corn
- Cream of chicken soup
- Cream of mushroom soup
- Evaporated milk
- Green beans: cut, French style
- Kidney beans
- Mandarin oranges
- Marinara sauce (for a base for scratch sauce)
- Olives: black, green
- Peaches
- Pineapple (I prefer chunks)
- Pinto beans
- Salsa
- Sweetened condensed milk
- Tomato paste
- Tomato sauce
- Tomato soup
- Tomatoes: whole, stewed, diced, crushed
- Tuna

BAKING GOODS
Store many of these in the freezer to keep them fresh longer.
- All-purpose flour
- Baking powder
- Baking soda
- Bouillon cubes/base: chicken, beef
- Brown sugar
- Chocolate: chips or bar
- Cocoa powder
- Cornstarch
- Granulated sugar
- Honey
- Nuts
- Peanut butter
- Powdered sugar
- Shelf-stable milk
- Vanilla
- Yeast

SNACK ITEMS
- Graham crackers
- Popcorn
- Potato chips
- Pretzels
- Tortillas
- Ritz crackers

PANTRY STAPLES

HERBS AND SPICES

- Basil
- Bay leaves
- Cayenne pepper
- Chili powder
- Cinnamon
- Crushed red pepper flakes
- Cumin
- Garlic powder
- Italian seasoning
- Lemon pepper
- Onion powder
- Oregano
- Paprika
- Parsley (dried)
- Pepper
- Rosemary
- Salt
- Seasoning salt
- Taco seasoning
- Thyme

RICE AND GRAINS

- Brown rice
- Bread crumbs
- Cornmeal
- Egg noodles
- Lasagna noodles
- Long-grain white rice
- Oats
- Pasta (penne, bowtie, spaghetti, macaroni, etc)
- Polenta
- Quinoa

DRY GOODS AND MIXES

- Bisquick
- Cereals
- Dry beans/lentils
- Italian dressing mix (great for slow cooker meals)
- Onion soup mix
- Pancake/waffle mix
- Vegetable soup/dip mix

OILS, SAUCES, VINEGARS, AND CONDIMENTS

- Balsamic vinegar
- BBQ sauce
- Coconut oil
- Ketchup
- Lemon juice
- Mayonnaise/Miracle Whip
- Mustard: yellow, Dijon
- Non-stick cooking spray
- Olive oil
- Red wine vinegar
- Rice vinegar
- Soy sauce
- Vegetable oil
- White vinegar
- White wine vinegar
- Worcestershire sauce

Savings Tip!

For your bulk staples, avoid the famous brands. They can cost you up to twice as much because you're paying for the advertising. And your family won't know the difference anyway!

LOVE YOURSELF SOME VEGGIES

how to prep and cook 'em

Vegetables—some people love 'em, and some people would rather have a spinal tap than sink their teeth into a noble Brussels sprout. (Okay, okay ... I'll admit they're not my favorite.) But I'm convinced that many who turn their noses up at veggies do it because they've never had veggies cooked the way they should be!

There's not much worse than a soggy, mushy, pile 'o green on your plate. So I'm throwing down the gauntlet. Take a look at the way you've been cooking veggies, and use the tips and tricks in this chart to turn out some lip-smacking plant parts your family will crave!

Notice that you don't need much water to cook veggies, and you should cook them only until they're crisp-tender (unless you're making mashed potatoes).

VEGGIE	GET IT READY	SAUTÉ	ROAST	STEAM (IN MICROWAVE)
ASPARAGUS	Wash. Break off woody ends. In the right spot, the spear will easily snap.	Melt butter in large pan over medium heat. Add asparagus & cook 3-4 min. or until tender. Add seasonings, cook 1-2 min., stirring constantly.	Preheat oven to 425°F. Toss asparagus with olive oil on baking sheet. Arrange in single layer. Bake in preheated oven until tender, 12-15 min.	Put in dish with 2 T. water. Cover. Cook at 100% power 3–5 min., rearranging once during cooking.
BEANS (FRESH)	Wash. Snap off ends & remove strings. Leave whole or cut into pieces. For French style, cut lengthwise.	Heat olive oil in skillet over medium heat. Cook, stir green beans & seasoning together until desired tenderness, 5-10 min.	Preheat oven to 400°F. Toss green beans with olive oil & seasonings on baking sheet. Spread in single layer. Roast until beans are slightly shriveled, 20-25 min.	Put in dish with 2 T. water. Cover. Cook whole or cut beans at 100% power for 8–12 min., French style for 7-10 min.
BROCCOLI	Wash. Remove outer leaves, trim tough stalks. Cut into florets or lengthwise into spears.	Heat olive oil in large skillet over medium heat. Add broccoli florets & sauté 5 min., stirring occasionally. Stir in seasonings. Cover, cook for 2-3 min., until crisp, tender, & bright green.	Preheat oven to 425°F. Toss broccoli on baking sheet with olive oil until lightly coated. Arrange in even layer across pan, season & bake for 18-22 min., tossing halfway, until florets have golden edges.	Put in a dish with 2 T. water. Cover. Cook at 100% power 5–8 min., stirring once during cooking.
CABBAGE	Tear off wilted outer leaves. Wash. Cut into wedges.	Melt butter in large skillet over medium-high heat. Add cabbage, seasonings, & saute for 10-15 min., stirring occasionally, until cabbage is tender & begins to brown. Season to taste & serve warm.	Preheat oven to 425°F. Brush both sides of cabbage with olive oil. Sprinkle seasoning & arrange on baking sheet. Roast for 15 min. Flip & continue roasting until golden, about 15 min.	Put in a dish with 2 T. water. Cover. Cook at 100% power 5–8 min., stirring once during cooking.

VEGGIE	GET IT READY	SAUTÉ	ROAST	STEAM (IN MICROWAVE)
CARROTS	Wash, trim, & peel or scrub well. Cut into slices or sticks.	Place sliced carrots, 1/3 cup water, & seasoning in large skillet. Bring to boil. Cover & cook over medium-low heat for 7–8 min., until just cooked. Add butter, sauté one minute until water evaporates & butter coats carrots.	Preheat oven to 400°F. Slice carrots diagonally in 1½-inch thick slices. Toss with olive oil & seasoning. Place in single layer on sheet pan & roast in oven for 20 min., until browned & tender.	Put in dish with 2 T. water. Cover & cook at 100% power 5–8 min. Stir once during cooking: 6–9 min. for slices, 5–7 min. for sticks.
CARROTS BABY (PACKAGED)	Wash and trim, if necessary.	Heat 1 T. butter with water in large skillet over medium heat. Add carrots, cover, & cook until softened, about 10 min. Remove cover & cook, stirring often for 5-10 min., until golden.	Preheat oven to 425°F. Toss carrots with olive oil & seasoning on baking sheet. Bake for 20-25 min., until carrots are fork tender. Flip halfway through.	Put in dish with 2 T. water. Cover & cook at 100% power 7–9 min. Stir once during cooking.
CAULIFLOWER	Wash. Remove outer leaves. Trim tough stalks. Cut into florets.	Cook in boiling water until tender; drain. Heat oil in large skillet over medium heat, add cauliflower. Cover skillet, cook, & stir occasionally until tender, 4-5 min. Increase heat & sauté until browned, 1-2 min.	Preheat oven to 450°F. Toss cauliflower with olive oil & seasoning on baking sheet. Roast until golden & tender, about 20 min.	Put in dish with 2 T. water. Cover & cook at 100% power 7–9 min. Stir once during cooking.
CORN	Cut kernels from cob, if using fresh. Can also used canned or frozen.	Melt butter in large skillet over medium heat. Add corn, salt, & pepper. Cook for 12-15 min. Stir frequently until corn is tender.	Preheat oven to 400°F. Pour corn onto baking sheet in single layer. Roast for 20-30 min. until golden & crunchy. Stir 1–2 times while roasting. For crunchier corn, turn oven off & leave pan of corn in oven for 15 more min.	Put in dish with 2 T. water. Cover & cook at 100% power 5–8 min. Stir once during cooking.
CORN (ON THE COB)	Remove husks. Scrub with stiff brush to remove silk and rinse.	Melt butter in large skillet over medium to medium-high heat. Add corn & cook, turning every few min., until golden brown, about 6 min.	Preheat oven to 350°F. Place corn husks directly on the oven rack & roast for 30 min. or until corn is soft.	Put in a dish with 2 T. water. Cover & cook at 100% power, rearranging once during cooking. 3–5 min. for 1 ear, 5–7 min. for 2 ears, 9–12 min. for 4 ears.
LEEKS	Wash well. Remove tough outer leaves & trim roots from base. Slit lengthwise & wash again to remove sand. Slice.	Heat olive oil & butter in large skillet over medium-high heat. Add leeks & coat with oil & butter. Add seasonings. Reduce heat to medium, stir frequently & cook until caramelized, about 20-25 min.	Preheat oven to 400°F with pan inside. Toss leeks with olive oil & seasoning. Arrange cut side down on hot baking sheet & cover loosely with foil. Reduce oven temperature to 300°F. Bake until leeks are lightly browned on cut sides & tender, about 90 min.	Put in a dish with 2 T. water. Cover & cook at 100% power 4–6 min. Stir once during cooking.

VEGGIE	GET IT READY	SAUTÉ	ROAST	STEAM (IN MICROWAVE)
MUSHROOMS 	Wipe with a damp towel or paper towel to remove all soil. Slice or leave whole.	Heat olive oil & butter in large skillet over medium heat. Cook & stir with seasonings until lightly browned, about 5 min. Reduce heat to low & simmer until tender, 5-8 more min.	Preheat oven to 425°F. Coat a sheet pan with cooking spray. Arrange the mushrooms in single layer on pan. Toss with butter & seasonings. Bake for 15-20 min. until mushrooms are tender. Stir once halfway through cook time.	Place thick-sliced mushrooms in microwave-safe bowl. Cover & cook at 100% power 2–3 min. Stir once during cooking.
ONIONS 	Pull off loose papers. Dice or cut into rings or strips.	Melt butter in skillet over medium-high heat. Add onions. Sauté 8 min. until golden brown. Stir frequently. Stir in seasonings; sauté 2 more min.	Preheat oven to 450°F. Toss onions with oil on foil-lined baking sheet; season. Roast until onions are tender, 25-30 min, Stir 2-3 times & rotate baking sheet halfway through.	Peel & cut slice from root to create flat bottom. Cut 1-inch deep recess on top, fill with 2 T. butter. Season with salt & pepper. Place onion in microwave-safe container, cover, & cook at 100% power until tender, about 6–8 min.
PARSNIPS	Wash, trim, & peel or scrub well. Cut into slices.	Heat oil in large skillet over medium heat. Add parsnips & seasonings. Sauté on medium to low heat until tender & transparent. Add oil as needed. When parsnips begin to look done, add butter. Sauté until slightly browned.	Preheat oven to 400°F. Peel parsnips & cut into 1-inch chunks. Toss with oil, seasoning & spread on large baking sheet in single layer. Roast, turning parsnips over 1-2 times, until parsnips are tender in center and browned on the outside, 25-35 min.	Cut parsnips into large chunks. Place in microwave-safe container with 2 T. water. Cover with lid or plastic wrap with steam holes. Cook at 100% power until tender, about 4–6 min.
PEA PODS, SNOW OR SUGAR SNAP	Wash and remove tips & strings.	Heat olive oil in large skillet over medium-high heat. Add peas & seasonings. Sauté, tossing occasionally for 3-5 min., until peas are crisp tender.	Preheat oven to 450°F. On baking sheet, toss peas with oil & seasoning. Bake for 10-12 min. or until desired tenderness.	In microwave-safe dish, combine peas with 1 T. water. Cover & cook high at 100% power 6–10 min. Stir once half-way through cooking.
PEPPERS, BELL 	Wash, remove seeds, stems, & membranes. Cut into rings or strips.	Heat oil & butter in hot saucepan over medium heat. Combine peppers, seasonings, & sauté for 2 min. Reduce heat to medium-low & continue cooking. Stir occasionally, until peppers soften.	Preheat oven to 450°F. Place cut & seeded bell peppers on prepared baking sheet. Drizzle with olive oil & coat well. Sprinkle bell peppers with seasonings & roast until tender & charred about 20 min.	Cut peppers into strips, place in microwave-safe container with 2 T. water. Cover & cook at 100% power 2 min. per cup of peppers or until crisp-tender. Stir during cooking.
POTATOES	Wash, peel, remove eyes, sprouts, & green areas & cut into quarters or cubes.	Heat butter & olive oil in large skillet over medium heat. Arrange potato slices in single layer. Cook without stirring for 5 min., or until have begun to brown on bottom. Sprinkle with seasoning, flip the potatoes, & cook 5 min. until tender.	Preheat oven to 400°F. Cut potatoes in half or quarters & place in bowl with olive oil & seasoning; toss until potatoes are well coated. Transfer to sheet pan & spread out into one layer. Roast for 45-60 min. or until browned & crisp, flipping twice.	Place potato quarters in microwave-safe dish. Add water & cover. Microwave at 100% power 8–10 min. or until tender. Drain.

VEGGIE	GET IT READY	SAUTÉ	ROAST	STEAM (IN MICROWAVE)
SPINACH	Wash, drain, remove stems & any pieces that look withered or spoiled, then tear into pieces.	Heat olive oil in large skillet on medium high heat. Add spinach to pan & coat with olive oil & seasonings. Cover pan, cook for 1 min., uncover & turn spinach over again. Cover pan & cook for another min.	Preheat oven to 425°F. Toss together spinach, olive oil on baking sheet. Roast until wilted, about 2 min. Season with salt & pepper.	Place spinach & water in microwave-safe bowl. Cover & cook at 100% power until vegetable starts to wilt, about 30 sec. to 2 min.
SQUASH: ACORN	Wash, cut in half lengthwise, remove seeds.	Melt butter in large skillet over medium heat. When hot, add squash cubes in single layer & cook without stirring for 5 min. Stir to turn cubes, cook another 5 min., sprinkle on brown sugar (optional), stir to mix well, & cook 5 more min. or until squash is tender.	Preheat oven to 375°F. Place 1-inch acorn squash slices on baking sheet in single layer, then brush both sides with butter. Roast squash for 25 min. on first side, then flip each slice over & bake for another 15-20 min., until soft.	Lay squash halves cut-side down on microwave-safe dish. Cover & cook at 100% power for 10 min., or until softened & fork-tender.
SQUASH: BANANA, BUTTERNUT, OR HUBBARD	Wash, cut in half lengthwise, remove seeds.	Melt butter in large skillet over medium-high heat. Add squash & salt. Cook, stirring occasionally, until squash is tender & lightly browned, about 15 min.	Preheat oven to 400°F. Toss butternut squash with olive oil & seasoning. Arrange on baking sheet. Roast until tender & lightly browned, 25-30 min.	Lay squash halves cut-side down on microwave-safe dish. Cover & cook at 100% power for 10–12 min., or until softened & fork-tender.
SQUASH: PATTYPAN, YELLOW OR ZUCCHINI	Wash, cut off ends, slice. Do not peel.	In large skillet over medium-low heat, heat olive oil. Add squash & seasoning. Increase heat to medium. Cook, stirring occasionally, until just cooked through & beginning to brown, about 10-15 min.	Preheat oven to 400°F. Spray cooling rack with nonstick spray & place on rimmed baking sheet. Toss squash with oil, seasoning, then arrange squash on top of cooling rack on prepared baking sheet. Do not overlap spears. Bake until tender, about 12-15 min.	Cut squash in half (the long way). Place squash halves cut-side down on a microwave-safe dish. Cover with plastic wrap. Cook at 100% on high for 5 min., or until tender.
SQUASH: SPAGHETTI	Wash, cut in half lengthwise, remove seeds.	Melt butter in large skillet over medium heat. Add baked or roasted squash to skillet & cook until hot. Season with salt & pepper.	Preheat oven to 350°F. Cut squash in half lengthwise, scoop out seeds with spoon. Place on baking sheet, cut side up & sprinkle with salt & pepper. Bake at 350° for 1 hour until tender. Cool 5 min., then gently run fork in squash to separate into strands.	Cut squash in half (long way). Place squash halves cut-side down on microwave-safe dish. Add about 1-inch of water. Cook at 100% power 20 min. until you can shred the flesh with fork.
SWEET POTATOES	Wash, peel, cut off ends and woody pieces. Cut into cubes or quarters.	Heat oil in large skillet over medium heat. Cut into cubes. Cook, stirring, until starts to soften, 8-10 min. Add seasonings. Cook, stirring, until water evaporates & potatoes are tender, about 10 min.	Preheat oven to 425°F. Add peeled & cubed sweet potatoes. Toss with olive oil & seasonings, spread out in even layer on pan. Bake for 25-30 min., flipping potatoes every 10 min.	Place potato on microwave-safe plate. Cook at 100% power 5 min., turning halfway through. If potato isn't fork-tender at 5 min., microwave in 30 sec. increments.

how to tell when

VEGGIES ARE RIPE

ARTICHOKES

Heavy for size, tight leaves, that squeak when rubbed against each other

ASPARAGUS

Bright color, tight heads, firm, smooth stalks of even thickness

AVOCADOS

Pale yellow or green under the stem (it looks like a little belly button; pick it off to check the color underneath) If very firm and light green ready to eat in 5 days

BEETS

Deep color, firm, fresh tops, avoid scaly tops, wilted leaves, or hairy roots (indicates woody flesh)

BELL PEPPERS

Heavy for size, firm, shiny, uniform, bright color

BROCCOLI

Bright-green color, tight florets, firm stems

BRUSSELS SPROUTS

Bright-green heads, compact leaves

CABBAGE

Heavy for size, firm, compact

CARROTS

Firm, smooth, evenly colored, avoid hairy growths

CAULIFLOWER

Creamy white color, tightly packed heads; avoid spotted, yellowed, or flowering florets

CELERY

Green leaves and stalks, firm, unblemished

CHIVES

Firm, dry, rich in color

CORN

Bright-green husks, moist (but not slimy) silk, plump (but not dry) kernels

CUCUMBERS

Uniform darker green in color, firm, no soft or mushy spots

EGGPLANTS

Heavy for size, smooth, shiny, give slightly to the touch (smaller eggplant is less bitter)

GARLIC

Firm, plump, dry; avoid green sprouts

GREEN BEANS

Slender (no bulging), firm, snap but do not bend

GREEN ONION

Firm white bulbs, crisp green tops

KALE

Deep-green leaves, crisp (smaller leaves are more tender)

LEEKS

Slender, firm, tightly rolled tops

LETTUCE

Uniform green color, fresh, crisp leaves

LEAFY GREENS

Uniform green color, fresh, crisp leaves

MUSHROOMS

Fresh, plump, firm, avoid mushrooms that are slimy or spotted

ONIONS

Ivory color, firm, small to medium size (larger ones tend to be woody)

PARSNIPS

Firm, dry, pointy tips, free from blemishes

PEAS

Ripe green color, plump, peas feel full and don't rattle; avoid peas that look dry

PEPPERS

Vivid color, heavy for their size, and firm

POTATOES

Smooth skin, firm, avoid potatoes with sprouts, green discoloration/ spots, soft spots, bruises

RADISHES

Bright-red color, fresh green tops, firm roots without blemish

RHUBARB

Pink or red stalks (no green), firm

SUMMER SQUASH

Taut, shiny, unblemished skin

SWEET POTATOES

Firm, unwrinkled skin, avoid those with cuts or bruises

TOMATILLOS

Green flesh (no yellow), green husks (no brown)

TOMATOES

Heavy for size, firm skin, light give to the touch, fragrant, earthy smell at stem end

TURNIPS

Choose small, young turnips, heavy for their size, firm, without any nicks or cuts. If greens are attached, they should be brightly colored

WINTER SQUASH

Heavy for size, intact stem, no cuts or soft spots

how to tell when

FRUIT IS RIPE

APPLES

Firm, deep color, heavy for its size, naturally shiny

APRICOTS

Soft but not mushy, fragrant

BANANAS

Green if you'll eat it in a few days, bright yellow if you'll eat it right away; avoid those with splits, bruises, or spots

BLUEBERRIES

Firm, dry, and intact; deep blue color with a faint white sheen; avoid berries that are red or green

CANTALOUPE

Cream/light gold in color; the end opposite stem should be slightly soft; melon should have a sweet, aromatic scent; heavy for its size; avoid ones that are green, bruised, cracked, or wet

CHERRIES

Dark in color, firm, shiny, and plump with intact stems

CRANBERRIES

Dark red color; avoid fruit that is soft, bruised, or shriveled

FIGS

Plump and soft with intact, bent stem; avoid cracked or dry fruit

GRAPEFRUIT

Heavy for its size; nicely rounded; firm but slight give to the touch; smooth, thin skin; fully colored

GRAPES

Firmly attached to stems; firm, plump, and heavy for their size; avoid grapes with brown spots, soft spots, bruises, wrinkles, or mold

HONEYDEW MELON

Heavy for its size; smooth, uniformly colored skin; melon should have sweet, aromatic scent; avoid dented, cracked, bruised, or wet melons

KIWI

Slight give when squeezed; shouldn't be mushy or hard; avoid kiwifruit that is bruised, wrinkled, or has soft spots

LEMONS

Heavy for size, smooth, well-shaped, and fragrant; evenly colored

LIMES

Heavy for size, smooth, well-shaped, and fragrant; evenly colored

MANGOES

Fully colored, slightly soft but still quite firm to the touch, fragrant at the stem end

ORANGES

Heavy for size with firm, smooth skin (color isn't important; a slight green tint or brown specks do not affect taste or quality)

PAPAYA

Smooth skin that is at least half yellow, slightly soft when squeezed

PEACHES, NECTARINES

Deep color, fragrant, slightly soft to the touch but firm; avoid those with green color

PEARS

Pears need to ripen on the counter; "check the neck" for ripeness by giving the area around the stem a gentle squeeze

PINEAPPLE

Heavy for size, plump, uniform size and color all the way to the top, deep-green leaves that pull out easily, sweet aroma at stem (smells pineapple-esque!); avoid soft spots, brown/dry leaves

PLUMS

Firm but not hard, plump, shiny, deep color with a white or gray sheen

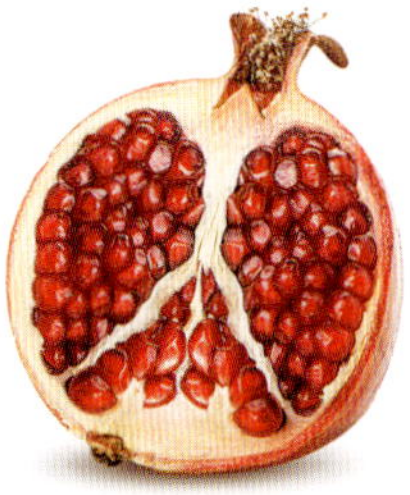

POMEGRANATES

Heavy for size, cracks in skin (indicates plump seeds); avoid those with mold in the cracks

STRAWBERRIES

Uniformly red (no green or yellow), shiny, fresh green tops, fragrant

WATERMELON

Heavy for size, firm, smooth rind, sounds hollow when thumped, a flattened yellow area on one side where it ripened on ground

Savings Tip!

If you have berries that are getting pretty ripe, blend them and pour into ice cube trays for smoothies or a sweet treat later.

KEEP IT FRESH LONGER

How to Store Food

	HOW TO STORE IT
APPLES	Store whole apples in a cool, dry place like your refrigerator's crisper drawer, preferably in individual bags. If you're planning to eat them soon, apples will keep just fine on your counter for 2-3 days. Sliced apples should be placed in an air-tight container in the fridge for up to 3 days. Sprinkle some orange or lemon juice on your sliced apples to help slow the browning process.
ASPARAGUS	Trim ends; store in the fridge upright, cut-end down, in a jar containing a few inches of water; The stalks will stay fresh for 2 weeks; trim ends again before cooking.
BANANAS 	Prolong their life by breaking up the bunch and wrapping individual bananas in plastic wrap. Or wrap the top of the banana cluster with plastic wrap to extend the life of the fruit by four or five days. Peel overripe bananas, put in a freezer bag, and freeze. (Keeping bananas in the fridge makes the peel go brown but actually slows ripening of the fruit.)
BREAD	Wrap in plastic or aluminum foil. These types of wrappings will trap in the bread's natural moisture to keep it from drying out and getting hard. To maintain freshness of soft-crust loaves, store in airtight plastic bags or wrap tightly in plastic wrap or foil and store at room temperature for no more than two days. Freeze extra bread. Don't put bread in the refrigerator.
BROWN SUGAR	Brown sugar should be stored in a cool, moist area in a rustproof container with a tight-fitting lid. It can also be stored in any type of resealable, moisture-proof plastic bag. If your brown sugar keeps getting dry, try throwing in a couple of marshmallows or a slice of bread; the brown sugar will absorb the moisture. The quality of brown sugar is best when consumed within six months of purchase and opening.
CANTALOUPE	Store whole melon in the fridge for as long as 4 days; tightly cover cut melon or keep it in an airtight container for as long as 2 days.
CARROTS 	Trim off the green ends before putting them in the fridge, but don't peel them. Submerge carrot sticks or baby carrots in a tightly covered container of water in the fridge.

	HOW TO STORE IT
CELERY	Keep the bunch tightly wrapped in foil in the fridge. Submerge celery sticks in a tightly covered container of water in the fridge.
CHEESE	Keep it tightly wrapped in the fridge. Shred it before you freeze it or it will get crumbly when thawed. Avoid touching the cheese with your fingers; the oils on your hands will cause it to grow mold faster.
CILANTRO	Cut the cilantro stems and place stem-down in a jar with a few inches of water, almost like cut flowers. Cover the leaves loosely in an upside-down plastic bag (unsealed). Store in refrigerator for up to two weeks. Change the water if it becomes discolored.
CRANBERRIES	Refrigerate as long as 4 weeks in an airtight container or wrap.
FRUIT	If fruit goes soft before you can use it, freeze it. Wash it well, cut off stems, and freeze whole, sliced, or chopped in freezer bags.
GARLIC 	Store at room temperature with good ventilation. Don't remove the papery husk until you're ready to use the clove.
GRAPES	Keep in the fridge for as long as 1 week in a covered container.
LEMONS/LIMES 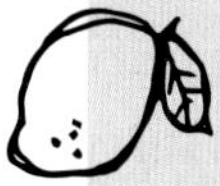	Can be refrigerated for 2 weeks.
LETTUCE	Wash thoroughly with water, dry the leaves, and store them in the fridge in a clean plastic bag with a few paper towels to absorb any remaining moisture.
MANGOES	Ripen at room temperature in a brown paper bag; refrigerate ripe fruit for as long as 5 days.

	HOW TO STORE IT
MUSHROOMS	Store unwashed in a paper bag or damp cloth bag in the fridge for 2 days.
ONIONS 	Store at room temperature with good ventilation. A great hack that's sure to turn heads, store onions in the legs of clean pantyhose; tie a knot between each onion and hang the whole contraption.
ORANGES	Keep in the fridge for as long as 2 weeks.
PEACHES	Ripen at room temperature in a brown paper bag; refrigerate ripened fruit for 2 to 4 days.
PEARS 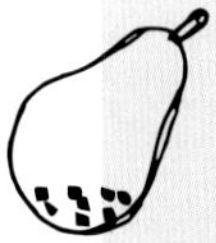	Ripen at room temperature in a brown paper bag; refrigerate ripened fruit as long as 2 to 3 days.
PEAS	Tightly wrap and store in the fridge for 3 days.
PEPPERS, SWEET OR HOT	Store in a covered container in the fridge for 5 days.
PINEAPPLE	Cut off leaves; store upside down at room temperature or store in the fridge in an airtight container for 2 days.
PLUMS	Ripen at room temperature in a brown paper bag; refrigerate ripened fruit as long as 2 to 3 days.
POTATOES	Store in a paper—not plastic—bag in a dark, cool, well-ventilated place. Do not refrigerate. To prevent buds and sprouts, put an apple in the bag with the potatoes.

	HOW TO STORE IT
TOMATOES 	Store at room temperature until fully ripened. Then store on a plate in the fridge. Bring them to room temperature before serving them. Do not wash until you're ready to use or serve them.
VEGETABLES	Don't store them in the same crisper drawer as fruits. The fruits produce gas that acts as a ripening hormone, causing veggies to spoil sooner. Store in a mesh bag or poke holes in a plastic bag to provide ventilation. Most vegetables can be refrigerated as long as 2 weeks.
WATERMELON	Store whole melon in fridge as long as 4 days. Tightly wrap cut melon and refrigerate as long as 3 days.

FOOD HACKS

Fun food tricks that will save you time and effort

	COOL TRICKS
AVOCADO 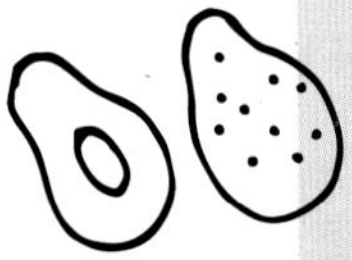	Toss sliced or cut avocado with lemon or lime juice to keep it from turning brown as quickly. To get a green avocado to ripen quickly, keep in a closed paper sack on your counter; it will ripen in 1-3 days. You can also ripen it more quickly by putting it in a bowl with bananas; the gas from the bananas will ripen the avocados.
BOILING WATER	Add salt to your water to get it to boil faster.
CAKE MIX	Use milk instead of water to make your cake taste homemade; use buttermilk to make it even richer and creamier. For a rich, moist cake, add an extra egg and stir in a dollop of mayo.
COTTAGE CHEESE	Flip the container upside down in the fridge to create an airtight seal against the lid, which makes it last longer! Blend to substitute for ricotta.
DENTAL FLOSS (no, not to eat)	Use unscented, unflavored dental floss to cut soft foods like quick breads, cake rolls, cinnamon roll dough, and soft cheese.
EGGS 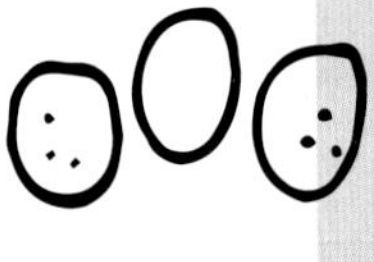	To tell if your eggs are still fresh, fill a glass bowl with water and put the egg gently in the water. If it floats, it's too old to use; toss it out. If it sinks to the bottom and stands on its end, it's perfect for hard-boiling. If it sinks to the bottom and lays on its side, it's very fresh (great to scramble, fry, or use in recipes).

	COOL TRICKS
GRATER	Don't eat this. Spray your grater with nonstick spray before using it to make clean-up a cinch!
GRAVY	To fix lumpy gravy, pour it through a strainer or toss it in the blender. To fix watery gravy, combine equal parts flour or cornstarch and water, mix into a slurry, and whisk into gravy, whisking until gravy thickens.
HAMBURGERS 	Put a thumbprint in the middle of your patty; it will stay flat while it cooks instead of curling up at the edges.
HASH-BROWN POTATOES	Get them perfectly crisp by cooking them in a waffle iron sprayed with nonstick cooking spray.
HERBS	Make herb butter by chopping up herbs, mixing with softened or melted butter. Place in an ice cube tray, and freeze.
ICE CREAM	Store the ice cream carton upside-down in a sealed gallon zip-top bag to keep it fresh longer.
KIWI FRUIT	Make a fast job of peeling by running a spoon between the hairy skin and the fruit.
LEMONADE	To avoid watering down lemonade, put lemon slices in a muffin tin, fill with water, freeze, and use to cool your drinks.
LEMONS AND LIMES 	To get the most juice, roll it on the counter firmly with the palm of your hand; cut and squeeze; use a fork to pop any remaining pieces of pulp. A pair of sturdy tongs will also help you get every last drop.

	COOL TRICKS
MARSHMALLOWS	Store unopened in the freezer or in an airtight freezer bag.
MASHED POTATOES	Sprinkle a few pinches of baking powder on top of potatoes before you mash them. The baking powder will act as a leavening agent to increase fluffiness.
MUSHROOMS	Mushrooms are like sponges. Avoid washing sliced mushrooms so they don't absorb all the water.
PANCAKES 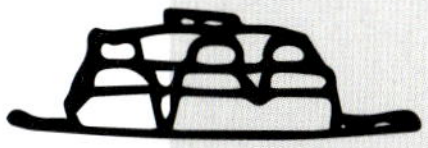	Squeeze pancake batter from an empty ketchup bottle to keep it from slopping all over. Squeeze batter into cookie cutters for creative shapes.
PB&J SANDWICHES	Build a little "moat" of peanut butter around the edges to keep jelly from dripping out.
SANDWICHES 	With butter, jelly, mayonnaise, and other spreads, be sure to coat the bread crust-to-crust for maximum flavor. Cut your sandwiches on the diagonal for a nice presentation and easier eating experience.
SOUR CREAM	Flip the containers upside down in the fridge to create an airtight seal against the lid, which makes them last longer!
WINE	Leftover red and white wines can be frozen to use in cooking later. No need to thaw before using, as it will thaw almost as soon as it hits the hot pan.

Savings Tip!

If you have salsa that's too watery, drain out some liquid into a dish, then use the liquid to cook rice. Easy Latin-inspired rice!

SEASON IT WITH WHAT?

tips & tricks on how to add herbs & spices

There are dozens and dozens and dozens of spices—but many don't regularly show up in most home-cooked dishes, and too few people know about them. If you're a bit of a spice novice, here's a quick guide to what they are, how they taste, and what they're usually used for. Unless otherwise noted, I'm describing ground spices.

	HOW IT TASTES	WHAT IT'S USED FOR
ALLSPICE 	A mixture of cinnamon, cloves, and nutmeg	Common in baked goods; also used in stews and to season jerky
ANISE SEEDS 	Tastes like black licorice	Used with meat, in cabbage dishes, in some fruit desserts, gelatins, dairy products, and candies
BASIL 	Fresh basil is bold, often sweet, sometimes a bit peppery with a hint of anise	Gives a distinctive taste to Italian-inspired sauces, pestos, pasta dishes, salads, and pizza. Varities also found in Thai, Indonesian, and Vietnamese cuisine
BAY LEAF 	Can develop a minty pine flavor with hints of black pepper	Adds a subtle bitterness to make heavy soups, chilis, and stews more balanced and tasty
CARDAMOM 	A blend of sweet (like ginger) and spicy (like pepper)	Most commonly used in baked goods; also used in bean and curry dishes
CAYENNE PEPPER 	Hot, smoky, and pungent	Commonly used in barbecue rubs and sauces; also used in meat, cheese, bean, and egg dishes to add a kick of heat

	HOW IT TASTES	WHAT IT'S USED FOR
CHILI POWDER 	Hot, spicy, and peppery	Commonly used in chili and other soups and stews; also used in meat dishes and marinades
CHIVES 	Mild onion flavor, with a hint of garlic	Often (but not always) a garnish with omelettes, potato dishes, casseroles, and soups; also complements fish and most vegetables
CILANTRO 	Refreshing, citrusy, and tart with a mild spicy flavor similar to parsley	Cilantro adds flavor to salads, salsa, pesto, sauces, dips, and dressings. Heat weakens its flavor, so it's often used raw
CORIANDER 	Earthy, tart, and sweet	Best when toasted, ground, and used in curry, spice rub, marinade, chili, sauces, and soups. Found in Spanish, Mexican, Latin, and Indian cuisines
CLOVES 	Strong and pungent	Commonly used in barbecue dishes, chili, baked beans, cakes, fruit desserts, and seasonal drinks (such as cider or wassail)
CUMIN 	Spicy, pungent, and slightly bitter	Used in Mexican and Indian dishes
CURRY 	A blend of many ground spices; can range from mild to hot	Commonly used in Indian and Asian dishes; also used in sauces, stews, and meats

	HOW IT TASTES	WHAT IT'S USED FOR
GARLIC POWDER 	Sweeter and less assertive than fresh garlic	Increases flavor in meat and veggies as well as snacks like roasted nuts and popcorn. Great for dry rubs, spice blends, and garlic bread
GINGER 	A blend of sweet and hot	Commonly used in baked goods like ginger spice cake or ginger snap cookies; also used in meat dishes, marinades, and stir-fry
ITALIAN SEASONING 	Savory, earthy, and slightly minty in flavor with a very subtle sweetness	Fragrant all-purpose seasoning used in a wide variety of dishes: pasta, dressing, spaghetti sauce, garlic butter, meatballs, fish, and chicken
MUSTARD 	Hot, spicy, tangy	Dry mustard is used in salad dressings and meat, cheese, and egg dishes. Mustard seeds flavor meat dishes, boiled vegetables, and pickles & relishes
NUTMEG 	Sweet and slightly spicy aroma	Commonly used in baked goods; also used in eggnog, custard, and sauces
ONION POWDER 	Has the main flavor notes of regular onions but without the crunch or liquid	Substitute one tablespoon of onion powder for one medium chopped onion. One tablespoon of dried minced onion equals ¼ cup minced raw onion
OREGANO 	Peppery, pungent, sharp, aromatic. Smells like pizza or tomato sauce	Oregano is commonly associated with Italian-inspired dishes like pasta and pizza. It's also common in Greek, Turkish, Filipino, and Latin American cuisines

	HOW IT TASTES	WHAT IT'S USED FOR
PAPRIKA 	Can range from sweet and mild to bitter and hot	Sweet paprika is used for meat rubs or on potato salad. Smoked paprika adds a mild smokey flavor to stews, potatoes, and dry rubs. Hot (Hungarian) paprika is perfect in goulash but adds heat to any dish
PARSLEY 	Light, fresh, clean and peppery taste with a touch of earthiness	Used in everything from soups to sauces. As a garnish, fresh parsley can be added to soups, dips, creamy potato dishes, casseroles, and more
RED PEPPER FLAKES 	Spicy, dry, earthy	Use for added heat. Sautee with onion to spice up broccoli. Add to salad dressing or infuse it in oil for a tasty homemade touch
ROSEMARY 	Woodsy and aromatic with flavors of pine, pepper, and sage	Widely used herb, popular with chicken, lamb, pork, steaks, and fish. Also goes well with many sides like potatoes and mushrooms
SAGE 	Earthy, peppery with a hint of citrus and pine	Pairs well with garlic, rosemary, and bay leaf. Stands up to heavy dishes and rich meats like pork and lamb
TARRAGON 	Bittersweet, tingly flavor of citrus or licorice	Commonly used with chicken, seafood, in marinades, dressings, and French bernaise sauce. Pairs with acidic flavors like vinegar or lemon
THYME 	Similar to oregano, earthy and herbal	Pairs well with eggs, tomatoes, cheese, omelets, poultry and stuffing

Savings Tip! If you're fortunate to live near Latin or Asian grocery stores, you can often find amazing deals on fresh herbs and dried spices.

CONVERSIONS MADE EASY

Truth: If I was on "Who Wants to Be a Millionaire" and my million-dollar question was "How many teaspoons are in a tablespoon?" you'd better believe I would need to phone a friend. Lucky for you, consider this section your phone-a-friend for recipe conversions!

You may not think you need to worry about conversions in a standard recipe—but if you're ever going to double or triple or half a recipe, think again! No one wants that deer-in-the-headlights stare when the recipe you're cutting half calls for 1 tablespoon of something. (No, I don't have a half-tablespoon measuring spoon either.) I have gathered up the best, most helpful conversions for you, so you can cook like a champ without needing to do any crafty mental math!

SPOONS & CUPS CONVERSIONS

TSP TEASPOON	TBSP TABLESPOON	OZ OUNCE (DRY)	FL OZ (LIQUID)	ML MILLILITERS	C CUP	PINT (LIQUID)	QUART (LIQUID)	GALLON (LIQUID)
3	1	0.5	1/2	15	1/16	1/32	-	-
6	2	1	1	29.5	1/8	1/16	1/32	-
12	4	2.1	2	59	1/4	1/8	1/16	-
18	6	3.1	3	89	3/8	-	-	-
24	8	4.2	4	118	1/2	1/4	1/8	1/32
36	12	6.3	6	177	3/4	-	-	-
48	16	8.3	8	237	1	1/2	1/4	1/16
96	32	16.7	16	473	2	1	1/2	1/8
-	64	33.4	32	946	4	2	1	1/4
-	256	66.8	64	1893	16	8	4	1

DRY ADD

dash	1/16 teaspoon
pinch	1/8 teaspoon
1/3 cup	5 tablespoons + 1 teaspoon

LIQUID

FL OZ FLUID OUNCE	TSP TEASPOON	TBSP TABLESPOON	C CUP	ML MILLILITERS	PT PINT	QT QUART	GAL GALLON
1/2	3	1	1/16	15	1/32	-	-
1	6	2	1/8	29.5	1/16	1/32	-
2	12	4	1/4	59	1/8	1/16	-
3	18	6	3/8	89	-	-	-
4	24	8	1/2	118	1/4	1/8	1/32
6	36	13	3/4	177	-	-	-
8	48	16	1	237	1/2	1/4	1/16
16	96	32	2	473	1	1/2	1/8
32	-	64	4	946	2	1	1/4
64	-	256	16	1893	8	4	1

DRY

OZ OUNCE	G GRAM	TSP TEASPOON	TBSP TABLESPOON	C CUP
0.5	14	3	1	1/16
1	28	6	2	1/8
2.1	57	12	4	1/4
3.1	85	18	6	3/8
4.2	113	24	8	1/2
6.3	170	36	13	3/4
8.3	227	48	16	1
16.7	454	96	32	2
33.4	907	-	64	4
66.8	1814	-	256	16

TEMPERATURE

FAHRENHEIT	CELCIUS
250°F	120°C
275°F	135°C
300°F	150°C
325°F	163°C
350°F	177°C
375°F	190°C
400°F	204°C
425°F	220°C
450°F	232°C
475°F	246°C
500°F	260°C

If using a fan (convection):
Reduce oven temperature by 25°.
To convert F to C: Subtract by 32° and divide by 1.8.
To convert C to F: Multiply by 1.8 and add 32°.

Don't have it? Improvise!

MAKING IT WORK: SUBSTITUTIONS

The key to shelf cooking is using what's in your pantry and freezer without having to make a last-minute dash to the grocery store for something you need. And the secret to doing that is to get creative with substitutions.

Don't have any sour cream? No problem—toss some cottage cheese and plain yogurt in the blender. Need some sweetened condensed milk? Make your own with white sugar, powdered milk, and water. Have a recipe that calls for tomatillos? Don't stress: use some good ol' plum tomatoes and a dash of lemon juice! And what on earth is tahini? Just reach for your jar of peanut butter.

You get the drift. There are great substitutions for almost any ingredient you can think of, and I've listed 253 ingredients you can easily find substitutes for—everything from the ordinary (like brown sugar and breadcrumbs) to the more exotic (like that blasted tahini). Keep in mind that a substitute might change the taste, moisture content, or texture of a dish. But in almost all cases, you'll get something very similar to the original. I've given tips where appropriate to help you avoid disappointment.

HOW TO USE THIS TABLE:
Ingredients you want to find a substitute for are listed in the left column; they're in alphabetical order to make it easy. The suggested substitutions—often more than one suggestion—are listed in the right column. Easy! If you don't see a measurement listed in the first column, you can swap out the same amount. In other words, if your recipe calls for 1 C. white wine, you can use 1 C. apple juice instead; you can switch out 1 T. soy sauce for 1 T. Worcestershire sauce. If there is a measurement listed, pay attention to the measurements of the substitutions. That's all there is to it! So hit those shelves!

SUBSTITUTIONS

FOOD ALLERGIES:
We've got you covered! Check the table for substitutions for everything from eggs to flour and dairy.

PHONE A FRIEND:
After consulting this list (and Google), if you still need something, consider trading ingredients with a neighbor instead of running back to the store.

WHAT ARE YOUR FAVORITE SUBSTITUTIONS?
Share (and get ideas) in our Shelf Cooking Facebook Group!
www.facebook.com/groups/shelfcookingcommunity

INGREDIENT	SUBSTITUTIONS
A	
Aioli	roasted garlic mayonnaise
Almond Extract	vanilla extract (use a little more)
Allspice (1 tsp)	½ tsp. cinnamon + ¼ tsp. ginger + ½ tsp. cloves ½ tsp. cinnamon + ½ tsp. cloves ½ tsp. cinnamon + ½ tsp. nutmeg + ¼ tsp. cloves
Apple, chopped (1 cup)	1 C. chopped pear + 1 T. lemon juice 1 C. chopped Asian pear 1 C. chopped quince
Applesauce	pumpkin puree mashed bananas sweet potato
B	
Bacon	turkey bacon smoked ham canadian bacon (less fat) pancetta smoked sausage imitation bacon bits
Baking mix (Bisquick) (3 cups)	3 C. pancake mix 3 C. biscuit mix 3 C. flour + ⅓ C. powdered milk + 1 T. baking powder + 1 tsp. salt + ½ C. shortening
Baking powder, double-acting (1 teaspoon) *rule: 1 teaspoon for every 1 cup flour in baking*	¼ tps. baking soda + 5/8 tsp. cream of tartar ⅓ tsp. baking soda + ½ tsp. cream of tartar ¼ tsp. baking soda + ½ C. buttermilk (reduce liquid in recipe by ½ C.) ¼ tsp. baking soda + ½ C. yogurt (decrease liquid in recipe by ½ C.) ¼ tsp. baking soda + ½ tsp. lemon juice or vinegar in milk to make ½ C. (decrease liquid in recipe by ½ C.) 1½ tsp. single-acting baking powder

INGREDIENT	SUBSTITUTIONS
Baking soda (1 teaspoon) *rule: ¼ teaspoon for every 1 cup flour in baking*	4 tsp. baking powder
Beans, Green	asparagus broccoli okra wax beans
Beer	1 C. chicken broth 1 C. white grape juice 1 C. apple cider or apple juice 1 C. water
Beet	1 C. carrots (sliced or grated)
Biscuit mix	3 C. flour + 1/3 C. powdered milk + 1 T. baking powder + 1 tsp. salt + ½ C. shortening 3 C. pancake mix
Blue cheese	feta cheese
Blueberries	red currants raisins huckleberries bananas (in baked goods) dates (in baked goods)
Brandy (¼ cup)	¼ C. white grape juice ¼ C. apple cider or apple juice ¼ C. water
Breadcrumbs dry (1 cup)	1 C. crushed cracker crumbs 1 C. Panko 1 C. matzo meal 1 C. crushed cornflakes 1 C. crushed croutons 1 C. ground oats 1 C. crushed potato chips 1 C. potato flakes 1 C. crushed rice cakes 1 C. Grapenuts 4 slices bread, crumbled

INGREDIENT	SUBSTITUTIONS
Brown Sugar light (1 cup packed)	1 C. white sugar + 1/4 C. molasses (decrease liquid by 1/4 C.) 1 C. white sugar 1 1/4 C. powdered sugar
Brown Sugar dark (1 cup packed)	1 C. light brown sugar + 1 T. molasses 1 C. granulated sugar + 2 T. molasses
Butter, salted *rule: don't use spreads or low-fat butter in baking*	7/8 to 1 C. hydrogenated fat (shortening) + 1/2 tsp. salt 7/8 C. lard + 1/2 tsp. salt 1 C. margarine 7/8 C. oil + 1/2 tsp. salt
Butter, unsalted (1 cup)	1 C. shortening 7/8 C. oil 7/8 C. lard
Buttermilk (sour milk) (1 cup)	1 C. milk + 1 T. vinegar (white or cider) or lemon juice (let stand 10 minutes before using) 1 C. milk + 1 1/2 to 1 3/4 tsp cream of tartar (let stand 10 min. before using) 1 C. mild-flavored soy milk + 1 T vinegar (white or cider) or lemon juice (let stand 5 min. before using) 1 C. plain or low-fat yogurt 1 C. sour cream 1 C. water + 1/4 C. buttermilk powder 2/3 C. plain yogurt + 1/3 C. milk 1 C. sour cream (in baking) 1 C. molasses (in batters that also call for baking soda)

C

INGREDIENT	SUBSTITUTIONS
Cake Flour (1 cup)	1 C. minus 2 T. all-purpose flour
Canola Oil	Corn oil Soybean oil Peanut oil Safflower oil Cooking spray (for greasing pans)
Capers	Chopped green olives Chopped dill pickles
Cardamom ground (1 teaspoon)	1/2 tsp. cinnamon + 1/2 tsp. nutmeg 1/2 tsp. cinnamon + 1/2 tsp. cloves 1 tsp. cinnamon 1 tsp. cloves 1 tsp. ground anise
Carrot	parsnip (cooked) jicama (raw) celery (raw or cooked) turnip (cooked) kohlrabi (cooked or raw) broccoli (cooked) cauliflower (cooked or raw)
Cayenne Pepper	jalapeño pepper serrano pepper cherry pepper habanero pepper
Celery	carrots bok choy jicama (raw)
Chickpeas	lima beans
Chili sauce (1 cup)	1 C. tomato sauce + 1/4 C. brown sugar + 2 T. vinegar + 1/4 tsp. cinnamon + dash of ground cloves + dash of allspice
Chives, finely chopped (2 teaspoons)	2 tsp. finely chopped green onion tops
Chocolate Chips, semisweet (1 ounce)	1 oz. sweet cooking chocolate 1 oz. unsweetened chocolate + 4 tsp. sugar 1 oz. semisweet chocolate chips + 1 T. shortening or oil
Chocolate, unsweetened (1 square or 1 ounce)	3 T. cocoa powder + 1 T. butter or margarine 3 T. carob powder + 2 T. water

INGREDIENT	SUBSTITUTIONS
Cilantro	Italian parsley + dash of lemon juice parsley + dash of lemon juice celery leaves dill basil
Cinnamon	allspice nutmeg
Cocktail Sauce (1 cup)	1 C. ketchup + 1/4 C. horseradish + 1 T. lemon juice
Cocoa powder, natural unsweetened (3 tablespoons)	1 oz. (square) chocolate (decrease fat called for in recipe by 1/2 T.) 3 T. Dutch-processed cocoa + 1/8 tsp. cream of tartar, lemon juice, or white vinegar 3 T. carob powder
Coconut (1 Tablespoon, grated, dry)	1½ T. fresh grated coconut 1 T. grated Brazil nut 1 T. grated macadamia nuts 1 T. chopped nuts
Coconut Cream, canned	1 C. heavy cream or whipping cream
Coconut milk, canned	1 C. whole milk 1 C. coconut cream (higher in highly saturated coconut oil) 1 C. milk + 1/4 tsp. coconut extract (much lower in fat) 1 C. chopped coconut + 1 C. hot water or milk; blend at high speed
Coriander Seeds	caraway seeds cumin
Cornflake Crumbs	breadcrumbs panko cornmeal crushed crackers crushed corn chips crushed pretzels

INGREDIENT	SUBSTITUTIONS
Corn syrup, light (1 cup)	1¼ C. granulated sugar + 1/3 C. liquid (use water or whatever liquid is called for in the recipe) 1 C. honey (sweeter) 1 C. molasses 3/4 C. light corn syrup + 1/4 C. molasses 1 C. maple-flavored syrup
Cornstarch (for thickening) (1 tablespoon)	2 T. all-purpose flour 2 T. granulated tapioca 4 tsp. instant tapioca 1 T. potato or rice starch 1 T. arrowroot
Cottage cheese	1 C. farmer's cheese 1 C. ricotta cheese (higher in fat) 1 C. buttermilk cheese 1 C. tofu
Couscous	rice
Cracker crumbs	dry bread crumbs ground oats matzo meal
Cranberries, dried	raisins (not as tart) dried currants dried cherries
Cream, half-and-half	1/2 C. whole milk + 1/2 C. light cream 7/8 C. milk + 1 T. butter or margarine 1 C. evaporated milk, undiluted 3 T. oil + enough milk to equal 1 C. 1/2 C. coffee creamer + 1/2 C. milk
Cream, heavy (36% to 40% fat) *rule: substitutions for heavy cream can be used in baking but will not whip*	3/4 C. milk and 1/3 C. butter or margarine 1 C. light cream 2/3 C. buttermilk plus 1/3 C. oil 1 C. evaporated skim milk 1 C. milk 1/2 C. milk + 1/2 C. cottage cheese 1 C. pureed cottage cheese 1/2 C. ricotta cheese + 1/2 C. nonfat yogurt beaten until smooth (cannot be heated) 1 C. yogurt (do not use in dishes that are heated; it will curdle)

INGREDIENT	SUBSTITUTIONS
Cream cheese	1 C. pureed cottage cheese 1 C. plain yogurt, strained overnight in a cheesecloth 1 C. Neufchâtel (lower in fat and moister) ½ C. ricotta + ½ C. yogurt ¾ C. tofu + ¼ C. margarine + 1 T. lemon juice 1 C. buttermilk cheese
Cream of tartar (1 teaspoon)	3 tsp. lemon juice 3 tsp. vinegar
Croutons	tortilla chips, crumbled oyster crackers chow mein noodles whatever nuts/seeds are in the pantry
Cumin (1 teaspoon)	½ tsp. caraway seeds 1 tsp. chili powder

D

INGREDIENT	SUBSTITUTIONS
Dates, dried	raisins dried figs fresh dates (not as sweet)
Dill seed	celery seed caraway seed dill leaves

E

INGREDIENT	SUBSTITUTIONS
Egg (1 whole) (3 T. or 1.7 oz.)	3 T. mayonnaise ½ tsp. baking powder + 1 T. vinegar + 1 T. liquid (in baking) 1 egg in every 3 can be replaced with 1 T. cornstarch in baking soften 1 T. unflavored gelatin in 3 T. cold water; add 3 tsp. boiling water; cool and beat until frothy; add to recipe (reduce other liquid by 2 T.) ¼ C. silken tofu, pureed ½ banana mashed with ½ tsp. baking powder
Egg noodles	linguine fettucine spaetzle
Egg roll, wrappers	phyllo (bake; do not fry) rice paper (thinner, makes crispier roll)
Eggplant	zucchini portobello mushroom okra
Evaporated milk	1 C. light cream 1 C. half-and-half

F

INGREDIENT	SUBSTITUTIONS
Fennel seed	caraway seed anise seed dill cumin
Feta cheese	blue cheese
Fish sauce (1 teaspoon)	1 tsp. Worcestershire sauce 1 tsp. light soy sauce
Flour, all-purpose (for thickening) (1 Tablespoon)	1½ tsp. cornstarch, arrowroot starch, potato starch, or rice starch 1 T. granular tapioca 1½ tsp. whole wheat flour + ½ tsp. all-purpose flour
Flour, all-purpose (1 cup)	1 C. + 2 T. cake flour 1 C. minus 2 T. unsifted all-purpose flour 1½ C. bread crumbs 1 C. rolled oats ⅓ C. cornmeal or soybean flour + ⅔ C. all-purpose flour ½ C. cornmeal, bran, rice flour, rye flour, or whole- wheat flour + ½ C. all-purpose flour ¾ C. whole-wheat flour or bran flour and ¼ C. all-purpose flour 1 C. rye or rice flour ¼ C. soybean flour and ¾ C. all-purpose flour
Flour, as a coating for frying	Cornstarch Tapioca starch

INGREDIENT	SUBSTITUTIONS
Flour, wheat	barley flour (replace up to ½ of wheat flour in a recipe) buckwheat flour (replace up to ½ of wheat flour in a recipe) oat flour (makes baked goods moister, chewier, and more crumbly) brown rice flour (replace up to ¼ of any wheat flour in a recipe) soy flour (replace up to ¼ wheat flour in a recipe; increase the liquid; reduce oven temp. by 25°) wheat germ (replace up to ⅓ of wheat flour in a recipe)

G

INGREDIENT	SUBSTITUTIONS
Garlic (1 clove, small)	⅛ tsp. garlic powder ¼ tsp. instant minced garlic ¼ tsp. granulated garlic ½ tsp. garlic flakes ½ to 1 tsp. garlic salt (reduce amount salt called for in recipe) ½ tsp. garlic juice
Garlic salt (¾ teaspoon)	1 medium-size clove or ½ tsp. minced fresh garlic + pinch of salt
Golden syrup (1 cup)	⅔ C. light corn syrup + ⅓ C. molasses ½ C. honey + ½ C. light or dark corn syrup ½ C. honey + ½ C. maple syrup 1 C. light corn syrup
Graham cracker crumbs (1 cup)	1½ C. chopped nuts + ⅛ C. sugar 1 C. chocolate wafer crumbs 1 C. vanilla wafer crumbs
Grapefruit juice	pineapple juice orange juice
Grapes	kiwi fruit blueberries
Grapeseed oil	corn oil soy oil sunflower oil peanut oil safflower oil

INGREDIENT	SUBSTITUTIONS
Green onions, fresh (½ cup chopped)	½ C. chopped onion ½ C. chopped leek ½ C. chopped shallots ½ C. chopped chives (raw)

H

INGREDIENT	SUBSTITUTIONS
Hazelnuts	almonds macadamia nuts pecans walnuts Brazil nuts
Herbs, fresh (1 tablespoon)	1 tsp. dried ground herbs 1 tsp. dried crumbled herbs
Hoisin sauce	¾ C. pitted prunes + 2 C. water + 1 T. crushed garlic + 1½ T. soy sauce; simmer for 10 minutes ¼ C. soy sauce + ¼ C. plum sauce + 1 tsp. flour + dash five-spice powder + dash garlic powder + sugar or honey to taste apple butter sweet bean sauce (spicier)
Hominy	dried beans (in stew and soup) potatoes barley grits
Honey (1 cup)	1¼ C. granulated sugar + 1/3 C. liquid (use water or liquid called for in recipe) 1 C. light molasses 1 C. light or dark corn syrup 1 C. maple syrup
Honeydew melon	cantaloupe crenshaw melon
Horseradish	2 T. bottled horseradish 1 T. wasabi for sauce use Dijon mustard, spicy brown mustard, horseradish mustard. If ground, ground mustard in equal parts

I

INGREDIENT	SUBSTITUTIONS
Italian seasoning	1 tsp. basil + 1 T. fresh or dried parsley + ½ tsp. oregano

INGREDIENT	SUBSTITUTIONS
J	
Jalapeño pepper	serrano pepper yellow wax chile pepper cayenne pepper fresno chile pepper
Jicama	water chestnuts turnip Jerusalem artichoke tart apple
K	
Kale	collard greens Swiss chard cabbage napa cabbage (do not boil) mustard greens spinach
Kefir	yogurt (thicker and more tart)
Ketchup (1 cup)	1 C. tomato sauce + ½ C. sugar + 2 T. vinegar 1 C. tomato sauce + ¼ C. sugar + ¼ C. vinegar + 1 tsp. salt + ¼ tsp. ground cloves
Kidney beans	pinto beans chili beans red beans
Kiwi fruit	gooseberries papaya strawberries pears
L	
Lard, for frying	bacon fat vegetable oil shortening
Lard, in baked goods	shortening vegetable oil butter (4 T. lard = 5 T. butter) margarine (4 T. lard = 5 T. margarine)
Lemon juice (1 tablespoon)	1 T. bottled lemon juice 1 T. fresh lime juice 1½ tsp. vinegar

INGREDIENT	SUBSTITUTIONS
Lemon, whole (1 medium)	2 T. lemon juice + 2–3 tsp. lemon zest 1 lime lemon grass grapefruit
Lemon zest (peel) (1 teaspoon)	½ tsp. lemon extract 2 T. lemon juice 1 tsp. lime zest
Lima beans	soybeans
Lime	lemon (weaker/less acidic, so use more lemon than you would lime)
Lime zest (peel)	1 tsp. grated fresh lemon zest
Liquid smoke	smoked paprika, smoke tea (or lapsang souchong), chipotle powder
M	
Mace	1 tsp. nutmeg (sweeter and milder) 1 tsp. allspice 1 tsp. cinnamon 1 tsp. ginger 1 tsp. pumpkin pie spice
Maple syrup (2 cups)	1 C. maple syrup (reduce liquid in recipe by ¼ C.) ¾ C. granulated white sugar + 1 tsp. pure maple extract 1 C. granulated white sugar
Margarine (1 cup)	1 C. shortening + ½ tsp. salt 1 C. butter ⅞ C. vegetable oil + ½ tsp. salt ⅞ C. lard + ½ tsp. salt
Mascarpone cheese (1 cup)	1 C. creme fraiche 1 C. sour cream 8 oz. softened cream cheese + ¼ C. whipping cream 8 oz. softened cream cheese + ⅛ C. whipping cream + ⅛ C. sour cream; blend until smooth 4 oz. softened cream cheese + ¼ C. butter + ¼ C. cream; blend to smooth 1 C. ricotta cheese, blend to smooth

INGREDIENT	SUBSTITUTIONS
Matzo meal	breadcrumbs cracker crumbs
Mayonnaise (in salads/salad dressings) (1 cup)	½ C. yogurt + ½ C. mayonnaise 1 C. yogurt 1 C. sour cream 1 C. cottage cheese pureed in blender
Mayonnaise (for sandwich spread)	mustard roasted garlic aioli yogurt mashed avocado
Milk, evaporated whole or skim	1 C. liquid whole milk 1 C. regular cream, whipping cream, or heavy cream
Milk, whole (1 cup)	1 C. reconstituted non-fat dry milk and 2 tsp. butter or margarine ⅔ C. evaporated milk + ⅓ C. water ½ C. condensed milk + ½ C. water 4 T. whole dry milk + 1 C. water 1 C. fruit juice (for use in baking) 1 C. potato water (for use in baking) ¼ C. non-fat dry milk + 2 tsp butter or margarine + ⅞ C. water 1 C. soy, almond, or rice milk 1 C. water + 1½ tsp. butter (for baking) 1 C. buttermilk + ½ tsp. baking soda (decrease baking powder in recipe by 2 tsp.)
Miso (1 tablespoon)	1 tsp. soy sauce
Molasses (1 cup)	1 C. honey, dark corn syrup, maple syrup, brown rice syrup, or barley malt syrup 1½ C. brown sugar ¾ C. brown sugar + 1 tsp. cream of tartar ¾ C. sugar, increase liquid by 5 T., decrease baking soda by ½ tsp. and add 2 tsp. baking powder to recipe
Mushrooms, cremini	white mushrooms shiitake mushrooms portobello mushrooms
Mushrooms, fresh	eggplant asparagus
Mushrooms, shiitake	cremini mushrooms enoki mushrooms white mushrooms oyster mushrooms
Mushrooms, white	cremini mushrooms oyster mushrooms (cook faster)
Mustard, dry (1 teaspoon)	1 T. prepared mustard ½ tsp. mustard seeds
Mustard, Dijon (1 tablespoon)	1 T. dry mustard + 1 tsp. water + 1 tsp. white wine vinegar + 1 T. mayonnaise + pinch of sugar
Mustard, yellow (1 tablespoon)	1 T. dry mustard + 1 tsp. water + 1 tsp. vinegar + 1 tsp. sugar mayonnaise (milder flavor) prepared horseradish sauce
N	
Naan	flour tortilla pita bread
Navy beans	great northern beans (larger) cannellini beans lima beans
Nectarines	peaches (not as sweet) apricots
Nuts, chopped, ground or whole	1 C. similar nuts (your favorite) prepared in the same way 1 C. rolled oats, browned (in baked products)
O	
Oats, rolled	quick-cooking oats (less chewy, take less time to cook) instant oats (less chewy, take less time to cook) steel-cut oats (chewier, take longer to cook) quinoa flakes rye flakes

INGREDIENT	SUBSTITUTIONS
Oats, steel-cut	rolled oats (less chewy, take less time to cook)
Oil (for sauteeing)	melted butter or margarine bacon drippings melted shortening or lard
Olive oil	corn oil peanut oil almond oil (for cold dishes)
Onion (1 small)	¼ C. chopped, fresh green onions (cook no longer than 1 minute) 11/3 tsp. onion salt 1–2 T. instant minced onion 1 tsp. onion powder 2 T. dried minced onion
Onion, red	Spanish onion green onion sweet onion
Onion flakes (1 tablespoon)	1 tsp. onion powder 1/3 C. chopped fresh onion
Orange, whole (1 medium)	6–8 T. orange juice + 2–3 T. orange zest 1 medium blood orange (less acidic) 1 medium mandarin orange kumquats grapefruit pomelo
Orange juice, freshly squeezed	reconstituted frozen orange concentrate pineapple juice grapefruit juice
Orange zest (1 tablespoon)	1 tsp. lemon juice ½ tsp. orange extract
Oreo cookies	chocolate graham crackers chocolate wafers (for pie crust) vanilla wafers (for pie crust)

P

INGREDIENT	SUBSTITUTIONS
Panko	breadcrumbs (not as crispy) cracker crumbs
Parmesan cheese, grated	½ C. grated Asiago cheese or grated romano cheese
Parsnip	carrot turnip celery root sweet potato
Peaches	nectarines (sweeter) papaya mango apricots
Peanuts	almonds (for nut butter) cashews (for stir-fry dishes)
Pearl barley	Arborio rice (not as chewy) orzo farro buckwheat
Pears, fresh	apples Asian pears quinces figs
Peas, black-eyed (dried)	split peas
Peas, fresh	edamame lima beans
Peas, split (dried)	black-eyed peas yellow peas
Peas, sugar snap	asparagus carrot snow peas
Peanut butter chips	butterscotch chips semisweet or milk chocolate chips

INGREDIENT	SUBSTITUTIONS
Pecans	walnuts
Pepper, white	1 tsp. black pepper
Pepperoni	1 oz. salami
Peppers, red bell (dried) (1 tablespoon)	3 T. fresh red bell pepper, chopped 2 T. chopped pimento
Peppermint (dried) (1 tablespoon)	¼ C. chopped fresh mint
Persimmon	plum pumpkin (in baked goods)
Pineapple	papaya
Pineapple juice	orange juice grapefruit juice
Pinto beans	chili beans red kidney beans
Pistachio nuts	blanched almonds pine nuts
Pita bread	flour tortilla naan
Plantain	bananas, underripe sweet potato potato (especially for frying)
Poblano pepper	anaheim chile serrano pepper (hotter) bell pepper (milder) canned chile peppers
Polenta, dry	cornmeal corn grits

INGREDIENT	SUBSTITUTIONS
Pomegranate juice	grenadine cranberry juice
Poppy seeds	sesame seeds
Potato	cauliflower (mashed) sweet potato parsnip jicama (mashed or baked) Jerusalem artichoke rutabaga (mashed or in stew)
Pot sticker wrappers	dumpling wrappers egg roll wrappers wonton wrappers
Poultry seasoning (1 teaspoon)	½ tsp. ground sage + ½ tsp. dried thyme + ½ tsp. dried rosemary
Prosciutto	country ham Black Forest ham lean bacon (blanch first in boiling water, drain)
Pumpkin	hubbard squash sweet potato acorn squash butternut squash
Pumpkin spice (1 teaspoon)	½ tsp. cinnamon + ¼ tsp. ginger + ⅛ tsp. allspice + ⅛ tsp. nutmeg
Pumpkin seeds	sesame seeds sunflower seeds squash seeds

Q

INGREDIENT	SUBSTITUTIONS
Quince	Asian pears crabapples Granny Smith apples Pippin apples Rhode Island Greening apples
Quinoa	wild rice brown rice couscous

R

INGREDIENT	SUBSTITUTIONS
Radish	jicama
Raisins	dried currants dried blueberries, cranberries, or cherries chopped, pitted prunes chopped dried apricots chopped nuts chopped dried figs (stronger flavor)
Refried Beans	black beans pinto beans
Rhubarb	cranberries tart apples tart cherries
Rice, basmati	long-grain rice jasmine rice (shorter, stickier grains)
Rice, brown	white rice (less fiber) wild rice quinoa
Rice, jasmine	basmati rice (longer grain, less sticky) long-grain rice
Rice, long-grain	medium-grain rice (stickier, less fluffy)
Rice, risotto	short-grain white rice medium-grain white rice pearl barley (chewier)
Ricotta cheese	goat cheese cottage cheese
Romano cheese	Parmesan cheese
Rutabaga	turnip (not as sweet) celeriac kohlrabi
Rye flakes	oatmeal

S

INGREDIENT	SUBSTITUTIONS
Saffron (1 teaspoon)	4 tsp. turmeric (for color, not flavor) 8 tsp. safflower red and yellow food coloring (for color, not flavor)
Salt (for seasoning)	citrus zest pepper herbs soy sauce
Salt, kosher	table salt (use half as much) pickling salt
Salt, sea	table salt kosher salt
Semisweet chocolate chips	chopped nuts peanut butter or other flavored chips chocolate candies chopped dried fruit
Serrano pepper	jalapeño pepper (milder) fresno chile (milder)
Sesame seeds	pumpkin seeds
Shallots, chopped	chopped onion chopped green onion chopped leeks
Shortening, melted (for frying)	olive oil vegetable oil clarified butter cooking spray
Shortening, solid (used in baking) (1 cup)	1 C. minus 2 T. lard 1 C. butter (if using salted butter, eliminated ½ tsp. salt from recipe) 1 C. margarine (eliminate ½ tsp. salt from recipe) 1 C. mashed bananas 1 C. applesauce 1 C. pureed prunes (in chocolate baked goods) ¾ C. apple butter + ¼ C. shortening 1 C. ricotta cheese (use to replace ¾ of the shortening in the recipe)

INGREDIENT	SUBSTITUTIONS
Sour cream (1 cup)	3/4 C. sour milk + 1/3 C. butter or margarine 3/4 C. buttermilk + 1/3 C. butter or margarine Blend until smooth: 1/3 C. buttermilk + 1 T. lemon juice + 1 C. cottage cheese 1 C. plain yogurt 1/2 C. cottage cheese + 1/2 C. plain yogurt 3/4 C. milk + 3/4 tsp. lemon juice + 1/3 C. butter or margarine 1 C. cottage cheese + 3 T. milk + 2 T. lemon juice
Sour milk (1 cup)	1 T. vinegar or lemon juice + enough milk to make 1 C.; let thicken for 5 minutes
Soy milk	cow's milk goat's milk oat milk (in both sweet and savory dishes) rice milk (in desserts) almond milk (in desserts)
Soy sauce (1/2 cup)	1/4 C. Worcestershire sauce + 1 T. water
Spearmint, dried (1 tablespoon)	1/4 C. chopped fresh mint
Spinach	Swiss chard beet greens kale turnip greens (discard stems) escarole
Sprouts	shredded lettuce grated carrots minced green onions
Squash	acorn squash butternut squash banana squash pumpkin green papayas
Sriracha	Tabasco sauce (not as sweet) sweet chili sauce cocktail sauce

INGREDIENT	SUBSTITUTIONS
Star anise, ground	ground anise seed ground fennel seed
Star fruit	melons lemon slices (as garnish)
Stock, beef or chicken (1 cup)	1 cube beef or chicken bouillon dissolved in 1 C. water
Strawberries	raspberries kiwi fruit guava
Stuffing mix (croutons only)	coarse breadcrumbs cornbread crumbs (softer) croutons rice
Suet	shortening butter chicken fat pork fat beef drippings
Sugar, brown (light) (1 cup firmly packed)	1 C. granulated sugar 1 C. granulated sugar + 1 T. molasses 2/3 C. dark brown sugar + 1/3 C. granulated sugar 1/2 C. liquid brown sugar 1 C. turbinado sugar
Sugar, brown (dark) (1 cup)	1 C. light brown sugar + 1 T. molasses 1 C. granulated sugar + 2 T. molasses
Sugar, powdered (1 cup)	1/2 C. granulated sugar + 1 T. cornstarch, blended in blender
Sugar, white (for any purpose) (1 cup)	1 C. corn syrup, decrease liquid called for in recipe by 1/4 C. (never replace more than 1/2 C. sugar called for in recipe with corn syrup) 1 1/3 C. molasses (decrease liquid called for in recipe by 1/3 C.) 1 C. caster (superfine) sugar 1 C. powdered (confectioners') sugar 1 C. light brown sugar, firmly packed 1 C. honey + 1/4 tsp. baking soda (decrease liquid in recipe by 1/4 C.)

INGREDIENT	SUBSTITUTIONS
Sugar, white (in baking)	1 C. honey + ¼ tsp. baking soda; decrease liquid in recipe by ¼ C. ¾ C. white sugar + ¼ C. powdered milk ¾ C. maple syrup + ¼ tsp. baking soda; decrease liquid in recipe by 3 T. 1¾ C. packed powdered sugar 1½ C. light corn syrup; decrease liquid in recipe by ¼ C. 1⅓ C. molasses +1 tsp. baking soda; decrease liquid in recipe by ⅓ C., reduce baking temperature by 25°F
Sunflower seeds	pumpkin seeds pine nuts peanuts
Sweet potato	yams (sweeter) mashed, cooked pumpkin
Sweetened condensed milk 1 14-oz. can	¾ C. white sugar + ½ C. water + 1 ⅛ C. dry powdered milk; bring to a boil and cook, stirring frequently, until thickened, about 20 minutes
Swiss chard	spinach beet greens turnip greens bok choy escarole mustard greens
T	
Tahini	peanut butter hummus
Tangelo	mandarin orange orange grapefruit
Tapioca, for thickening	1 T. flour
Tomatillos	green tomatoes + dash of lemon juice plum tomatoes + dash of lemon juice

INGREDIENT	SUBSTITUTIONS
Tomatoes, canned (1 cup)	1⅓ C. diced fresh tomatoes simmered 10 minutes
Tomatoes, fresh (2 C. chopped)	1 16-oz. can tomatoes 1 T. tomato paste 2 C. roasted red peppers 2 C. chopped tomatillos
Tomatoes, grape	cherry tomatoes teardrop tomatoes currant tomatoes
Tomatoes, green	cherry tomatoes teardrop tomatoes currant tomatoes
Tomato juice (1 cup)	½ C. tomato sauce + ½ C. water
Tomato paste	tomato sauce (use twice as much; decrease liquid in recipe) tomato puree (use twice as much; decrease liquid in recipe) + salt
Tomato sauce	¾ C. tomato paste + 1 C. water
Tomato soup (1 10¾-oz. can)	1 C. tomato sauce + ¼ C. water
Turmeric, ground	mustard powder mustard powder + pinch of saffron
Turnip	rutabaga (sweeter) kohlrabi parsnip carrot celeriac
V	
Vanilla bean (1 inch)	1 tsp. vanilla extract
Vanilla Extract, pure (1 teaspoon)	½ vanilla bean ½–1 tsp. other extract (such as almond, peppermint, lemon, or orange)

INGREDIENT	SUBSTITUTIONS
Vanilla wafer cookies	chocolate wafer cookies (for pie crusts) gingersnaps
Vanilla wafer crumbs	graham cracker crumbs chocolate wafer crumbs crushed gingersnaps crushed Oreo cookies
Vegetable oil for baking	applesauce fruit puree
Vegetable oil for frying	lard vegetable shortening
Vegetable shortening, solid	butter lard margarine
Vinegar, apple cider	white vinegar wine vinegar (do not use in pickles) malt vinegar
Vinegar, balsamic (1 tablespoon)	1 T. sherry vinegar or cider vinegar 1 T. red wine vinegar + 1 T. sugar or honey
Vinegar, champagne	white wine vinegar rice vinegar (not as mild) apple cider vinegar (not as mild)
Vinegar, red wine	white wine vinegar balsamic vinegar apple cider vinegar rice vinegar
Vinegar, rice	1 C. apple cider vinegar + pinch of sugar 1 C. white wine vinegar ¾ C. white vinegar + ¼ C. water
Vinegar, white	cider vinegar lemon or lime juice brandy malt vinegar

INGREDIENT	SUBSTITUTIONS
W	
Walnuts	hazelnuts pecans pine nuts (in pesto)
Wasabi	ground dry mustard + enough water to make a paste
White sugar (1 cup)	1 C. brown sugar 1¼ C. powdered sugar ¾ C. honey ¾ C. corn syrup
Wine, red	1 C. beef broth 1 C. cranberry juice + 2 tsp. vinegar 1 C. grape juice 1 C. water
Wine, white	chicken broth apple juice white grape juice water
Wonton wrappers	dumpling wrappers egg roll skins pot sticker wrappers
Worcestershire sauce	bottled steak sauce soy sauce
Y	
Yeast, active dry (1 tablespoon)	1 yeast cake, compressed 1 package active dry yeast 1 T. instant or fast-rising active yeast
Yogurt, plain	1 C. buttermilk (in baked goods, dressings, and sauces) 1 C. sour milk (in baked goods, dressings, and sauces) 1 C. cottage cheese blended until smooth (not as tart) 1 C. sour cream (higher in fat)
Z	
Squash, zucchini	yellow crookneck squash eggplant carrot pumpkin

don't waste a thing:

STORE, FREEZE, & REHEAT

FREEZING & REHEATING

I'd like to introduce you to Freezer and Leftover...your new best friends! Give up boring, frozen food and sad, wet leftovers. Master the art of making stored food taste as fresh as the day you got it!

FREEZING FOOD

Shelf cookers love their freezers! Follow our comprehensive tips to master your freezer.

PAGE 100

STORE IT RIGHT

This section will help you maximize how long things last in the fridge and freezer.

PAGE 106

THAWING & REHEATING

Let's teach you how to thaw and cook all of that delicious frozen food safely, while making it taste yummy.

PAGE 116

LEFTOVERS

Re-use it, re-heat it, re-invent it! Make yesterday's meal into today's masterpiece.

PAGE 120

simple tricks on

HOW TO FREEZE FOOD

LET'S TALK ABOUT FREEZER BURN

How can something burn if it's frozen?

Oh, it can. And it does. And if you've ever seen it (or tasted it), you know it.

Freezer burn is damage to frozen food that's caused by air (oxidation), dehydration, and water evaporation (which continues after food is frozen unless you do something to stop it). Water that evaporates forms ice crystals in and on the food. Freezer burn changes the flavor, color, and texture of the food.

Food that has been freezer burned often has a layer of "frost" directly on the food. It looks "off." It looks (and is) dry. Freezer-burned meat usually looks grayish white and dry like it's been overcooked. If air reaches meat while it's frozen, it can become rancid.

Food that has been freezer burned is safe to eat. It's just not very good.

The single most important thing you can do to prevent freezer burn is to provide an airtight, moisture-proof barrier between your food and whatever container it's in. Here's a list of things that if done consistently, will help prevent freezer burn.

THE MOST IMPORTANT THING TO DO

You must provide an airtight, moisture-proof barrier between your food and whatever container it's in to prevent freezer burn.

Ziploc

IMPORTANT TIPS TO FREEZING FOOD

COOL FOOD BEFORE PUTTING IT IN THE FREEZER

Not only will you prevent evaporation, but you will avoid partially thawing the foods around it. The best practice is to put it in the fridge for a couple of hours before you put it in the freezer.

SET YOUR FREEZER TO THE RIGHT TEMPERATURE

That should be obvious, but you'd be surprised how many freezers aren't quite cold enough. Keep yours at 0°F (-18°Celsius).

AVOID SELF-DEFROSTING FREEZERS

Sure, they're a lot handier, but the way they "defrost" is by fluctuating the temperature, allowing the frost to melt. When the frost melts, the water molecules in frozen food also melt and start to evaporate. The result? The dreaded freezer burn.

KEEP YOUR FREEZER ABOUT 75 PERCENT FULL

How does that help? Stuff stays colder—all that frozen food keeps the food and the freezer colder (bonus: it also saves on energy). If the power goes out, as sometimes happens, the stuff in your freezer will stay cold longer if it's full or almost full. If you don't have enough food yet to accomplish that task, no worries: use ice to fill some of the empty spaces. On the other hand, don't stuff it full—there should be a little bit of room for air circulation around frozen items.

USE FREEZER CONTAINERS AND WRAP FOOD TIGHTLY

Don't skimp here. Investing in some good-quality containers can protect your food. Look for containers that have a moisture-vapor barrier for optimum protection. You should not freeze foods in bread wrappers, plastic wrap, food storage bags, or Styrofoam trays with plastic wrap. Not if you want to eat it later. However, you can wrap foods in plastic wrap, foil, or freezer paper before putting them in an appropriate freezer container to add a layer of protection.

USE THE RIGHT SIZE OF CONTAINER

Whatever you store your food in—rigid containers or freezer bags—should be almost full. Leave only enough room (half an inch should do) for the food to expand a little as it freezes. Push all the air out of the freezer bag before you seal it. If you use freezer paper, wrap it tightly enough to touch all the surfaces of the food.

REPACK FROZEN FOODS AFTER YOU OPEN THE CONTAINER

When using store-bought frozen foods (such as veggies, pasta shells, or fish sticks), repack what you don't eat the first time using all the tips above. Never return these foods to the freezer in their partially empty original bags or containers.

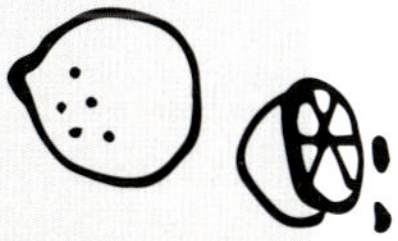

ADD CITRIC ACID TO FRUIT BEFORE FREEZING IT

Add a solution that contains citric acid or vitamin C, such as Fruit Fresh, to your fruit to prevent oxidation, which destroys nutrients.

BLANCHE GREEN VEGETABLES

Boil green veggies—beans, peas, broccoli, asparagus, and so on—for 30 seconds, then immediately plunge them in ice water. This helps prevent freezer burn and keeps them from going brown in the freezer.

FREEZE FOODS IN LIQUIDS

This works especially well for cooked foods; if any evaporation does occur, it will be from the liquid, not from the food. Simply use an appropriate container and cover the food with broth, sauce, or good old water. (Use the broth or sauce when you reheat it, or just drain the water off.)

KNOW WHEN TO TOSS FROZEN FOOD

Hopefully, you're able to prevent freezer burn and rotate your food wisely. If there's something that lingers in the freezer too long, though, toss it. While that magic number can vary with different types of food, as a general rule, nothing should stay in your freezer longer than about nine months.

Brilliant Tip

If you're unsure of what meals can be frozen, take a walk through your grocery store's frozen aisle. If they can be frozen there, they can be frozen at your house.

WHAT TO KEEP IN THE FRIDGE

DO REFRIGERATE

VEGGIES

- Asparagus
- Broccoli
- Brussels sprouts
- Cabbage
- Carrots
- Cauliflower
- Celery
- Corn on the cob
- Green beans
- Green onions
- Herbs
- Lettuce
- Mushrooms
- Peas
- Radishes
- Summer squashes (zucchini, crook-neck, straight-neck, yellow, pattypan)

FRUIT

- Apples
- Apricots
- Blackberries
- Blueberries
- Cherries
- Figs
- Grapes
- Raspberries
- Strawberries
- Any fruit you've cut should be refrigerated.

Brilliant Tip

Not sure how to choose the perfect fruits and veggies? Check out our tips on page 60

DO NOT REFRIGERATE

VEGGIES BEFORE YOU CUT THEM

- Bell peppers (red, green, yellow)
- Cucumbers
- Eggplant
- Garlic
- Ginger root
- Jicama
- Onions
- Potatoes
- Pumpkins
- Sweet potatoes
- Tomatoes
- Winter squashes (acorn, buttercup, butternut, banana, Hubbard, pumpkin, spaghetti)

FRUIT BEFORE YOU CUT THEM

- Avocados
- Bananas
- Cantaloupe
- Grapefruit
- Kiwi fruit
- Lemons
- Limes
- Mangoes
- Nectarines
- Oranges
- Papayas
- Peaches
- Pears
- Plums
- Pineapple
- Pomegranates
- Watermelon

tips and tricks to

STORE FOOD PROPERLY IN FREEZER

	HOW TO	TIPS/TRICKS
AVOCADOS 	Cut in half or mash. Store in freezer bags. Lasts 5–6 months.	Frozen avocado works best in foods in which it is blended, such as guacamole.
BACON 	Wrap individual slices in waxed paper OR roll up in a pinwheel shape. Freeze on cookie sheet overnight Transfer frozen bacon to freezer bags or plastic airtight containers. Lasts up to 6 months.	Bacon can be thawed in the refrigerator, in cold water, or in the microwave. Never thaw at room temperature. Bacon is ready to cook when the slices can be separated.
BANANAS 	Peel before freezing (they are hard to peel after being frozen). Freeze whole, mashed, or cut into slices. Place whole or mashed bananas in freezer bags/plastic airtight containers. Freeze banana slices on a cookie sheet, then transfer to a bag or airtight container. Best if used within 2–3 months.	Bananas are mushy after freezing, so use them in smoothies or baked goods.
BAR COOKIES AND BROWNIES 	Wrap unsliced bars or brownies tightly in plastic wrap and again in foil. Should last up to 3 months.	Thaw at room temperature.

	HOW TO	TIPS/TRICKS
BREAD 	If you won't be using the whole loaf, slice it before freezing. Take care not to crush the loaf in the freezer. Lasts up to 6 months.	Let thaw for 2–3 hours at room temperature. Can also be heated in the oven if you want to serve it hot; heat at 350°F for up to 10 min.
BREAD DOUGH 	Shape kneaded dough in ball. Wrap well in moisture-proof, airtight wrap. Lasts 3 months in freezer.	Thaw overnight in the fridge or for 2 hours at room temp. Bring to room temperature before shaping into loaves.
BUTTER 	Freeze in original wrapping placed in an airtight bag or tightly wrapped in foil. Lasts 4–6 months.	Thaw overnight in the refrigerator.
BUTTERMILK 	Fill plastic drink cups half full. Place on cookie sheet in freezer overnight. Transfer frozen blocks to freezer bags or plastic airtight containers. Lasts up to 3 months.	Before using thawed buttermilk, stir well.
CAKE 	Freeze cake before frosting it. Wrap tightly in plastic wrap. Lasts up to 2 months.	Don't frost cake while it's still frozen; frost it while it's still partially chilled.

	HOW TO	TIPS/TRICKS
CHEESE, BULK 	Store block cheese in its original packaging, wrapped tightly in plastic wrap or heavy-duty aluminum foil. Hard cheeses (Gouda, cheddar, and Swiss) last 6 months. Soft cheeses last 1 month.	Thaw overnight in the refrigerator. Cheese can become crumbly when thawed; to minimize, thaw slowly in the refrigerator for 24 hours.
CHEESE, GRATED 	Place grated cheese in freezer bags. Toss with a little flour or cornstarch to keep cheese from sticking together. Lasts up to 6 months.	Thaw at room temperature or in the refrigerator.
CHEESE, SLICED 	Wrap cheese slices in moisture-proof wrapping, such as plastic wrap, aluminum foil, or freezer paper. Put wrapped cheese slices in a freezer bag or container and seal well. Lasts up to 6 months.	Cheese can become crumbly when thawed; to minimize, thaw slowly in the refrigerator for 24 hours.
CHICKEN 	Raw pieces last 9 months. Whole chicken lasts 1 year. Cooked chicken lasts 2-6 months.	Can be thawed in the refrigerator, or in the microwave. Never thaw at room temperature.
CHOCOLATE 	Place the original box in a heavy-duty plastic freezer bag, seal it tightly and freeze. Lasts up to 18 months.	Can be thawed in the refrigerator, or in the microwave, or thaw at room temperature.

	HOW TO	TIPS/TRICKS
CITRUS, SLICED 	Stack individual slices between pieces of freezer, waxed, or parchment paper in a plastic airtight container. Last up to 6 months.	No need to thaw if used in drinks. Thaw for 30 minutes at room temperature to use as a garnish.
CITRUS, WHOLE 	Wash and pat dry. Freeze whole in freezer bags. Last up to 6 months.	Thaw at room temperature. Thawed citrus fruit will be mushy.
CITRUS JUICE 	Fill freezer-safe containers ¾ full to allow for expansion. Can be frozen in plastic drink cups then transferred to freezer bags. Lasts 8–12 months.	Thaw at room temperature.
CITRUS ZEST 	Place in small mounds on a plate or tray. Freeze for several hours. Transfer to small freezer bags. Lasts up to 6 months.	No need to thaw before using.
COOKIE DOUGH 	Put dough in cookie-sized balls on a tray, freeze, then transfer to plastic airtight container. Lasts up to 3 months.	Take out as many balls of dough as desired and thaw in the refrigerator. The best cookie dough for freezing is dough that is dense, including chocolate chip, peanut butter, sugar, gingerbread, shortbread, and brownies.

	HOW TO	TIPS/TRICKS
COOKIES 	Wrap cooled cookies individually in plastic. Place wrapped cookies in an airtight container. Last up to 1 month.	To refresh crisp cookies after thawing, bake unfrosted cookies at 300 for a few minutes.
CREAM CHEESE 	Leave in original foil packaging to last longest. Opened cream cheese should be transferred to an airtight container before freezing. Lasts up to 2 months.	Thaw in the refrigerator.
EGGS 	You can freeze whole eggs, or freeze the yolks and whites separately. You can also freeze your eggs using different containers such as muffin tins. Lasts up to 1 year.	Let the eggs thaw in the refrigerator overnight.
FRUIT 	Keep in a tightly-sealed freezer zip bag. See page 102 for more Lasts up to 18 months.	Freezing changes the texture of most fruit. Frozen fruit works best in baked goods or blended drinks. Use frozen fruit instead of ice for a more flavorful smoothie. Also works well in ice cream and sorbet recipes.
GARLIC 	Can be frozen whole, chopped, minced, or in olive oil. Mix with just enough neutral-flavored oil to coat. Freeze overnight on a cookie sheet. Transfer to freezer bags or plastic airtight containers. Lasts up to 1 month without losing flavor.	Freezing garlic alters the texture (it gets mushy when thawed) but not the flavor. Garlic can be thawed at room temperature.

	HOW TO	TIPS/TRICKS
HERBS 	Method 1: Wash, pat dry, and chop before freezing; spread on parchment paper on a tray or cookie sheet; cover with plastic wrap; when frozen, store in airtight bag. Method 2: Freeze overnight in olive oil or water in ice cube trays; transfer frozen cubes to a freezer bag or airtight container. Lasts up to 1 year.	Can be used in soups, sauces, and stews. Thaw at room temperature. No need to thaw cubes for sauces, stews, and soups.
JAM 	Freeze in glass airtight container. Lasts up to 1 year.	Thaw overnight in the refrigerator.
MEAT 	Do not freeze in original container; wrap tightly in freezer paper, parchment paper, or plastic wrap and secure with tape if needed If cooked lasts up to 3 months. Uncooked lasts 6 months to 1 year (quality diminishes. after 3 months).	Thaw overnight in the refrigerator.
MILK 	Milk can be frozen in its original plastic container; the divets on the side allow for expansion when frozen. If freezing milk in another container, fill container ¾ full, leaving room for expansion. Lasts up to 3 months.	Thaw overnight in the refrigerator. Before using thawed milk, shake it well to evenly distribute the solids.
MUSHROOMS 	Rinse off and pat dry. Freeze in freezer bags Last for up to 1 year.	Larger and meatier mushrooms take longer to thaw.

	HOW TO	TIPS/TRICKS
NUTS 	Shell nuts before freezing Store in a plastic, airtight container. (metal causes nuts to spoil). Last for up to 8 months.	Frozen nuts can be added directly to recipes without thawing first. To thaw, spread nuts out on a towel to absorb any moisture as they thaw.
ONIONS 	Chop raw onion. Store in freezer bags. Best if used within 3–6 months.	Can be used in cooked dishes without thawing first. You can also freeze caramelized onions.
PASTA, UNCOOKED 	Freeze in a single layer on a cookie sheet for 1 hour. Transfer to freezer bags or plastic airtight containers. Lasts up to 1 month.	Frozen pasta can expand by 50 percent, so allow plenty of space in the pot. Wait until the water is at a full boil before putting frozen pasta in the pot to avoid mushy pasta that sticks to itself. Add 2-3 minutes cooking time for pasta that is still frozen.
PASTA, COOKED 	Cook the pasta for 2 minutes less. Allow the pasta to cool for 5 minutes. Stir a little olive oil through the pasta so all pieces are slightly coated. Place pasta on a baking sheet lined with parchment; place in freezer until frozen. Transfer to serving-size airtight containers. Lasts up to 2 weeks.	Can be thawed in the microwave. Can be thawed in a colander; run tepid water over the pasta until thawed. Can be thawed in a pot; to reduce mushiness, cook frozen pasta in sauce.
PESTO 	Freeze overnight in ice cube trays. Transfer frozen cubes to a freezer bag or plastic airtight container. Last up to 3 months.	Thaw at room temperature or in the refrigerator.

	HOW TO	TIPS/TRICKS
PIE 	Cool completely to room temperature before freezing. Wrap tightly in plastic wrap. If pie has a filling that would stick to the plastic wrap, freeze it overnight before wrapping. Lasts up to 3 months.	Thaw in the refrigerator or at room temperature.
POTATO CHIPS 	Place the potato chip bag directly in the freezer. Last up to 1 year.	Once thawed chips are exposed to sunlight and air, they lose their flavor and texture fairly quickly, so thaw only what you plan to eat.
POTATOES, RAW 	Peel and blanch in boiling water for 5 minutes. Immerse in cold water for 10 minutes. Freeze in freezer bags. Lasts up to 1 year.	Because potatoes are only blanched but not cooked, they can be boiled, roasted, fried, or baked. No need to thaw before using in dishes.
POTATOES, MASHED 	Mash with cream cheese before freezing (8 oz. cream cheese to 2 lbs. potatoes). Store in freezer bags. Lasts up to 1 month.	Thaw at room temperature, in the microwave, or in the oven. Stir frequently while thawing to incorporate the moisture.
POTATOES, DICED/SHREDDED 	Soak diced or shredded potatoes in cold water to remove excess starch. Blanch potatoes in boiling water for 3 minutes; drain, rinse in cold water, drain again, squeeze in a towel to remove all moisture; spread potatoes on a baking sheet and place in freezer for 1-2 hours. Transfer serving-size portions into freezer bags or containers. Last up to 1 year.	Soaking potatoes in cold water before boiling helps prevent brown discoloration.

	HOW TO	TIPS/TRICKS
RICE, COOKED 	Cool completely to room temperature. Freeze in freezer bags or plastic airtight containers. Lasts up to 6 months.	To heat, add a little water and microwave until heated through.
SANDWICHES 	Assemble sandwich with filling. Do not put condiments on sandwich before freezing (lettuce, pickles, sprouts, tomatoes, jam, or jelly); dress the sandwich after thawing. Wrap tightly in plastic wrap Placed wrapped sandwich in freezer bag. Last up to 3 months.	Thaw in the refrigerator overnight. Fillings that freeze well: Deli meats, Tuna salad, Chicken salad, Hard cheeses, Nut butters. Do not freeze egg salad filling, as freezing makes the eggs rubbery.
SAUSAGE 	Wrap the original packaging in freezer wrap. Lasts 2 months.	Thaw overnight in the refrigerator.
SPINACH 	Store in freezer bags. Lasts up to 9-12 months.	Great for lasagna, casseroles, and smoothies.
SOUP AND STOCK 	Ladle portions into freezer bags and squeeze out excess air. Lasts 3–4 months.	Too little air (space) in a container does not allow room for expansion; too much space increases the risk of freezer burn.

	HOW TO	TIPS/TRICKS
SOUR CREAM 	Whip before freezing to evenly distribute moisture. Lasts 4–6 months.	Thaw in the refrigerator. Stir in 2 T. of cornstarch and whip after thawing to evenly distribute moisture and return to a creamy consistency.
VEGETABLES 	Keep in a tightly sealed freezer zip bag. See page 102 for more. Lasts up to 18 months.	For hot meals like pastas or soups, frozen veggies can be added as-is during the cooking process. To use raw vegetables in a room-temperature dish, allow them to thaw out before use. Or you can roast them in the oven for a tasty side dish!
WHIPPED CREAM 	Place in dollops on parchment-lined tray or baking sheet. Freeze just long enough for the dollops to get firm enough to handle easily. Transfer to a freezer bag or plastic tairtight container. Lasts up to 2 months.	Thaw at room temperature for 20 minutes. Thaw in the refrigerator for 1–2 hours. Can be placed directly on dessert to thaw.
YOGURT 	Leave in its own container, an airtight container, an ice-cube tray, or in a zipped freezer bag. Lasts up to 2 months.	Yogurt has a lot of water content, so when you freeze it expect a result like ice, which is great for smoothies or other cold recipes. To make frozen yogurt you can scoop like ice cream, add sugar (more sugar means softer frozen yogurt), and a little half-and-half or mascarpone wouldn't hurt either.

Brilliant Tip

Teach your kids how to bag food, and the process can go even faster!

reheat, reheat, reheat!

THAWING YOUR FOOD

"Mmmm...I can't wait to eat this soggy frozen pizza!" Said no one, ever.

Okay, so now you have all this delicious (and valuable!) food in your freezer...how the heck do you re-heat it, so it doesn't look and taste like yesterday's socks?

Simple! We've got a few methods that will help you thaw your food in easy, safe ways! Use our guides and charts in this section to help you navigate all of that delicious frozen food, and let's get thawing and reheating!

BEST METHODS FOR THAWING FOOD

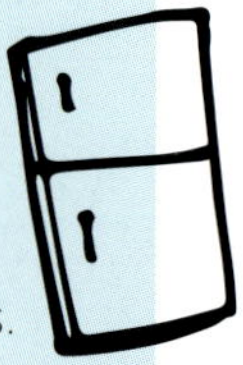

IN THE FRIDGE
The safest way to thaw food, but you will need to plan ahead!

ON THE COUNTER
This method is only safe for a few foods–fruits, breads, and pastries.

IN THE MICROWAVE
So fast and convenient! Just check our tips so the food doesn't dry out and thaw unevenly.

IN COLD WATER
This method is best for a variety of foods. Check out our tips for best steps and methods.

NEVER EVER EVER EVER EVER!
The only way food-borne bacteria can hurt you is if you eat it. No amount of frugality is worth getting sick. If you think your food—fresh or frozen—may be unsafe, throw it away.

FOOD YOU CAN COOK WITHOUT THAWING

FROZEN FRUIT

Eat these straight out of the bag, toss in the blender, or add them to what's cooking!

FROZEN VEGGIES

Add them to whatever meals you are cooking for quick added flavor!

FROZEN SOUP

Easy peasy! Just adjust your cooking time depending on how you warm it up.

PREPARED MEALS

Casseroles, pizza, lasagna, and baked pastas all bake beautifully from frozen state with adjusted cooking times! Pro tip: Walk the freezer aisle at the store for ideas as to what can be baked from frozen!

THINNER CUTS OF MEAT

If it's precooked (such as lunch meat), you can put it on your sandwich frozen, and it will be thawed and ready by lunchtime!

BREADS

Whether it's a loaf of white bread, french bread, waffles, pancakes, french toast, breadsticks, or even bread crumbs, breads of all kinds freeze beautifully. Pop in the toaster or oven to make them feel fresh and brand new.

TIPS FOR BAKING FROZEN FOOD

- Add about 50 percent to the cooking time. In other words, a dish that takes an hour to bake will take about an hour and a half to bake when frozen.
- Turn the oven down 25 degrees so the edges don't get overcooked and the middle has time to catch up.
- If cooking in the oven, cover with foil.

BASIC METHODS FOR THAWING FOOD

IN THE FRIDGE

This is the safest way to thaw food, but unfortunately it can take a while, so you have to plan ahead. Some tips:

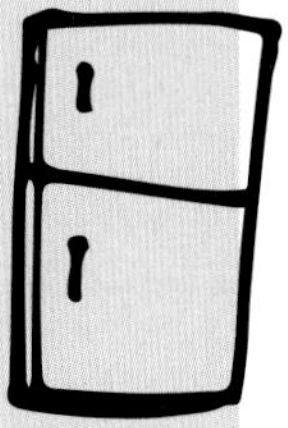

- If possible, keep the food in its original container or freezer container.
- Put the food on a plate or small tray to catch any liquids as it thaws.
- Avoid the coldest areas of your fridge--usually toward the front will be best.
- Give it a little space for air circulation to help it thaw more quickly.
- Give it plenty of time. A pound of beef or chicken will take 12 hrs. Give 24 hrs for 2-5 pounds.

ON THE COUNTER

In most cases, thawing food on the counter is only safe for fruits, breads, and pastries (2-4 hours). But it should be avoided for meat, fish, or veggies.

IN THE MICROWAVE

We love the speed of the microwave, right? A pound of ground beef takes 12 hours in the fridge, 9 minutes or so in the microwave. So convenient. But thawing in the microwave can dry out our food while cooking it unevenly. If time is of the essence, here are some ways to maximize your microwave thawing:

- Whenever possible, keep the food in its original container or freezer container.
- Put the food on a plate or small tray to catch any liquids as it thaws.
- Cook the food as soon as you thaw it. Don't give bacteria time to grow.
- Check it at intervals to see how it's doing. Some foods thaw more quickly than the defrost setting indicates.

BASIC METHODS FOR THAWING FOOD

IN COLD WATER

This method works best for fruit, vegetables, sauces, dairy products, cooked meals, and meat. Plan 30 to 45 minutes for every pound. (Frozen veggies thaw almost instantly.)

- Put the food in a sealed, watertight container.
- Put the container under cold water in a bowl, pot, bucket, or your sink. Make sure the water stays cold.
- Put a plate on top of it to hold it down.
- Drain off water every 20-30 min (being sure the water goes directly down the drain).
- Replace it with fresh cold water until the food is completely thawed.
- If you thaw meat in the sink, sanitize the sink.

IN THE SLOW COOKER

The advice on whether or not to put frozen meat in a slow cooker is mixed. The USDA recommends thawing your meat in the refrigerator before starting a slow cooker recipe. Otherwise, the frozen meat might take too long to cook to a safe temperature (above 165°F).

However, many cooking sources say you can cook frozen meat in a Crock-Pot, but you might need to increase the cooking time. As a general rule, chicken cooks faster than meats with more connective tissue and fat, so chicken will get to a safe temperature faster. Consider cutting your frozen meat into small pieces before adding it to the slow cooker. Frozen roast and frozen raw ground beef are NOT recommended for the crockpot, so thaw or cook those first to be safe.

FREEZER TIP

If you plan to utilize your freezer (which we highly recommend!), consider investing in a vacuum sealer. For less than $100 you can get a quality machine that will save you thousands in the long-run. See my favorite items linked at ShelfCooking.com/Amazon.

Brilliant Tip!

Vacuum sealers are good for more than preserving food! You can pickle or marinate in minutes, make your own yogurt pops or ice pops, or seal your toiletries when packing for a trip.

the truth about LEFTOVERS

Some people love leftovers, some won't eat them at gunpoint. Look, I get it! There's a good reason for all the resistance. Nobody likes eating the same thing for days on end (ooh me! me! pick me!), and for others, they think leftovers are just gross. And let's be honest, they sure can be—unless you do them the right way!

DID YOU KNOW . . . The average American household wastes over 30% of the food they obtain. THIRTY. PERCENT. That's ⅓ going straight into the trash! (And that's just an average!) Worse yet, the United States as a whole wastes more than $160 billion in food a year, according to the United States Department of Agriculture. That's billion. With a B.

Buckle up, I'm going to say it: If you are not eating leftovers, you are wasting food, and ultimately doing yourself, the environment, and your family a disservice. If we all made the effort to reduce our waste, even if only by half, think of how much better off our world would be!

The good news? Leftovers don't have to taste terrible! Here are some of our best tips for getting your leftovers to taste just as good as—if not better than—the food did when you first served it. (Yes, you read that right!)

CREATE MAGIC WITH LEFTOVERS: FIVE GREAT TIPS

1. HEAT IT LIKE YOU MEAN IT

Don't just microwave it! Broil, air fry, saute, or bake to bring some crisp and texture back!

2. ADD SEASONINGS, SPICE, OR SOMETHIN' NICE

Flavors fade, so add some seasonings and make it super tasty!

3. ADD MOISTURE

Things are going to dry out, so adding some liquid is KEY.

4. TOP IT OFF

Add some toppings to give your leftovers new life. Yum!

5. REPURPOSE

See our awesome charts for lots of ideas!

LEFTOVER TIP 1: HEAT IT! JUST HEAT IT!

I am weirdly obsessed about the temperature of my food and drinks. If hot food isn't scald-your-mouth hot and cold drinks aren't hurt-your-teeth-and-bash-your-head-in cold, I'm not interested. So please do me a favor—get in there and HEAT your leftovers! And don't think the microwave is your only option, though it is right up there with disposable diapers when it comes to convenience. Use the full array of what's available and use the following tips.

MICROWAVE IT

I know, I know, no one has fifteen minutes to wait for leftovers to heat properly on the stove when you're so hungry you are about to eat the toddler that's screaming at your left leg! If leftovers take forever to fix, you'll find yourself opting for expensive convenience food instead. So learn to love your micro. Here are the basics:

- Put a wet paper towel over your food. Not only does it keep the stuff from drying out, it prevents nasty splatters all over the microwave.
- If you're heating a large chunk of whatever, cut it into smaller pieces so it cooks more evenly.
- Only heat the portion you know you will eat. The fewer times you re-heat food, the better.
- Make sure it's heated thoroughly. Heat it. Stir it. Rotate it. Flip it. Then heat again if needed.
- After your food is nice and heated, take it to the next level: toast it, broil it, or pan-fry it. It adds a little crunch, browns the crust, stiffens the soggy, and helps it feel like a fresh meal.

BROIL IT

If it hasn't happened already, it's time to meet your broiler. It's the high-heat setting in your oven that lets you toast something quickly and intensely. The heat comes off the coils at the very top of the oven. You can broil all kinds of leftovers, including:

- French fries
- Bread
- Sandwiches (flip it over halfway through)
- Pizza
- Anything topped with melted cheese
- Anything topped with a crumb topping
- Anything breaded or fried

Use your imagination and experiment! Whatever you're crisping up in the broiler, remember:

- Heat it first in the microwave or on the stove, then use the broiler to crisp it up or brown the top as a last step. The broiler is so intense that you'll never be able to heat food all the way through before it starts to burn on the top.
- Use a microwave- and oven-safe dish so you don't have to transfer it. Fewer dishes to wash!
- If you want that golden crust, top your food with a little cooking oil, cooking spray, or melted butter. The key words here are "a little."
- Broiling focuses heat on the TOP of the food. That's all. If the bottom, sides, or middle need to be toasted, you should do it on the stove.
- Keep a constant eye on your food under the broiler. A few seconds can mean the difference between perfectly toasted and a roaring oven fire.

CRISP IT

In a frying pan you can, of course, fry, but you can also stir-fry, sauté, and toast food in it. Some of the best leftovers to refresh in a frying pan include pizza (it makes the crust crispy again), burritos & chimichangas, pasta, and large cuts of meat (steak, chicken, pork chops, etc.).

Consider heating the food in the microwave first, even if only partially. You want to get the center warm without burning the outside. To oil, or not to oil—that is the question. It depends on the food and your personal taste. Using a little oil (you don't want to deep-fry!) will slightly brown the outsides and crisp them up a bit.

Another great tool is an air fryer! It's a great way to get a beautiful, crisp texture on both raw and reheated food.

USE A SAUCEPAN

This is the perfect way to heat things like soup, sauce, pasta, shredded meat, and anything else you don't want to crisp or brown. A few tips:

- Use the right size pan for the food you're reheating. Too big? You risk scorching. Too small? The stuff will take forever to heat.
- Restore the food to its original consistency by adding liquid—water, chicken or beef stock, milk, cream, or butter. Leftovers can be nasty if they get dried out.
- Use a whisk, spoon, spatula, or tongs (good for pasta and meat) to stir and turn the food frequently so it gets evenly heated.
- Keep the heat moderate. You want to warm the food slowly and evenly.

LEFTOVER TIP 2: ADD SEASONINGS, SPICE, OR SOMETHIN' NICE

This is me, officially giving you permission to get adventurous with those boring leftovers! You do NOT have to eat them as they currently are. Flavoring your leftovers with some fun herbs, spices, and even sauces will kick them up a notch (or ten!). Here are some essentials from the Jordan Test Kitchen:

- Salt and pepper are essential, obviously. Do not disregard the power of a pinch of salt!
- A little more of whatever herbs or spices you originally used in the dish.
- Crystalized lemon or lime—this stuff is magical! (or a squeeze of lemon or lime juice, if that's what you've got!)
- Red pepper flakes (adds a little kick!)
- A sauce that matches the cuisine style.
- Even a little extra onion or garlic can go a long way!
- Consider getting creative with blended seasonings. Some of my favorite blends: garlic + rosemary, Italian blend, lemon + herb, zesty southwest, or create your own by getting creative with what you have!

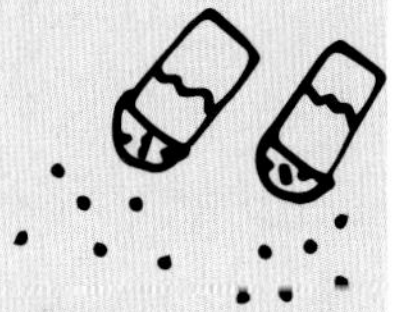

LEFTOVER TIP 3: ADD MOISTURE

Dry mashed potatoes? Stir in some melted butter and a little milk. Dry rice? Add a tablespoon of water before you reheat it. Dry, crusty bread? Dip it in soup, spread melted butter on it, or wrap the bread in a damp paper towel and nuke it for 10 seconds. Moisture = magic! Consider any of the following to moisten things up:

- Salsa
- Sour cream
- Salad dressing
- BBQ sauce
- Mayonnaise/mustard/ketchup
- Pasta sauce
- Oil and/or vinegar
- Tabasco/Sriracha
- Teriyaki/soy sauce
- Lemon or lime juice (fresh or bottled)
- Butter
- Beef or chicken broth
- Milk or cream

LEFTOVER TIP 4: TOP IT OFF

Time for the cherry on top! A little topper seals the deal and adds some sorely needed texture to otherwise boring leftovers. Try some of these topping ideas:

- Cheese! Toss cheese on just about anything to kick it up a notch, especially when you broil it for a second in the oven. Parmesan, cheddar, mozzarella, you name it. Don't forget about crumbled cheese like feta, blue cheese, or even queso resco (my personal fave)
- Crushed tortilla or corn chips
- Crushed potato chips or crackers
- Bread or cornflake crumbs (especially great mixed with a little melted butter)
- Tortilla strips
- Nuts—sliced, slivered, candied, chopped, you name it
- Onion straws
- Croutons
- Sunflower seeds (shelled)

Savings Tip!

Vegetable trimmings can be re-used to create a tasty stock. When you have things like ugly veggies, carrot tops, ends of onions, herb stems, corn cobs, leftover greens, or tomato cores, put them in a zip-top bag in the freezer. When you're ready, defrost these items you usually throw away, throw them into a big pot, and cover with water. Simmer for a couple of hours and strain for a veggie stock to rival the best expensive store brands.

LEFTOVER IDEAS

tips & tricks on how to repurpose food

True story...one of my biggest pet peeves in life is repeating something too often. If I love a song, I will actually change the radio station when I hear it come on, just so I don't get sick of it! I love having a big closet of clothes so I can mix and match in order to rarely repeat outfits. The same goes for my food! It's okay (nay, encouraged) to get creative and reinvent your leftovers! Here are a few ideas to get your creative juices flowing. And please note—these are just a few of zillions of things you can do with these items!

	LEFTOVER	REPURPOSE
	bread	Chop it up and toast or bake into croutons Dry it out, place in food processor to create breadcrumbs Re-use in a toasted or baked sandwich Cube it and mix into a breakfast casserole Let it soak up the custard in a bread pudding Soak in egg, cinnamon, and nutmeg for yummy french toast Mix into a meatloaf Use it for a stuffing (not just for Thanksgiving)
	cake	Cut it into individual portions and freeze it Make cake balls—blend the frosting and cake, roll into balls (add a little bit of flour if needed to make it stiff enough), and insert sucker sticks
	chicken, grilled	Chicken salad sandwiches Dice it for soup Add it to a casserole Use it to make tacos, burritos, or enchiladas Make a chicken stir-fry Stir in some sauce and serve it over rice
	chicken, rotisserie	Chicken pot pie Chicken noodle soup BBQ chicken tacos Chicken salad sandwiches Chicken quesadillas Chicken wraps Chicken tortilla soup Chicken-fried rice Chicken/pasta salad Chicken tacos/enchiladas Chicken burritos/taquitos Hawaiian haystacks Chicken and dumplings BBQ chicken pizza White chicken chili

LEFTOVER		REPURPOSE
	chips	Crush them to use on top of casseroles Use corn chips to make taco salad If the chips are in mini-bags, make Walking Tacos: add favorite taco toppings to the bag of chips
	cole slaw	Put it on a sandwich (shredded pork, chicken, BBQ beef, etc.) Tuck it in a taco (steak, chicken, or halibut) Egg rolls Stir it into any salad Throw it on hot dogs
	fruit	Make smoothies/make-ahead smoothie bags to pop in freezer Put chunks of fruit in ice cube trays, fill with water and freeze
	ham	Toss it with veggies to make ham-fried rice Ham and potato soup Casseroles Omelets Scrambled eggs Chef salad Ham sandwiches Breakfast muffins
	hamburgers	Chop it up & make hamburger soup Cheeseburger casserole Chili (that's how Wendy's does it) Make mini sliders with different toppings

LEFTOVER	REPURPOSE
 rice	Fried rice Add to a soup Mexican rice Add to meatballs Add to a meatloaf Rice fritters
 sandwiches	Cut into individual portions and freeze Deconstruct and use bread to make croutons/breadcrumbs Use the slices of meat and cheese to make roll-ups Chop up the meat and cheese to use in scrambled eggs, omelets Use in breakfast egg muffins Bread the sandwiches and bake them! You've heard of the famous Monte Cristo sandwiches? That's what they are: breaded and served with berry jam.
 soda	Make a cake! Mix 12 ounces of soda and 1 boxed cake mix; bake as directed. That's all there is to it! If you use light-colored soda (like Sprite or 7Up), use a light-colored cake mix (like vanilla or yellow). If you use a dark-colored soda (like Coke), use a dark-colored cake mix like chocolate or Devil's food. Easy peasy!
 veggie trays	Freeze separate veggies in baggies to use later Separate into small lunch bag size portions Use them in stir-fry dishes Roast the veggies (brush on a little olive oil) You can even make your own baby food—cook the veggie and put it in the blender until smooth

the ultimate choose-your-own adventure:

BUILD YOUR OWN RECIPES

Build-Your-Own Recipe

SMOOTHIES

TOSS IT ALL IN THE BLENDER AND BLEND UNTIL SMOOTH, OR PREPARE IN BAGS AND FREEZE FOR A LATER DATE

ITEM		USE ONE OR MORE
fruit		strawberries mangos oranges raspberries blueberries blackberries peaches cherries grapes apples
bananas		no substitute. bananas have a rich, creamy texture that blends well and thickens up smoothies.
veggies		spinach carrots cucumbers avocados
yogurt		greek plain vanilla flavored
liquid		fruit juice milk ice
add-ins		chia seeds acai berries coconut oil flax seeds wheatgrass cayenne goji berries (soaked) turmeric cinnamon spirulina Emergen-C™

Build-Your-Own Recipe

SALAD

ITEM		USE ONE OR MORE
		CHOP IT UP AND TOSS IT IN A BOWL OR INDIVIDUAL CONTAINERS FOR EASY LUNCHES
greens		arugula nappa cabbage escarole romaine iceberg frisee & chicory green leaf red leaf lettuce bibb butter lettuce boston lettuce
veggies		beets radicchio red onion bell peppers carrots radish whatever you have in the kitchen!
fruits		berries apples grapes pear avocado pomegranates mandarin oranges anything on hand!
protein		chicken breast turkey shrimp cheese chickpeas black beans egg tofu hamburger meat pulled pork
dressing		use your favorite bottle from the store or save some money by making your own! (see page 215 or 264)
toppings		crunch: seeds nuts croutons bacon bits chow mein noodles fresh herbs: parsley basil cilantro mint chives

Build-Your-Own Recipe

TRADITIONAL SALSA

ITEM		CHOOSE ONE

CHOP BY HAND OR IN A FOOD PROCESSOR, OR BLEND IN A BLENDER UNTIL IT'S THE CONSISTENCY YOU LIKE

ITEM		CHOOSE ONE
tomatoes		2 large fresh tomatoes 6 roma tomatoes, chopped 1 large can whole tomatoes, diced 1 large can chopped tomatoes, diced 2 10-ounce cans tomatoes with green chilis and onion
onion		½ yellow onion, chopped ½ red onion, chopped ½ sweet onion, chopped
peppers		1 red bell pepper, finely diced 1 green bell pepper, finely diced
heat		1 jalapeño, chopped 1 Anaheim chile, chopped *remove seeds to decrease the heat
liquid		Juice of 1 lime Juce of 1 lemon
extras		Use all the following: 1 tablespoon olive oil 1–3 cloves garlic 1 bunch chopped cilantro 1 teaspoon cumin 1 teaspoon salt ½ teaspoon black pepper 1 teaspoon sugar chili powder (optional, to taste)

Build-Your-Own Recipe

FRUIT SALSA

ITEM		CHOOSE ONE
	CHOP UP WHAT YOU WANT FOR YOUR SALSA:	
fruit		*Pick one, peel & pit as needed:* 2 cups chopped fresh pineapple 2 cups chopped mango 1 orange + 2 kiwi 2 cups chopped watermelon
onion		½ red onion, coarsely chopped ½ yellow onion, coarsely chopped *with mango:* 2/3 cup chopped green onion *with watermelon:* ¼ chopped onion
veggies		½ cup red bell pepper, chopped ½ cup green bell pepper, chopped 1 avocado, coarsely chopped
heat		1 jalapeño, chopped 1 anaheim chile, chopped *remove seeds to decrease the heat
liquid		juice of 1 lime *with watermelon:* 2 tablespoons balsamic vinegar juice of 1 lemon
spices		use as many as desired: salt and pepper garlic salt fresh cilantro, chopped fresh parsley, chopped

Build-Your-Own Recipe

MUFFINS

ITEM — **PICK ONE**

PICK YOUR INGREDIENTS AND FOLLOW DIRECTIONS BELOW

grain

2 cups white flour
1½ cups whole-wheat flour
1 cups white flour + 1 cup whole-wheat flour
1 cups white whole-wheat + 1 cup white flour
1 cup oat flour + 1 cup white flour
1 cup rye flour + 1 cup white flour
2 cups Bisquick
2 cups alternate flours: rice, almond, buckwheat, potato, soy, corn, tapioca, quinoa

sweetener

¾ cup white sugar
¾ cup packed brown sugar
½ cup honey
½ cup maple syrup
¾ teasoon stevia
⅜ cup fruit puree (banana, fig, papaya)

salt

½ teaspoon salt

leavening

3 teaspoons baking powder
1½ teaspoons cream of tartar + ¾ teaspoon baking soda
¾ teaspoon baking soda + ¾ teaspoon cream of tartar + ¾ teaspoon cornstarch
1½ cups buttermilk + ¾ teaspoon baking soda (eliminate liquid)
1½ cups sour milk + ¾ teaspoon baking soda (eliminate liquid)
1½ cups plain yogurt + ¾ teaspoon baking soda (cut liquid to 1 cup)
1½ teaspoons cream of tartar + ¾ teaspoon baking soda
1½ teaspoons lemon juice + ¾ teaspoon baking soda
1½ teaspoons vinegar + ¾ teaspoon baking soda

binder

1 egg
½ medium banana, mashed
¼ cup buttermilk
¼ cup applesauce
¼ cup plain yogurt

ITEM		PICK ONE
liquid		1 cup milk ½ cup evaporated milk + ½ cup water 1 cup water + ⅓ cup dry milk powder 1 cup plain yogurt 1 cup sour cream 1 cup water + 1 Tablespoon butter 1 cup almond milk 1 cup soy milk 1 cup coconut milk 1 cup heavy white cream 1 cup evaporated milk
oil		¼ cup vegetable oil ¼ cup alternative oil: canola oil, corn oil, coconut oil, olive oil, sesame oil, flaxseed oil ¼ cup butter ¼ cup buttermilk ¼ cup applesauce ¼ cup mayonnaise ¼ cup mashed fruit
add-in	 	1 cup raisins 1 cup finely chopped, pitted dates 1 cup chopped nuts ¾ cup dried cranberries + ½ cup chopped nuts 1 cup fresh or frozen blueberries 1 cup cinnamon chips 1 cup chocolate chips ¾ cup peeled, diced apples + ¼ teaspoon cinnamon ¾ cup dried pears or apricots, diced ¾ cup prunes, diced ¾ cup grated carrots + ¾ cup chopped walnuts ¾ cup crushed pineapple (drained) + ½ cup sweetened shredded coconut 1 cup mashed bananas + ½ cup chopped nuts 1 cup canned pumpkin + ½ teaspoon pumpkin pie spice + ½ cup nuts 1 cup grated cheese + ¼ cup crisp, cooked, crumbled bacon

DIRECTIONS

Use your selected ingredients and assemble in the order below:

1. Preheat oven to 400° F.
2. In a large bowl, combine grain, sweetener, salt, and leavening.
3. In a small bowl, combine binder, liquid, and oil. Pour into the mixture in the large bowl and mix with a fork only until all ingredients are moistened. The batter will be lumpy.
4. Stir in add-ins; do not beat.
5. Generously grease 12 muffin cups, or use paper cupcake liners instead. Fill cups ¾ full with batter. Bake 18-25 minutes or until golden and toothpick comes out clean when poked in the center. Immediately remove from muffin tin and cool on wire racks.

Build-Your-Own Recipe

PASTA

ITEM		USE ONE OR MORE
		COOK PASTA ACCORDING TO PACKAGE DIRECTIONS, ADD EVERYTHING ELSE TO PASTA AS DESIRED AND ENJOY!
noodle		spaghetti, linguini, macaroni, rigatoni, zucchini, spaghetti squash, carrot noodles, black bean pasta, whatever your family loves!
veggie		broccoli, bell peppers, peas, mushrooms, sliced asparagus, zucchini, steamed kale, spinach
protein		steak, ground beef, chicken, pork, chorizo, lentils, quinoa, anything left over!
sauce		use your favorite store-bought jar or or make your own sauce using one of our recipes on pp. 258, 259, 260, or 262
topping		bread crumbs, cornflakes, lemon zest, chili flakes, butter, herbs, cheese, more cheese!

Brilliant Tip!

If using meat, cook that first. Then par-cook your vegetables separately, and finish it by mixing it all together with sauce in a sauté pan with your almost-cooked pasta.

Build-Your-Own Recipe

LASAGNA

ITEM		USE ONE OR MORE

LAYER IN A PAN & BAKE AT 350° FOR 1 HOUR OR UNTIL NOODLES ARE SOFT & SAUCE IS BUBBLY, OR FREEZE FOR LATER

lasagna noodles		you can also use any pasta (layered baked pasta is totally delicious)
meat		ground beef ground pork turkey sausage grilled sausage grilled chicken sauteed shrimp
sauce		marinara sauce alfredo sauce bolognese (meat) sauce pesto
cheese		mozzarella ricotta Parmigiano-Reggiano
vegetables		zucchini bell pepper onions squash carrots mushrooms
topping		broccoli fresh herbs mixed veggies crispy prosciutto ham

Build-Your-Own Recipe

TORTILLA SOUP

ITEM		PICK ONE
oil		1 tablespoon virgin olive oil 1 tablespoon vegetable oil
onion		½ onion, chopped 1 tablespoon onion powder
garlic		3 large cloves, minced ½ teaspoon garlic powder
veggies		2 cans diced tomatoes with chilis (pulse in blender) 1½ cups corn (drained if canned)
beans	 	2 cans black beans, rinsed & drained 2 cans kidney beans, rinsed & drained 2 cans chickpeas, rinsed & drained
meat		2 cups cooked shredded beef 2 cups cooked shredded chicken 2 cups cooked shredded pork
flavor liquid		4 cups chicken broth 4 cups vegetable broth 4 cups water + 4 teaspoons bouillon 4 cups water + 4 bouillon cubes

ITEM		AMOUNT
seasonings		1 teaspoon ground cumin 2 teaspoons chili powder salt & pepper to taste
add-ins		1 jalapeño, diced and seeded ¼ cup cilantro, chopped 1 lime, juiced 2 cups cooked long-grain rice
toppings		6" corn tortillas 1 avocado, diced ½ cup sour cream 1 cup shredded cheese

DIRECTIONS

1. Cut six 6" tortillas into 1/4" strips. Fry in oil in a frying pan over medium-high heat until crisp. Sprinkle with salt. Set aside.
2. Heat oil in a large pot over medium heat. Add onion. Sauté until soft, about 3-5 minutes. Add garlic and sauté for 1 to 2 minutes. Add veggies, beans, meat, liquid and seasonings; simmer for 10 minutes. Add salt and pepper to taste.
3. Top with tortilla strips and other desired ingredients; serve immediately.

Freeze it!

Allow soup to cool, then store flat in zip-top baggies in the freezer (without the tortilla strips). Thaw in the fridge overnight.

Build-Your-Own Recipe

CREAM SOUP

ITEM | **CHOOSE ONE**

---

butter or oil

⅓ cup butter
3 tablespoons olive oil
3 tablespoons vegetable oil

---

onion

½ cup onion, chopped

---

thickener

3 tablespoons flour
3 tablespoons cornstarch

---

seasonings

As many as you like, starting with
½ teaspoon of salt & pepper

onion powder	thyme
garlic powder	parsley
basil	tarragon
oregano	chives
Italian seasoning	cilantro
chicken bullion	paprika

---

cream

Pick one, or combine all
add 1 cup at a time until you reach
your desired creaminess

milk	evaporated milk*
heavy cream	sour cream
half & half	plain greek yogurt

* don't bring to rapid boil or it will curdle!

---

flavor liquid

4 cups-6 cups stock or broth
(chicken, beef, vegetable)
Can add
¼ cup dry red or white wine
(for additional flavor if desired)

ITEM	AMOUNT
add-ins	Add as many as you like: 2 cups cooked chopped mushrooms 1½ cups potato, chopped, diced & cooked 1½ cups broccoli, cooked & finely chopped 1½ cups cauliflower, finely chopped cooked 1½ cups cream-style corn 1 cups cooked chicken, shredded/chopped 1½ cups diced tomatoes with juice 1½ cups chopped cooked asparagus + ½ teaspoon nutmeg 1 cup cooked pasta (add at very end, after everything else has simmered) Cooked meat (sausage, diced ham, ground beef, or diced chicken)
toppings	shredded cheese (Parmesan is a favorite!) cream cheese diced green onions scallions chives bacon bits parsley cilantro

DIRECTIONS

This cream soup will turn out deliciously no matter what flavor you choose:

1. In a large saucepan over low heat, melt butter; add onion and cook until onion is browned. Pour in stock.

2. Stir in thickener and seasonings; blend well.

3. Pour in milk gradually, whisking; cook, stirring constantly, about 5 min or until soup is thickened.

4. Stir in add-ins until heated through and cheese is melted. Add toppings as desired.

Build-Your-Own Recipe

MEXICAN-INSPIRED DISH

ITEM		PICK ONE
tortilla		flour tortillas
meat		shredded beef shredded chicken shredded pork
rice		white rice Spanish/Mexican rice brown rice
beans		black beans pinto beans refried beans
shredded cheese		cheddar Monterey-jack colby-jack jalapeño-jack queso fresco cotija
toppings		salsa sour cream guacamole chopped tomatoes sliced olives shredded cheese shredded lettuce

DIRECTIONS

Regardless of how you prepare your dish, here are some important tips to remember as you assemble:

1. Cook (or reheat) the meat, rice, and beans before assembling any of the following dishes.

2. When assembling burritos, chimichangas and taquitos place fillings—meat, rice, beans, cheese—near one side down the length of the tortilla; leave a little room at the top, bottom, and side. Fold the top and bottom over the filling. Fold the side nearest the filling over the filling; continue rolling/folding until all the filling is securely tucked in.

3. If you freeze or refrigerate, garnish with toppings after reheating.

FOR TACOS: Assemble as desired. Pro-tip: Start with refried beans to help the other toppings stay put better on the shell!

FOR TOSTADAS: Preheat broiler. Lay tortilla flat on a baking sheet, spread beans first, top with rice, meat, and cheese. Broil until cheese is melted! Add desired toppings!

FOR QUESADILLAS: Warm tortilla in a pan on the stove, add desired fillings and cheese. Allow cheese to melt then fold the tortilla over and add additional toppings. Larger flour tortillas are the best, but any tortilla will do.

FOR NACHOS: Preheat oven to 325 °F. Spread a layer of tortilla chips on a baking sheet. Sprinkle other desired toppings over chips evenly (meat, rice, beans, and cheese), bake until the cheese is melted. Add desired toppings and serve!

FOR BURRITOS: Assemble as desired. See how much you can fit in your tortilla when you wrap it up! Eat warm or bake in the oven and add toppings.

FOR CHIMICHANGAS: Add desired filling. Fry or bake until golden brown and crispy. To serve, garnish with toppings.

FOR TAQUITOS: For best results, warm tortillas before adding 2 T. of filling into tortillas. Roll up tightly, use toothpicks to keep them closed. Fry or bake until golden and crispy! Serve with rice and toppings of choice.

Build-Your-Own Recipe

FRIED RICE

ITEM		PICK ONE
oil		vegetable oil canola oil light/refined olive oil peanut oil
eggs		no substitute
sauce		soy sauce (recommended!) can add any others as well: oyster sauce teriyaki sauce toasted sesame oil umami sauce
veggies		Pick any mix of fresh & frozen chop veggies small to ensure they all cook the same! bell peppers green onions green peas carrots mushrooms pineapple kimchi edamame
meat		shrimp, chopped bacon, cooked and chopped sausage, cooked and crumbled ham, cooked and chopped chicken, cooked and chopped pork, cooked and chopped lunch meat, chopped

ITEM		AMOUNT
seasonings		Add as many as desired, to taste: salt & pepper garlic garlic powder dried ginger minced ginger scallions (garnish/topping) cilantro (garnish/topping)
cooked rice		any kind of rice works well cold, cooked rice works even better

DIRECTIONS

This is a perfect clean-out-your fridge recipe—delicious every time!

1. In a skillet, heat a little oil with a small amount of soy sauce over medium heat. Break egg into skillet and whisk with a fork until egg is cooked. Remove egg from skillet.

2. Add more oil and seasonings to skillet, and cook veggies until soft; add the ones that are quickest to cook at the end. Add meat. Heat through.

3. Push veggies and meat to the side of the skillet. Add more oil and the rice. Cook until the rice is heated through. Add egg at the end and season with plenty of soy sauce.

NOTE: At any one of these steps, use just enough oil to keep foods from sticking to the skillet and to lightly coat the ingredients.

Freeze it!

Spread your just-cooked rice evenly over a cookie sheet and allow to cool. Scoop into plastic bags and store flat in freezer. Reheat in the microwave or skillet.

Build-Your-Own Recipe

PIZZA AND CALZONES

Start with the dough—I offer you three below—slap on some sauce, sprinkle with shredded cheese, choose your toppings, and bake! Let's start with pizza, and you'll find the calzone variations on the next page.

DOUGH OPTIONS

STYLE	INGREDIENT	DIRECTIONS
NO FAIL CRUST	1 teaspoon active dry yeast 1½ cups warm water 4 cups flour 1 teaspoon kosher salt ⅓ cup olive oil plus more for drizzling	Sprinkle yeast over water; let stand for a few minutes or until bubbly. Combine flour and salt in bowl of mixer; turn mixer on low and drizzle in ⅓ C. oil. Add the yeast mixture. Mix just until combined; dough should be sticky. Lightly coat mixing bowl with oil; form dough into ball and roll around bowl to coat with oil; cover tightly with plastic wrap; let rise for 1–2 hours. Roll dough to ¼ inch thickness. *Dough can be refrigerated for as long as 4 days; bring to room temperature before shaping.*
TWO-INGREDIENT CRUST	1¾ cups self-rising flour 1 cup plain or Greek yogurt	In a medium bowl, combine flour and yogurt; mix well. Knead on a lightly floured surface until smooth and elastic, about 5 minutes. Roll dough to ¼ inch thickness. Makes 1 large or 2 small pizzas. *Dough can be refrigerated for as long as 2 days; bring to room temperature before shaping.*
CAULIFLOWER CRUST *Cutting carbs? This crust is more work but virtually no carbs.*	1 head cauliflower, broken into florets ½ cup mozzarella cheese, shredded ¼ cup Parmesan cheese, grated ½ teaspoon oregano ½ teaspoon kosher salt ¼ teaspoon garlic powder 2 eggs, slightly beaten	In a food processor, pulse florets to a fine texture. Steam, drain well, and cool. In a large bowl, combined steamed cauliflower and remaining ingredients; mix well. Cover baking sheet with parchment paper; form cauliflower mixture into a round shape about ¼ to ½ inch thick in center of the sheet.

ITEM		PICK ONE
dough		no fail crust two ingredient crust cauliflower crust
sauce		pizza sauce (jar or homemade) marinara sauce (jar or homemade) alfredo sauce tomato sauce + minced garlic + olive oil pesto (jar or homemade) barbeque sauce
cheese		mozzarella buffalo mozzarella provolone cheddar fresh-grated Parmesan bleu fontina Gruyere ricotta gouda
meats	 	pepperoni browned ground beef thinly sliced steak browned sausage sliced salami cubed ham shredded chicken, plain or barbecue buffalo chicken bacon, cooked and crumbled panchetta shrimp, crab, or lobster
additional toppings	 	tomatoes, sliced or chopped mushrooms, sliced black olives, sliced spinach or arugula, chopped onions, caramelized onions, chopped or sliced sweet onions, chopped or sliced red onions, chopped or sliced green onions, sliced green, red, yellow peppers, sliced marinated artichoke hearts, sliced fresh basil leaves chopped broccoli pineapple

DIRECTIONS

PIZZA*

1. Preheat oven to 475°F or 500°F—the hotter the oven, the crisper the crust.

2. Pizza can be baked in a pizza pan, inverted baking sheet, or on a pizza stone. For best results, cover the pan or stone with parchment paper; you can also sprinkle the pan or stone with a little cornmeal or flour.

3. Bake for 5 minutes. If using parchment paper, slide it out from under the crust. Rotate pizza; bake 5 additional minutes or until crust is golden brown and cheese is melted and browned in places.

4. Remove from oven and let cool slightly before slicing.

* For cauliflower crust pizza, first bake crust for 20 minutes at 400°. Then add toppings and bake for 10 more minutes. Cauliflower crusts should always be pre-baked from scratch.

CALZONES:

1. Let dough rest for ½ hour in an oiled bowl covered with a towel. After the dough has risen and rested, punch it down and divide it into balls.

2. Stretch each ball out into a round shape, ¼ to ½ inch thick. Spread sauce on half of each calzone to within 1 inch of the edge. Sprinkle cheese over the sauce.

3. Cover cheese with desired toppings. Fold the side of the dough over to create a half-moon-shaped calzone; using fingers or a fork, pinch and seal the edges.

4. Calzones can be baked on a baking sheet or pizza stone; sprinkle with cornmeal and arrange the calzones on the sheet or stone. Bake at 475–500°F for 12–15 minutes, or until the crust is a light golden brown. Serve with marinara sauce or pizza sauce for dipping.

MAKE AHEAD, FREEZE FOR LATER

TO FREEZE: Let pizza cool completely, wrap in tin foil or plastic wrap and store in an airtight container. It will keep for 3-6 months.

TO THAW: Remove from the freezer and re-heat, covered, in an oven-safe container until toppings are warm and melted.

take something plain and dress it up nice!

NAKED RECIPES

when you're in a fowl mood

NAKED CHICKEN

Why did the chicken cross the road? To get dressed up because it is BORING when it's naked! That might be a terrible joke. But it's also the truth!

You might have steered away from chicken breasts—or had a less-than-awesome experience with them—because of their tendency to turn out dry and tough instead of moist and tender. That can especially happen with boneless, skinless breasts. But here are a few things you can do to ensure moist, tender, delectable chicken every time, as well as more than twenty ways to prepare plain ol' chicken breasts and transform them into something incredible!

CHICKEN TIPS

- Put a piece of parchment paper over chicken breasts while they're baking; it acts like a "skin" to hold in the juices.
- Sear the chicken breasts in a hot skillet just until golden, no more than a couple of minutes on each side. Heat the skillet and the cooking oil before you put the chicken in the pan. You're not trying to cook them through—just give enough of a sear to seal in the juices. Then transfer to a baking pan and bake as directed in the recipe.
- Dredge the chicken in a mixture of flour, salt, and pepper, shaking off the excess. You'll get a very light crust that will help retain the juices.
- Use a meat mallet, rolling pin, or the bottom of a small frying pan; pound chicken breasts until they're all the same thickness—that way you don't end up undercooking some and overcooking others in the same pan.
- Resist the urge to keep "checking on" the chicken, whether it's in a skillet, in the oven, or on the grill. You'll disrupt the cooking process and end up cooking the living daylights out of it.
- Avoid overcooking chicken—the main culprit in dry, tough meat. Generally, chicken is "done" when it's no longer pink in the middle and the juices run clear. If you want to be sure, use a meat thermometer; the center should be at least 165°F.

20 WAYS TO PREPARE CHICKEN BREASTS

If you've got chicken breasts in your fridge or freezer just begging to be cooked, try one of these 20 scrumptious ways of preparing them. All suggestions below call for 4 boneless, skinless chicken breast halves unless otherwise noted. Enjoy!

STYLE	TOP IT/MIX IT WITH	HOW TO PREPARE IT
SUGARY SPICED CHICKEN	Make a marinade by combining ¼ cup brown sugar 2 tablespoons paprika 1 tablespoon garlic powder 1 teaspoon oregano ½ teaspoon pepper ¼ teaspoon salt	Put chicken breasts in the marinade and shake to coat chicken. Chill for 2–3 hours or overnight. Discard marinade. Bake on a lined baking sheet in a 425°F oven for 20–25 minutes. Slice chicken into strips and add to a salad, a bed of veggies, or serve over baked potatoes.
7-UP CHICKEN	Make a marinade by combining 1 cup vegetable oil ¼ teaspoon garlic powder 2 cups 7-Up 1 cup soy sauce 1 teaspoon horseradish Pour into a gallon-size zip-top bag	Put chicken breasts in the marinade and shake to coat chicken. Chill overnight. Discard marinade. Sauté, bake, or grill the chicken. Dice or shred and serve over rice or on your favorite toasted bun!
CHICKEN AND RICE CASSEROLE	Mix together: 2 cups long-grain rice 1 can cream of mushroom soup 1 can cream of chicken soup 1 cup water 1 teaspoon oregano 1 ounce package onion soup mix 1-2 cups veggies (optional)	Combine rice, soup, and desired veggies (optional) and pour into a greased 9x13 baking dish. Season chicken with salt and pepper, arrange over rice mixture. Sprinkle with onion soup mix. Cover tightly with aluminum foil. Bake at 350°F for 1 hour and 15 minutes. Garnish with parsley, if desired.
CHICKEN ROLLUPS	8 ounces cream cheese 4 tablespoons softened butter ½ cup finely diced celery 2 tablespoons minced onion ½ teaspoon salt ¼ teaspoon pepper 3 cans refrigerated crescent rolls Optional: breadcrumbs, melted butter	Dice the cooked chicken. Mix chicken with all ingredients except rolls. Place spoonful of chicken mixture on each roll; seal shut; bake at 375°F for 10 minutes. If desired, can be rolled in breadcrumbs or dipped in melted butter before baking.

STYLE	TOP IT/MIX IT WITH	HOW TO PREPARE IT
HAWAIIAN CHICKEN	Make a marinade by combining ¼ cup reduced-sodium soy sauce ¼ cup pineapple juice ¼ cup packed brown sugar 2 tablespoons ketchup 1 tablespoon fresh grated ginger 3 cloves minced garlic 1 teaspoon sesame oil Pour into a gallon-size zip-top bag, reserving ¼ cup of the mixture	Put chicken breasts in marinade and chill for 1 hour or overnight. Turn occasionally to coat chicken. Drain and discard marinade. Over a medium-high grill, cook chicken 5–6 minutes on each side until done, basting with reserved marinade. Serve over rice.
CHICKEN PESTO SANDWICH	For pesto, combine in a food processor 1 cup fresh basil leaves 3 cloves peeled garlic 3 tablespoons pine nuts ⅓ cup grated Parmesan cheese salt and pepper to taste While motor runs, drizzle in ⅓ cup olive oil until well blended. Pour into a gallon-size zip-top bag.	On 4 toasted baguettes, layer shredded cooked chicken, ½ cup pesto, Greek yogurt, sliced tomatoes, arugula, and sliced mozzarella cheese.
THAI CHICKEN	2 tablespoons unsalted butter 4 cloves garlic, minced ½ cup yellow onion, diced salt & pepper, to taste 1 carrot, shredded ½ cup shredded cabbage 3 green onions, chopped ¼ cup peanuts, chopped 2 tablespoons cilantro, chopped Peanut sauce on page 266 butter lettuce (optional)	Make the peanut sauce, stir until smooth, and set aside. Heat oil in skillet over medium heat. Add diced chicken, garlic, onions, salt and pepper and cook until chicken is cooked. Add carrots, cabbage, and green onions; cook for 2 more minutes. Add sauce to pan, cilantro, toss everything until combined. Serve in lettuce wraps, buns, or over rice. Garnish with peanuts and green onions.
RITZY BAKED CHICKEN	1 cup Ritz crackers, crumbled garlic powder (to taste) ½ teaspoon seasoning salt ¼ cup Parmesan cheese plain yogurt	Combine cracker crumbs, garlic powder, seasoning salt, and Parmesan cheese. Dip chicken in plain yogurt to coat, then in cracker crumb mixture. Bake on a greased cookie sheet at 350°F for 45 minutes to an hour. Serve with mashed potatoes.

STYLE	TOP IT/MIX IT WITH	HOW TO PREPARE IT
SALSA VERDE CHICKEN ENCHILADA CASSEROLE	⅓ cup chopped fresh cilantro 1 cup sweet corn 1 cup black beans 3 ounces cream cheese ½ teaspoon each: chili powder and ground cumin salt and pepper, to taste ½ cup chopped onion 1 teaspoon minced garlic green enchilada sauce on page 269 12 corn tortillas, quartered 1 cup shredded cheddar cheese	Preheat oven to 425°F. Cook, shred chicken. Mix 2 T. cilantro, corn, beans, cream cheese, spices, onion, & garlic. Add mixture to chicken. Reduce heat; simmer 15 min. In 9X13 pan, spread thin green enchilada sauce layer. Place 16 tortilla quarters over sauce, then ½ chicken mixture, cheese. Repeat layers. Top with tortillas and remaining sauce. Sprinkle with cheese. Bake 15 min. Top with salsa, guacamole, sour cream, olives.
CHICKEN SALAD SANDWICHES	¾ cup Miracle Whip or mayo ½ pint heavy cream 1 cup diced celery 1 cup green grapes halved ½ cup almonds 1½ tablespoon fresh parsley 1 can chunk pineapple	Mix Miracle Whip and cream; fold in remaining ingredients with cooked chicken (shredded or cut into bite-size pieces). Season with salt and pepper. Serve in croissants, pita pockets, or on a bed of lettuce.
CANDIED CHICKEN	1½ cup brown sugar ½ cup ketchup ¼ cup chopped onion ¼ cup mustard 1 tablespoon Worcestershire sauce ½ teaspoon salt	Mix all ingredients and add ¾ cup water. Season chicken with salt and pepper and dredge in flour; brown in oil in skillet. Transfer chicken to a greased baking dish; cover with sauce. Bake, covered, at 350°F for 2¼ hours; remove cover during last 15 minutes. Serve over rice with pineapple.
CHICKEN DIVAN	2 heads broccoli (steamed until tender) 3 cans cream of chicken soup 1½ cups mayonnaise 1½ teaspoon lemon juice ¾ teaspoon curry ¾ cup breadcrumbs 1½ tablespoons melted butter ¾ cup shredded cheese.	Arrange steamed broccoli in greased 9 x 13 pan. Top with cooked chicken cut into bite-size pieces. Combine soup, mayo, lemon juice, and curry; pour over chicken. Combine breadcrumbs and melted butter; sprinkle on top. Bake at 350°F for 30 minutes; top with cheese for the last 5 minutes. Serve over rice or egg noodles.
BAKED LEMON CHICKEN	Combine ⅓ cup chicken broth 4 tablespoons lemon juice 1 tablespoon honey 2 teaspoons minced garlic 1 teaspoon italian seasoning 1 teaspoon salt ¼ teaspoon pepper	Brown chicken in a skillet in 3 tablespoons butter just until browned, about 3 minutes on each side. Transfer to a greased casserole dish. Pour sauce over chicken. Bake at 400°F for 30 minutes, spooning sauce from the pan over the chicken every 5–10 minutes while cooking. Serve with rice, pasta, quinoa, or potatoes.

STYLE	TOP IT/MIX IT WITH	HOW TO PREPARE IT
CHICKEN KABOBS	4 cups chopped veggies (bite size chunks: zucchini, yellow squash, bell peppers, mushrooms, cherry tomato, onion) Dressing or marinade of choice	Place veggies in large bag; add ½ the dressing. Place cubed chicken in separate bag; add remaining dressing. Seal and marinate for 3-4 hours in the refrigerator. Remove bags; skewer, alternating chicken and veggies. Preheat grill to about 425°F. Cook for 4-5 minutes on each side, flipping once. Remove from grill. Serve immediately with rice, pasta, side salad, or toasted roll.
SUN-DRIED TOMATO CREAM SAUCE	½ cup chopped sun-dried tomatoes tomato cream sauce on page 262 Parmesan cheese optional: cheesy garlic bread, pasta, rice	Add sliced chicken to heated skillet with butter over medium-high heat. Cook 2-3 minutes per side until cooked through. Remove chicken from skillet and make sauce. After blending sauce, return to pan and add sun-dried tomatoes and chicken; simmer until heated through. Delicious over pasta, rice or over cheesy garlic bread!
BARBECUE CHICKEN	2 tablespoons olive oil 2 teaspoons chili powder ½ teaspoon onion powder ½ teaspoon garlic powder ½ teaspoon oregano 1 teaspoon salt 1 cup barbecue sauce	Combine all ingredients but bbq sauce then coat chicken. Spray skillet with nonstick cooking spray; cook chicken, covered, over medium-high heat for 5 minutes on each side. Pour bbq sauce over the chicken and cook for an additional 3–5 minutes, basting with bbq sauce as the chicken finishes cooking. Shred and serve on rolls, buns, or rice.
BREADED RANCH CHICKEN	¼ cup melted butter ¾ cup grated Parmesan cheese ¾ cup crushed cornflakes 1 envelope Ranch salad dressing mix **This recipe uses 8 chicken breast halves*	Dip each chicken breast in melted butter. Roll in mixed cheese, cornflakes, and Ranch mix. Bake uncovered in a greased 9 x 13 dish at 350°F for 1 hour. Serve with rice or potatoes.
CHICKEN TENDERS IN MUSTARD SAUCE	Combine: ½ cup whole-grain mustard 2 tablespoons fresh chopped tarragon ½ ounce lemon juice 1 clove minced garlic ½ teaspoon paprika ½ teaspoon pepper ¼ teaspoon salt	Mix all ingredients well. Add chicken tenders to mustard sauce; stir to coat chicken. Bake, covered, at 425°F for 20 minutes or until chicken is cooked through. Serve with potatoes: mashed, steak fries, baked, etc.

STYLE	TOP IT/MIX IT WITH	HOW TO PREPARE IT
RAID THE GARDEN CHICKEN	1 clove minced garlic ¼ cup butter (divided) 1 small sliced yellow squash 1 small sliced zucchini squash ½ cup thinly sliced green pepper ½ cup thinly sliced red pepper ¼ cup thinly sliced onion 2 tablespoons flour ½ teaspoon salt ¼ teaspoon pepper ¾ cup chicken broth ½ cup half-and-half	Cut chicken in strips; sauté chicken and garlic in 2 tablespoons butter until chicken is cooked, 10–12 minutes. Add veggies; cook until crisp-tender. Remove from pan. In same pan, melt remaining butter; stir in flour, salt, and pepper to make a smooth paste; gradually add broth. Bring to a boil, then cook and stir for 2 minutes or until thickened. Stir in cream and heat through. Add chicken and veggies and stir until well-mixed. Serve over pasta of your choice.
SLOW COOKER CREAMY CHICKEN NOODLE SOUP	4 cups low sodium chicken broth 5 medium carrots, peeled & diced ½ medium onion, diced 2 ribs celery, diced 2 teaspoons dried thyme 2 teaspoons dried parsley 1 teaspoon salt ¼ teaspoon black pepper 1 cup heavy cream 2 tablespoons flour 3 cups wide egg noodles or other short pasta	Add broth, chicken, carrots, onion, celery, thyme, parsley, salt, and pepper to a slow cooker. Cook 7-8 hours on low or 3 hours on high, until vegetables are tender. Turn slow cooker to high. Whisk together cream and flour; add to the slow cooker with noodles. Cover and cook for 10-20 min., until noodles are cooked and soup has thickened slightly. For a thicker soup, whisk together more cream and flour. The soup thickens as it sits.

chicken kabobs on page 157

nothing fishy about it

NAKED SALMON

Salmon is one of the easiest, fastest things you can prepare—and there's no one "right" way to do it. One of the most important things to remember is to keep the salmon fresh. If you can, eat it the same day you buy it. If that's not possible, you can keep it tightly wrapped in plastic in the coldest part of the fridge for a day or two—no longer! You can also freeze it for up to six months. Thaw it in the fridge overnight.

Not only is salmon one of the easiest and tastiest things you can cook, but it's also one of the most versatile. Try the following:

SALMON TIPS

- **BROIL IT.** Put the seasoned salmon on a sheet pan on the top rack of the oven—about three inches from the red-hot broiler. Don't get distracted; it will be done in about three minutes. If you want the center a little more done, turn off the broiler and let the salmon sit in the oven for three or four more minutes.
- **PAN-FRY IT.** Do this if you want a crunchy, crispy "crust." Put some butter or olive oil in a hot skillet over medium-high heat. Season the salmon with salt and pepper. Starting with the skin side up, cook for five or six minutes. Flip it and cook with the skin side down for an additional three minutes. That's all there is to it!
- **POACH IT.** This is your best option if you're adding sauce, making salmon cakes, or want a fat-free option. Bring water (or other liquid) to a simmer after tossing in a pinch of salt and a few peppercorns; slide the salmon into the water, cover the pan, turn off the heat, and let the salmon cook gently in the warm water for about twenty-five minutes.
- **GRILL IT.** Get the coals (or inside heat source) hot. Lightly coat the salmon with oil. Place it on the grill skin side down and cook for five minutes. Flip it and cook on the other side for another five minutes. Important tip: If the salmon sticks to the grill when you try to flip it, that means it's not quite ready to flip; cook it for another couple of minutes.
- **ROAST IT.** This is the best way to cook for a crowd—you can fit a lot more salmon on a baking sheet than you can in a pan or on a grill. Place the seasoned salmon skin side down on a lightly greased pan; bake at 400 °F for twelve to fifteen minutes. You don't need to flip it while baking (another plus!).
- **STEAM IT.** Here's a close cousin to roasting: Put the seasoned salmon on a piece of foil or parchment; wrap the foil or parchment around the salmon; place on a pan; and bake at 400 °F for twelve to fifteen minutes. The steam does all the work, and the salmon stays super moist!

14 WAYS TO PREPARE SALMON

If you've got salmon in your fridge or freezer just begging to be cooked—or you've just decided to get brave and pick some up at the store—here are 14 mouth-watering ways to prepare it. Unless otherwise indicated, the suggestions below are for 4 salmon fillets. Enjoy!

STYLE	TOP IT/MIX IT WITH	HOW TO PREPARE IT
GINGER GLAZED SALMON	Glaze ingredients: ⅓ cup water ¼ cup rice vinegar 4 cloves minced garlic 2 tablespoons brown sugar 1 tablespoon finely grated fresh ginger 1 teaspoon soy sauce	Season salmon fillets with a little salt; cook salmon on preheated grill or hot pan for 6–8 minutes per side, or until it flakes easily with fork. While salmon cooks, combine glaze ingredients in saucepan over medium heat; bring to boil, reduce heat, simmer until thickened, 2–3 minutes. Spoon glaze over salmon. Serve with rice, quinoa, veggies, or over a bed of greens.
TIN-FOIL SALMON	3 chopped tomatoes 1 medium chopped onion 2 tablespoons olive oil 2 tablespoons fresh lemon juice 1 teaspoon dried oregano 1 teaspoon dried thyme	Sprinkle salmon with some olive oil, salt, and pepper. In a medium bowl, add other ingredients. Place each salmon fillet on a sheet of tin foil; spoon tomato mixture over salmon, and seal each "packet." Place packets on baking sheet and bake at 400°F for 25 minutes. Transfer to plate to serve. Serve with rice, potatoes, or veggies.
SALMON BURGERS	1 tablespoon grill seasoning 1 tablespoon poppy seeds 3 tablespoons fresh chopped dill ½ cup softened cream cheese ½ cup sour cream 3 chopped green onions 1 teaspoon lemon juice Rolls, split and toasted Toppings as desired: sliced red onion, sliced tomato, leaf lettuce	Place chopped skinless salmon in food processor; pulse until coarsely ground. In a bowl, mix salmon with grill seasoning, poppy seeds, and dill. Form 4 patties; drizzle with olive oil. Cook burgers in oiled skillet 4–5 minutes per side. Combine cream cheese, sour cream, green onions, and lemon juice; use as garnish. Serve with your favorite rolls or buns.
SALMON WITH CURRY CREAM SAUCE	1 cup heavy cream 1 teaspoon mild curry powder 1 teaspoon lemon juice 2 pinches ground ginger	In a skillet, combine cream, curry, lemon juice, and ginger; bring to a boil over medium heat. Reduce heat to low and slide salmon fillets into the cream sauce. Cover and simmer about 12 minutes, flipping once or twice during cooking. Season with salt and pepper to taste. Serve over rice.

STYLE	TOP IT/MIX IT WITH	HOW TO PREPARE IT
BROWN SUGAR GLAZED SALMON	Glaze: 2 tablespoons olive oil ¼ cup brown sugar ¼ cup soy sauce 3 minced garlic cloves 5 tablespoons lemon juice 1 teaspoon salt ½ teaspoon pepper	Line baking sheet with foil; place salmon on foil, sprinkle with salt and pepper, and fold up the sides of foil around the salmon. In a small bowl, whisk glaze ingredients, and pour over salmon. Put a piece of foil on top and seal all edges. Bake at 350°F for 20–25 minutes. Remove top foil, baste with glaze, and broil 3–5 minutes until caramelized. Serve over rice or orzo pasta.
LEMON-DILL SALMON	¼ cup melted butter 5 tablespoons lemon juice 1 tablespoons dried dill ¼ tsp. garlic powder	Place salmon in a lightly greased baking dish. In a small bowl, mix butter and lemon juice; drizzle over salmon. Season with dill, garlic powder, and salt and pepper to taste. Bake at 350°F for 25 minutes. Serve over a bed of veggies, couscous, or quinoa.
SIMPLE SALMON SALAD	1½ cups cucumber chunks 1 cup red bell pepper chunks ½ cup sliced green onion 3 sliced hard-boiled eggs Dressing: juice of 1 lemon, black pepper to taste, mayo to taste **Uses 6 oz. salmon*	Pan-fry salmon and cut into chunks; mix with remaining ingredients. Mix dressing ingredients and toss with salad.
BROWN-SUGAR AND MUSTARD-GLAZED SALMON	1½ tablespoons brown sugar 2 teaspoons honey 1 tablespoon butter 2 tablespoons Dijon mustard 1 tablespoon soy sauce 1 tablespoon olive oil 2 teaspoons finely grated ginger	Melt brown sugar, honey, and butter in small saucepan; remove from heat and whisk in mustard, soy sauce, olive oil, and ginger. Let cool. Grill or bake salmon, brushing both sides with glaze during cooking. Serve over rice, veggies, or potatoes.

STYLE	TOP IT/MIX IT WITH	HOW TO PREPARE IT
CITRUS SALMON	¾ cup orange juice ¼ cup fresh lemon juice ¼ cup fresh lime juice ¼ cup chicken stock 1 clove minced garlic 2 tablespoons orange marmalade 2 tablespoons soy sauce 1 tablespoon rice wine vinegar 1 tablespoon brown sugar 1 tablespoon butter	In a medium saucepan, combine all ingredients and bring to a boil, stirring constantly. Reduce heat and simmer for 15–20 minutes, until glaze is syrupy. Add salt and pepper to taste. Brush both sides of salmon with olive oil and season with salt and pepper; grill, bake, or fry, brushing with the glaze while cooking. Serve over rice, veggies, or pasta.
BBQ SALMON	¼ cup oil ½ tablespoon lemon juice ½ tablespoon garlic powder ¼ cup teriyaki sauce ½ tablespoon Mrs. Dash seasoning ½ chopped onion	Combine all ingredients to make a marinade; marinate salmon for 2 hours in fridge. Remove from marinade and cook salmon as desired (grill, bake, broil). Serve with grilled/roasted veggies and rice.
SWEET & SPICY SALMON	1 tablespoon brown sugar 1 teaspoon kosher salt 1 teaspoon cumin 1 teaspoon chili powder ½ teaspoon black pepper honey (for drizzling)	Mix spices and rub on salmon that has been brought to room temperature. Bake at 450°F for 12–15 minutes. Drizzle with honey before serving. Serve with veggies and rice.
SALMON AND SUMMER VEGGIES	1 sliced cucumber 10–12 ounces halved cherry tomatoes 1 tablespoon lemon juice 2 tablespoons white balsamic vinegar 3 tablespoons olive oil Pinch sugar Salt and pepper to taste	Toss cucumber and tomatoes. Combine lemon juice, vinegar, olive oil, sugar, salt, and pepper; drizzle over veggies. Arrange veggies on serving plates. Fry salmon until golden and place each fillet on top of veggies. Serve over rice, veggies, or potatoes.

STYLE	TOP IT/MIX IT WITH	HOW TO PREPARE IT
SALMON CHOWDER	¼ cup butter 1 cup chopped onion ½ cup chopped celery 3 tablespoons flour 3 cup chicken broth ½ teaspoon salt 1 pound red potatoes cut into pieces 1 9-ounce package thawed frozen corn 2 cups half-and-half optional: 6 thick-cut bacon slices, cooked and crumbled	Sprinkle salmon with salt and pepper to season; bake on a foil-lined sheet at 400°F for 15 minutes. Flake into ½-inch pieces and set aside. Melt butter; sauté onion and celery for 5 minutes. Stir in flour until mixture is smooth; cook, stirring constantly, 1 minutes. Gradually whisk in chicken broth and cook over medium heat, stirring constantly, until thick and bubbly. Stir in salt, potatoes; simmer for 20 minutes. Stir in corn and half-and-half; cook 6 minutes or until heated through. Gently stir salmon into chowder. Top each serving with crumbled bacon if desired.
SALMON CAKES	1 cup panko breadcrumbs 1 small onion 1 clove minced garlic 2 finely sliced green onions ⅓ cup fresh dill 2 eggs ½ cup Parmesan grated or shredded ¼ teaspoon salt ¼ teaspoon pepper serve with sour cream or yogurt	Cook and flake salmon; set aside. Grate onion over breadcrumbs, allowing juices to soak into crumbs. Stir in remaining ingredients; fold in cooked, flaked salmon. Use ¼ C. mixture to form each patty. Drizzle oil over baking sheet and heat in 450 F oven, making sure oil covers sheet. Place patties on hot tray; spray surface of patties lightly with nonstick cooking spray. Bake at 450 F for 15 min; flip, spray surface with cooking spray, and cook 5 min longer. Serve over rice, mashed potatoes, or greens.

Freeze it!

Place uncooked salmon cakes on a baking sheet, then freeze until firm. Wrap each cake in plastic; transfer to zip-top freezer bags. Defrost overnight in the refrigerator before cooking.

let's go hog wild

NAKED PORK

There's more to the pig than just bacon. And while pork chops get a bum rap because people tend to overcook the living daylights out of them, it doesn't have to be that way. Buy thicker chops with the bone in for better flavor and moisture. Pig out with even more tried and true tips:

PORK TIPS

- **BRINE IT.** Pork is a lean meat. Brining is a simple way to seal the moisture in and to add flavor. It's simple, too. Just add 3 cups of water to a gallon zippered bag, along with ½ cup kosher salt, 3 tablespoons light brown sugar, and 2 minced cloves of garlic. Refrigerate pork in the bag for 30 minutes. Then remove pork from the brine and pat dry with paper towels.
- **PAN FRY IT.** Use a hot pan for the initial sear. This will give you a crisp crust without overcooking the center. Resist the urge to flip the chops too much. While you're searing, let the chop cook undisturbed for the cooking time described below. When you think it's done on that side, take a bashful peek. If you're right, flip it over and repeat.
- **BROIL IT.** Set the broiler to high. Pat pork chops dry. Toss with olive oil and season. Place pork chops on a sheet pan on the top rack of the oven—about three inches from the broiler element. Broil for 10-12 minutes flipping half-way through, until juices run clear and the meat thermometer reads 145°F.
- **POACH IT.** To keep pork extra-moist and to keep the pork's tenderness and flavor, cooking pork cuts that are naturally less tender, such as shoulder cuts, leg/ham cuts and pork shanks. Place meat in a saucepan or Dutch oven and cover with cold liquid. Slowly bring to a boil, skimming off the foam. Reduce the heat to low. Cover and simmer until meat reaches 145°F - 150°F doneness and juices run clear.
- **GRILL IT.** Bone-in rib and center-cut chops that are at least an inch thick are perfect for grilling because they're lean, but they can develop a crust. Brine your pork for 30 minutes to keep the meat moist and to help season the meat. Heat grill. Place pork on a hot grill and cover. Cook for about three minutes per side, or until grill marks appear. Move pork to the cooler part of the grill and cook, covered, flipping every few minutes, until the thickest piece reaches 145°F.
- **ROAST IT.** Pork loin, belly, and leg are the best cuts for roasting. Choose fresh-looking meat, preferably with thick layer of fat (for the best flavor). Bring pork to room temperature and pat dry. For every pound of pork, roast for 25 minutes, plus an added 25 minutes at 400°F. Cook until roast reaches internal temperature of 145°F. Let rest and serve.

15 WAYS TO PREPARE PORK

If you've got pork chops in your fridge or freezer just begging to be cooked, try one of these 15 ways of preparing them. All suggestions below are for 4 pork chops or 1 pound pork. Enjoy!

STYLE	TOP IT/MIX IT WITH	HOW TO PREPARE IT
STUFFED PORK CHOPS	Leftover stuffing or stuffing mix 1 can cream of mushroom soup ½ soup can of milk	Cut a slit in each chop, careful not to cut all the way through; stuff pocket with stuffing; arrange in greased baking dish; top with can of cream of mushroom soup mixed with milk; bake in 375°F oven for 45 minutes.
PORK CHOPS WITH MANGO SALSA	Salsa: 3 cups chopped mango 1 diced red bell pepper ½ small chopped red onion 4 thinly sliced green onions Juice of 1 lime 2 tablespoons olive oil Salt and pepper to taste Pork rub: 1 tsp cumin, sugar, ginger, salt ¼ teaspoon allspice	In an oven-safe skillet, sear chops in olive oil over medium-high heat until golden, 3 minutes per side. Bake in 425°F oven for 12 minutes or until cooked through. Let rest 5 minutes. Top with salsa.
BBQ PULLED PORK	6 ounces Coca-Cola 1 cup bbq sauce 2 tablespoons brown sugar 2 tablespoons apple cider vinegar 1 teaspoon garlic ½ teaspoon onion powder	Add pork to greased Instant Pot or slow cooker. Pour cola over, combine the remaining ingredients and pour over pork, reserve ½ cup. Slow cook on low for 6 hours or pressure cook on high for 45 minutes, natural release for 10 minutes, then vent. Remove from pot, shred, and add reserved bbq sauce. Serve on buns with coleslaw, over baked potatoes, rice, in tortillas, or even in a salad.
GARLIC GINGER PORK STIR FRY	2 tablespoons oil 4 cloves garlic 1 teaspoon ginger 3 cups veggies (snow peas, shredded carrots, sliced mushrooms, broccoli, bell pepper, etc.) 1 cup broth 2 tablespoons honey ¼ cup soy sauce 1 tablespoon chili paste 2 teaspoons sesame oil 2 teaspoons cornstarch Garnish with minced cilantro, green onions, crushed peanuts	Heat 1 tablespoon oil. Fry sliced pork over medium heat, until browned. Remove to a plate and cover to keep warm. Add remaining oil, garlic, ginger, and desired veggies, cook for 4-5 minutes until vegetables are crisp tender. Whisk broth, honey, soy sauce, chili paste, sesame oil, and cornstarch. Pour the sauce over the veggies and simmer for 1-2 minutes until sauce thickens. Add cooked pork, stir fry noodles or cooked rice, garnish with toppings and serve.

STYLE	TOP IT/MIX IT WITH	HOW TO PREPARE IT
GARLIC-ROSEMARY PORK CHOPS	Make glaze by combining: ½ cup melted butter 2 cloves minced garlic 1 tablespoon fresh rosemary, minced	Sear chops in olive oil until golden. Top with the garlic butter mixture. Bake in a 375°F oven for 15 minutes or until cooked through.
PINEAPPLE PORK	2 cloves garlic 1 red onion 2 red bell peppers 1–2 jalapenos 1 cup pineapple juice ½ cup soy sauce 1 pineapple, peeled and cored ¼ cup fresh cilantro or parsley for topping	Combine the pork, garlic, onion, peppers, jalapeno, pineapple juice, and soy sauce in a slow cooker for 4-5 hours on high or or a pressure cooker for 45 minutes on high, release for 10 minutes, then vent. Shred pork and drain off some of the juice. Grill pineapple on a hot skillet, serve pork and pineapple on a bun or over rice.
SWEET AND SPICY PORK	1-2 tablespoons sriracha 2 tablespoons soy sauce 2 tablespoons brown sugar ¼ teaspoon ground ginger 1 garlic clove, finely minced Toppings: chopped green onion, sesame seeds	Mix ingredients. Pour over thin-sliced pork and marinate for 20–60 minutes In a heavy skillet over high heat, heat vegetable oil until hot and shiny. Add pork in a single layer. Cook, undisturbed, for 1-2 minutes until you get a golden brown sear. Flip and repeat to finish. Top with toppings. Serve with rice noodles, rice, broccoli, or other veggies.
CRISPY BAKED PORK CHOPS	Combine: 1½ cups panko breadcrumbs ¼ cup olive oil ½ teaspoon garlic powder ¼ teaspoon onion powder ¼ teaspoon oregano ¼ teaspoon parsley flakes ¼ teaspoon paprika 2 teaspoons salt	Place chops 1 at a time in plastic bag with mixture and shake to coat. Cook on wire rack in 400°F oven until chops are cooked and coating is golden, 20–25 minutes.

STYLE	TOP IT/MIX IT WITH	HOW TO PREPARE IT
KALUA PULLED PORK	2 to 3 pound pork shoulder roast roast, trimmed 1 tablespoon liquid smoke Coarse sea salt	Rinse pork roast. Pat dry. Place pork in slow cooker. Pierce all over with fork. Rub in sea salt. Drizzle with liquid smoke. Set crock pot to low; cook about 8-12 hours and meat shreds easily with fork. Shred pork with two forks. Drizzle cooking liquid over the pork to keep from drying out. Use remaining liquid to make gravy. Serve with mashed potatoes, sweet potatoes, and rice.
PORK ENCHILADAS	1 cup sour cream 1 cup salsa verde ½ cup onion, chopped 2 cloves garlic, minced 2 teaspoons oil 1½ cups shredded cheese 1 4-ounce can chopped green chiles, drained 8 flour tortillas (6 inch)	Preheat oven to 350°F. Mix sour cream & salsa; set aside. Cook and stir onion & garlic in hot oil in large skillet on medium heat 4-5 minutes, until onions are crisp-tender. Stir in pork, 1 cup sour cream mixture, ½ cup cheese, & chiles. Spoon ⅓ cup pork mixture into each tortilla. Roll up. Place, seam-sides down, in greased 13x9 in. baking dish. Add remaining sour cream mixture & cheese. Cover. Bake 15-20 minutes. Serve with rice & black beans. Sprinkle with chopped tomatoes & sliced green onions.
SWEET AND SOUR PORK	Sweet and Sour Sauce on page 263 Salt & pepper to taste ¾ cup all-purpose flour ⅓ cup cornstarch 2 eggs, whisked 1 tablespoon minced garlic 1 cup white onions, chopped 2 cups red bell pepper, chopped 1 cup pineapple chunks 2 tablespoons sliced green onion ½ teaspoon sesame seeds	Combine sweet and sour sauce ingredients, set aside. Dissolve cornstarch in water. Season pork with salt & pepper. Coat pork in flour + cornstarch mixture, then into whisked egg, then into flour mixture. In medium pan, heat 2 cups oil over medium heat to 350°F. Fry battered pork until golden brown, 5-7 minutes. Clean pan. Heat 1 tablespoon oil over medium heat, add garlic and onions; stir-fry 30 seconds. Add peppers and pineapple; stir-fry 1 minute. Add pork and sauce. Bring sauce to boil; add cornstarch + water, stir until sauce thickens and covers pork and veggies. Garnish with green onions & sesame seeds. Serve over rice.
SUNDAY PORK ROAST	3-5 pounds. pork shoulder or butt roast 2 tablespoons vegetable oil 2 teaspoons salt 2 teaspoons black pepper 1 teaspoon garlic powder 2 medium onions, cut into chunks 2 pounds baby carrots 1 pound potatoes, cubed 1 cup apple juice 1 rosemary spring	Preheat oven to 450°F. Rub pork with oil. Mix salt, pepper, & garlic powder; sprinkle on pork roast. Place roast, fat side up, in roasting pan. Cook, uncovered, 30-45 minutes. Reduce heat to 350°F; cook for 60 minutes. Add onion, carrots, potatoes, & apple juice + seasonings. Cook 60-90 minutes, until veggies are tender and meat shreds easily with fork. Season with salt & pepper to taste. Serve hot.

STYLE	TOP IT/MIX IT WITH	HOW TO PREPARE IT
ASIAN SHREDDED PORK	1 pound pork shoulder or pork butt ⅓ cup soy sauce ¼ cup honey 2 tablespoons brown sugar 1 tablespoon sesame oil 1 tablespoon rice wine vinegar 1 tablespoon hoisin sauce 4-5 cloves garlic	Combine soy sauce, honey, brown sugar, sesame oil, rice wine, and hoisin sauce. Pour into slow cooker over pork. Add garlic cloves. Coat meat with the sauce, but it does not have to be completely submerged. Cook on high for 4-5 hours. Discard garlic cloves. Shred the pork (it should come apart easily) and then cook on high for another 30 minutes. Serve with rice, noodles or taco style. Garnish with green onion!
PORK CHOPS WITH ONION AND GRAVY	flour mixture: 1½ C flour ¼ teaspoon garlic powder ¼ teaspoon chili powder (reserve 2 tablespoons of mixture for gravy) 2 yellow onions, thinly sliced 2 tablespoons butter cream sauce: 1½ cups chicken broth ¼ cup heavy cream	Cover chops with flour mixture, and sear coated chops in ¼ cup olive oil over medium heat until golden, 5 minutes per side. Remove from skillet. Put onions in skillet; salt and pepper; cook in oil for 15–20 minutes or until caramelized. Stir in 2 tablespoons butter; melt. Sprinkle with reserved flour; cook 1 minute. Stir in cream sauce; simmer until thickened. Return pork chops to skillet; cook pork chops through, about 10 minutes.
PORK CARNITAS	4 pounds boneless pork roast 3 tablespoons salt 1 tablespoon ground black pepper 1 teaspoon dried oregano 1 large onion, chopped 5 garlic cloves, minced 4 tablespoons lime juice ½ cup orange juice 1 cup chicken broth 2 bay leaves	Pat pork dry with paper towel. Combine salt, pepper, & oregano; rub seasoning on pork. In the slow cooker, combine onion, garlic, broth, lime & orange juices, & bay leaves. Add pork. Cook on high for 5 hours (low for 7-8 hours). Shred pork with two forks. For crispy edges, transfer shredded pork to a baking sheet. Pour ½ cup of the juices on top of the meat; broil for 5-7 minutes, until golden brown. Serve over rice or in a tortilla with cheese and salsa!

home (cooking) on the range

NAKED ROAST BEEF

It's a common dilemma: roasts are, well, not exactly small. In fact, they're legendary for feeding a crowd. On those occasions when you dust off your culinary genius and cook a roast, you'll find some tips below. Depending on the size of the roast and the size of your family, you might have a lot of leftover roast beef.

And if your family is typical, there are only so many times they will greet slices of leftover beef on the dinner plate with a smile. What to do? NO WAY do you want to waste all that glorious beef! NO PROBLEM, there are lots of creative ways to repurpose it. Turn the page for lots of delicious and creative ways to use those leftovers!

COOKING THE ROAST

- Bone-in rib roasts give maximum flavor and visual effect, but most of the time it's better to save a few bucks and instead buy a top or bottom round roast.
- Look for dark red color, which indicates desirable aging, and a thick covering of fat, which adds flavor and prevents the meat from drying out during cooking. (You can always cut off fat before serving.) Sometimes you might find these labels on the meat:
    - USDA Select = slight marbling
    - USDA Choice = small to moderate marbling
    - USDA Prime = abundant marbling
- Always let the beef come to room temperature before you put it in the pan or oven.
- Season generously before cooking.
- Depending on your recipe, you may want to sear in a hot pan before you put it in oven or slow cooker.
- Monitor the meat temperature by investing in a quality meat thermometer. It takes away all the guesswork!
- After cooking, let the meat rest for 10-20 minutes. For best results, place it on a warm platter and tent it loosely with foil. Resting allows the muscle fibers to relax while redistributing the meat juices for maximum tenderness.
- During the resting period, the meat can rise in temperature up to 10 degrees. So pull it out about 10 degrees before you hit your target. These are good guidelines: Rare: 125°F, Medium Rare: 135°F, Medium: 145°F, Medium Well: 150°F, Well: 160°F
- If you're still not sure what to do, use an app like Roast Perfect to help guide you through the process.

The Pioneer Woman
by Hamilton Beach
TEMP
HOURS
WARM
LOW
HIGH
2
4
6
8
10

11 WAYS TO USE ROAST BEEF

If you've got a wad of leftover roast beef, here are eleven mouth-watering ways to use it—and not even the most determined detective in the family will recognize it as last Sunday's roast!

STYLE	TOP IT/MIX IT WITH	HOW TO PREPARE IT
SUNDAY ROAST	1 roast of your choice Carrots Potatoes, roughly cut 2 onions, cut in half Onion soup mix water	Add roast to the slow cooker, then add all veggies and potatoes. Mix the onion soup mix with 2 cups of water and pour on top of the roast. Cover and cook on low for 8-10 hours, or until tender and delicious!
EASY BBQ BEEF SANDWICHES	Leftover roast beef Water Barbecue sauce Coleslaw **I don't specify quantities--it all depends on how many sandwiches you want!*	Put desired amount of leftover beef in a saucepan; add enough water to moisten the beef. Heat on medium until warmed through. Stir in enough barbecue sauce to completely coat the beef; and simmer for 5 minutes. Serve on buns or toast, topping the beef with coleslaw.
FAJITAS	3 cups thinly sliced beef strips 2 thinly sliced green peppers 2 thinly sliced red peppers 1 thinly sliced yellow onion 1 tablespoon cayenne pepper 1 tablespoon paprika 1 tablespoon oregano 1 teaspoon salt 1 teaspoon pepper Corn or flour tortillas Optional toppings: salsa, sour cream, guacamole, cheese	In a skillet sprayed with nonstick cooking spray, combine beef, peppers, and onion. Mix the cayenne pepper, paprika, oregano, salt, and pepper and add to beef and veggies as they cook. Cook until veggies are crisp-tender. Serve in warm tortillas. Add toppings and serve with rice.
SIMPLE BEEF STEW	3 cups beef cut into bite-size cubes 6 cups water 3 beef bouillon cubes 1 large chopped onion 2 whole bay leaves 1 pound chopped carrots 2 pounds halved baby red potatoes 1 can corn 1 teaspoon thyme 2 teaspoon salt ¼ teaspoon pepper For roux: ½ cup butter ⅓ cup flour	In a large stock pot, combine all but roux ingredients. Bring to a simmer and cook about 30 minutes, or until carrots and potatoes are tender. To make roux, melt butter in small saucepan; whisk in flour and cook 5 minutes, stirring constantly. Stir roux into simmering stew; bring to a simmer again and cook an additional 10 minutes, stirring frequently, until stew is thick.

STYLE	TOP IT/MIX IT WITH	HOW TO PREPARE IT
SHREDDED MEXICAN BEEF	3 pound chuck roast salt & pepper, to taste 2 tablespoons vegetable oil 1¼ cup beef broth, divided 3-4 chipotle chilies in adobo 6 garlic cloves, minced 1½ tablespoons ground cumin 1 tablespoon dried oregano ¼ teaspoon ground cloves 3 bay leaves ¼ cup lime juice	Cut roast into portions. Season with salt & pepper. Sear meat in oil until browned in skillet over medium-high heat. Puree chiles, garlic, ¼ cup beef broth. Add remaining beef broth, chile puree, cumin, oregano, cloves, & bay leaves to beef in crockpot. Cook low 8-9 hours. Shred. Add lime juice. Stir. Cook low for 20-30 minutes. Strain. Serve in tortillas with toppings.
TERIYAKI BEEF STIR FRY	¼ cup soy sauce ½ cup water ¼ cup brown sugar 2 teaspoons minced garlic 2 teaspoons minced ginger 1 tablespoon honey 1 teaspoon toasted sesame oil 1 tablespoon + 1 teaspoon cornstarch 3 cups veggies of your choice 1 tablespoon vegetable oil Optional garnishes: sliced green onions and sesame seeds	Combine first 7 ingredients in small pot over med.-high heat. Stir & dissolve sugar, about 3 min. Bring to boil. Mix cornstarch & 2 T. cold water; add to sauce; boil for 1-2 min. until thick; set aside. Heat 1 tsp. oil in large pan over med.-high heat. Add veggies; season with salt & pepper. Cook 3-5 min. Add 2 T. water; cook until veggies are tender. Remove from pan; set aside. Wipe out pan. Heat remaining oil over high heat. Season thinly-sliced steak with salt & pepper. Cook for 2-3 min on each side until just cooked through. Add vegetables and sauce; cook for 2-3 min. over med.-high heat until warm.
SHEPHERD'S PIE	1 tablespoon olive oil ½ chopped onion 1 cup chopped mushrooms 2 tablespoons butter 2 tablespoons flour 3 cups. shredded or chopped beef 1 cup frozen veggies (any kind) 3 cups mashed potatoes shredded cheddar cheese	In large saucepan, sauté onion and mushrooms in oil for 3–5 minutes. Add butter; stir until melted. Sprinkle in flour; stir to combine. Gradually add beef broth and cook, stirring, until gravy thickens. Stir in beef and veggies; cook until heated through. Pour into lightly greased 9-inch-square baking dish. Smooth mashed potatoes over top, sprinkle with cheese. Bake at 400°F for 20 minutes until cheese is melted and slightly browned.
PHILLY CHEESESTEAK SANDWICHES	Vegetable oil Thinly sliced leftover beef Large sliced mushrooms Medium thinly sliced onion Chopped tomatoes Cream cheese Provolone cheese Rolls ** I don't specify quantities—it all depends on how many sandwiches you want!*	In a skillet over medium heat, season the beef with salt and pepper and cook in oil until heated through. Add onions and mushrooms; stir-fry until tender-crisp. Add tomatoes and cream cheese; heat through. Spoon onto rolls with a slice of provolone cheese.

STYLE	TOP IT/MIX IT WITH	HOW TO COOK IT
FRENCH DIP OVEN SLIDERS	5 tablespoons butter (divided) 1 large thinly sliced onion ¼ teaspoon thyme 12 slider buns cut in half 12 thin slices roast beef 12 slices provolone cheese ¼ teaspoon garlic powder 1 clove minced garlic 1½ cups beef broth 1 tablespoon Worcestershire sauce	Melt 2 tablespoons butter in large skillet; add onion, thyme, and salt and pepper to taste. Cook, stirring occasionally, until onions are caramelized, about 15 minutes. Place bottom half of buns on large baking sheet; top with beef, provolone cheese, caramelized onions, and bun tops. Melt 2 tablespoons butter; brush on top of buns and sprinkle with garlic powder, coarse salt, and parsley flakes. Bake at 350°F for 10–15 minutes, until cheese is melted. Serve with au jus for dipping: melt 1 tablespoon butter; add garlic and cook 1 minute; stir in beef broth, Worcestershire sauce, and salt and pepper to taste. Simmer until slightly reduced, about 10 minutes.
CREAMY SHREDDED BEEF ENCHILADAS	3 cups shredded beef 1 cup chopped onion 1 can (10-3/4 ounces) condensed cream of mushroom soup 1 cup sour cream 1 can (4 ounces) chopped green chilies 3 cups shredded cheddar cheese, divided 3 cans (10 ounces each) enchilada sauce, divided 12 flour tortillas (8 inches), warmed	Combine beef, soup, sour cream, chilies, 1 cup cheese and 1/2 cup enchilada sauce in a medium sized skillet; heat through. In each tortilla, put ¼ cup beef, cheese, and a little sauce. Roll up and put seam-side down in a greased 9x13 pan. Pour remaining sauce over the enchiladas and sprinkle with remaining cheese. Bake at 350° for 20–30 minutes or until bubbly.
BEEF POT PIE	Pie: 3 cups leftover roast 1 cup corn 1 cup chopped carrots 2 cups diced potatoes ½ cup frozen peas ½ cup green beans Gravy: ¼ cup + 2 tablespoons butter ¼ cup flour 3 cups beef broth ¼ teaspoon thyme ½ teaspoon onion powder ⅛ teaspoon garlic powder 1 prepared pie crust 1 egg yolk 1 tablespoon water	Combine pie ingredients and dump into a 12-inch baking dish. Set aside. Make gravy: In a medium skillet, melt butter; whisk in flour until there are no lumps; add remaining gravy ingredients and cook over medium-low heat for 5–7 minutes, stirring frequently, until thickened. Pour gravy over beef and vegetables. Top with pie crust; cut several slits in crust to vent steam. Whisk egg yolk and water; brush onto pie crust with pastry brush. Bake at 350°F for 1 hour. If crust gets too brown, cover with foil for remainder of time.

fajitas on page 174

beyond hamburgers

NAKED GROUND BEEF

Are your tried-and-true ground beef recipes more like tired and worn out? There are a lot of things to do with ground beef other than make hamburgers!

If you've got ground beef in your fridge or freezer just begging to be cooked, try one of these 19 scrumptious ways of preparing it. All suggestions below are for 1 pound of ground beef unless otherwise noted. Enjoy!

STYLE	TOP IT/MIX IT WITH	HOW TO PREPARE IT
EASY CHEESEBURGER SLIDER CASSEROLE	1 teaspoon ground cumin 1 teaspoon ground paprika 1 teaspoon garlic powder 1 teaspoon onion powder 2 tablespoons tomato paste 1 small onion, diced 1 bell pepper, diced 1-2 jalapenos, diced Glaze: ½ cup butter 2 tablespoons brown sugar 1 tablespoon Worcestershire sauce 1 tablespoon mustard 12 slices cheese 12 rolls	Preheat oven to 350°F. Brown meat in 1 tablespoon oil. Add veggies & spices to meat. Cut rolls in half. Place bottom halves in ungreased baking dish. Layer on meat mixture. Add cheese. Cover with roll tops. Heat glaze ingredients in saucepan over low heat. Pour glaze over rolls. Bake 20-25 minutes.
LASAGNA SOUP	2 tablespoon olive oil 1 large yellow onion, diced 5 garlic cloves, to taste, minced 4 ½ cups chicken broth 2 14.5-ounces cans petite diced tomatoes 2 ½ tablespoons tomato paste 2 tablespoons Italian seasoning 6.5 ounce pasta 1 ¼ cups shredded mozzarella cheese ½ cup Parmesan cheese 8 ounces ricotta cheese 2 tablespoons chopped fresh parsley, plus more for garnish Salt and pepper to taste	Heat oil; brown ground beef; season with salt and pepper. Add onion, saute about 3 minutes; add garlic. Combine next 4 ingredients. Bring to a boil and simmer for 20 minutes. Prep pasta according to package. Combine the 3 cheese mixture. Stir cooked pasta into soup with parsley. Add a large scoop of the cheese mixture to each bowl of soup as you serve; stir to melt the cheese.

STYLE	TOP IT/MIX IT WITH	HOW TO PREPARE IT
MANICOTTI	1 clove crushed garlic 2 cups cottage cheese 8 ounces shredded mozzarella cheese 1 teaspoon salt 1 cup mayonnaise (optional) 1 box cooked and drained manicotti shells 1 jar spaghetti sauce 1 teaspoon oregano Parmesan cheese	Brown ground beef and garlic; drain. Mix in cottage cheese, mozzarella cheese, salt, and mayo. Stuff into shells. Place shells in greased 9 x 13 pan. Pour sauce over shells; sprinkle with oregano and Parmesan cheese. Bake covered with foil at 350°F for 15 minutes; remove foil and bake 15 additional minutes.
EASY PORCUPINE MEATBALLS	½ cup cooked long grain rice ¼ cup onion, diced ½ teaspoon garlic powder 2 tablespoons fresh parsley 1 tablespoon Worcestershire sauce 1 egg sauce: 15-ounces can tomato sauce 1 cup water 2 tablespoon brown sugar 2 teaspoons Worcestershire sauce	In a bowl, combine meat with first 6 ingredients. Shape into 1½-inch balls. In a large skillet over medium-high heat, brown meatballs in oil; drain. Combine tomato sauce, water, brown sugar, and Worcestershire sauce; pour over meatballs. Reduce heat; cover and simmer for 1 hour.
SLOW-COOKER HAMBURGER STEW	3 peeled and chopped carrots 3 peeled and chopped potatoes 1 chopped onion 2 chopped stalks celery 1 can tomato soup 1 soup can water Salt and pepper to taste	Combine cooked, drained ground beef with other ingredients. Cook in slow-cooker for 3 hours on high or 6 hours on low. If desired, add 1 cup frozen peas ½ hour before the stew is done.
TACO BAKE	1 chopped onion 1 package taco seasoning mix 1 can tomato sauce 1 can drained corn 2 cups shredded cheese 2 cups bisquick 1 cup milk 2 eggs. Garnish: shredded cheese, chopped tomatoes, sour cream	Brown ground beef with onion until meat is done. Mix with taco seasoning, tomato sauce, and corn. Put in greased 9 x 13 pan. Top with shredded cheese. Mix Bisquick, milk, and eggs; pour over cheese. Bake at 350°F for 35 minutes; let cool 10 minutes before cutting. Top with garnishes as desired.
SLOW-COOKER BAKED BEANS	1 chopped onion 1 can rinsed and drained kidney beans 1 can drained green beans 1 can tomato sauce ½ cup ketchup 3 cans pork and beans 1 tablespoon brown sugar 1 teaspoon vinegar 2 teaspoons mustard 1 can drained pineapple tidbits	Brown ground beef and onion. Put in a slow-cooker with all other ingredients except pineapple; cook on low 3 hours. Stir in pineapple during last ½ hour.

STYLE	TOP IT/MIX IT WITH	HOW TO PREPARE IT
BEEF ENCHILADAS	Enchilada Sauce on page 268 Filling: 1 chopped green pepper 1 diced onion Shredded cheddar cheese 1 can sliced olives Corn tortillas	Make enchilada sauce according to instructions. Brown meat with onion, add green pepper, cook for 2-3 minutes. To assemble, dip each tortilla in sauce; fill with meat, cheese, and olices; roll. Place in a greased 9x13 pan. Pour remaining sauce over top with more cheese. Bake at 350°F until bubbly, about 20 minutes.
EGG ROLL IN A BOWL	1 sweet onion, diced 1 tablespoon sesame oil 1 tablespoon rice vinegar 2 teaspoons minced fresh garlic 1 teaspoon ground ginger ¼ cup low sodium soy sauce 16 ounce bag coleslaw mix ½ cup grated or "matchstick" carrots 2 green onions, thinly sliced Salt and pepper, to taste 1 tablespoon hoisin sauce (optional)	Heat large skillet over medium heat. Add ground meat. Cook stirring, until no longer pink. Drain. Add onion, sesame oil, and rice vinegar. Cook, for a few more minutes. Add garlic, ginger, soy sauce, hoisin sauce, coleslaw, and carrots. Cook, stirring, for 5-7 minutes, until cabbage wilts. Remove skillet from heat. Stir in green onions, season with salt and pepper. Serve with rice or chow mein noodles.
MEATBALLS IN SPICY SAUCE	Sauce: ½ cup brown sugar 1 can tomato sauce ¼ cup lemon juice ½ cup water ⅛ teaspoon garlic salt Meatballs: 1 peeled grated potato 1 finely minced onion 1 egg 1 teaspoon salt	Combine sauce ingredients in saucepan; bring to a boil, stirring constantly; reduce heat and simmer, uncovered, for 20 minutes. Meatballs: Combine ground beef with meatball ingredients and form into walnut-size balls. Cook at 500°F until meatballs are cooked through. Put meatballs in prepared sauce and heat through.
BEEF STROGANOFF	1 small chopped onion 1 can cream of mushroom soup 2 cups sliced fresh mushrooms 1½ cups sour cream	Brown ground beef with onion until meat is cooked. Stir in soup and mushrooms; cook over low heat until mushrooms are tender. Stir in sour cream and cook over low heat until heated through. Serve over rice, noodles, or toast.
POT OF GOLD	½ onion, diced 1½ cups water 10¾-ounce can tomato soup 2 cups cooked pasta 16 ounce can corn, drained 2 cups shredded cheddar cheese, divided Salt and pepper, to taste	Preheat oven to 350°F. In large skillet over medium heat, cook beef and onion. Mix in all ingredients except pasta; simmer 10 minutes. Add pasta; stir. Pour half mixture into greased 9x13 pan, top with 1 cup cheese. Layer remaining beef mixture; top with cheese. Bake covered for 20 minutes. Uncover; cook 5 minutes, until melted. Serve with bread, salad or vegetables of your choice.

STYLE	TOP IT/MIX IT WITH	HOW TO PREPARE IT
ASIAN GROUND BEEF	¼ cup brown sugar, packed ¼ cup reduced sodium soy sauce 2 teaspoons sesame oil ½ teaspoon crushed red-pepper flakes, or more to taste ¼ teaspoon ground ginger 1 tablespoon vegetable oil 3 cloves garlic, minced 2 green onions, thinly sliced ¼ teaspoon sesame seeds	In a small bowl, whisk together brown sugar, soy sauce, sesame oil, red pepper flakes and ginger. Heat oil in large skillet over medium-high heat. Add garlic and cook, stirring constantly, until fragrant, about 1 minute. Add ground beef and cook until browned, about 3-5 minutes, chopping beef as it cooks; drain excess fat. Stir in soy sauce mixture and green onions until well combined; simmer until heated through, about 2 min. Serve over rice, veggies, or noodles, or in lettuce wraps, egg rolls, or empanadas.
GROUND BEEF BISCUITS CASSEROLE	½ cup chopped onion salt and pepper, to taste ¾ cup water 14 ounce can tomato sauce 6 ounce can tomato paste 2 cups shredded mozzarella cheese 1½ cups veggies: peas, carrots, and corn (or any veggies you like) 16 ounce can refrigerated flaky-layer biscuits 1 tablespoon butter, melted ½ teaspoon oregano Salt and pepper, to taste	Preheat oven to 375°F. Spray 13x9-in. baking dish with nonstick cooking spray. In a large skillet over med.-high heat, cook and break up ground beef. Add onion; cook until translucent. Drain; season with salt & pepper. Add ¾ C. water, tomato sauce, tomato paste. Simmer on med.-low heat for 15 min. Spread half of the hot mixture in the baking dish. Add ⅔ cup mozzarella and vegetables. Top with ⅔ cup mozzarella, remaining meat mixture & cheese. Split biscuits in half. Place on top, overlapping, in 3 rows of 5. Brush melted butter and sprinkle with oregano. Bake until golden brown, about 25 min. Serve with noodles or salad.
MEXICAN CASSEROLE	4 bell peppers, diced (2 colors) 1 jalapeno ½ red onion, minced 2 cups frozen corn 2 teaspoons chili powder 2 teaspoons cumin salt and pepper, to taste 2 cups Mexican cheese 18–20 corn tortillas 16-ounces can refried beans 2 cups red Enchilada sauce (see page 268) Cilantro, guacamole, or sour cream for topping Salt and pepper, to taste	Preheat oven to 400°F. Heat oil in large skillet over med.-high heat; add onion and peppers; sprinkle with chili and cumin. Cook until outside of peppers are browned. Remove; set aside. Repeat process with corn, chili, and cumin; remove from heat once browned. Sprinkle both with salt. Grease a 9x13 pan. Cut tortillas into thin strips. Mix refried beans in a bowl with water for easy spreading. Spread some sauce in the pan. Layer: ½ tortilla strips, beans, ½ veggies, ½ sauce, ½ cheese. Repeat with rest of toppings. Cover with foil. Bake for 15-20 minutes, until sauce bubbles and cheese melts. Serve with guacamole, fresh cilantro, and sour cream.

STYLE	TOP IT/MIX IT WITH	HOW TO PREPARE IT
SWEDISH MEATBALLS	1 cup torn bread ½ cup canned milk 1 teaspoon nutmeg 1 large chopped onion 1 cup cooked rice 2 beaten eggs 1 teaspoon salt 1 teaspoon pepper gravy: 1 can cream of celery soup 1 can cream of mushroom soup 1 soup can milk	Mix all meatball ingredients with ground beef. Add meatballs to a large frying pan over medium heat. Bring to a boil and then simmer, covered, for 30 minutes. Mix gravy ingredients; pour over meatballs in pan. Cook, covered, for 30 minutes.
EASY BEEF AND POTATO CASSEROLE	4 pounds russets potatoes, peeled and sliced 1 pound ground beef 1 onion, diced 10 ounce can cream of chicken soup 12 ounce can evaporated milk ½ cup milk 2 teaspoons salt 1 teaspoon pepper 2 teaspoons onion powder 4 cups shredded cheddar cheese	Preheat oven to 350°F. In a large skillet over med.-high heat, brown ground beef with onions, ½ tsp of salt & pepper. Drain grease; set aside. In a bowl, whisk cream of chicken soup, evaporated milk, milk, 1 tsp. salt, ¼ tsp. pepper, & onion powder; set aside. In a greased 9x13" baking dish, layer ⅓ peeled, sliced potatoes & ⅓ ground beef mixture; top with 1 cup cheese. Sprinkle with salt & pepper. Repeat process 3 times. Pour milk mixture over the top. Cover dish with foil; bake for 1 hour. Check potatoes for tenderness. Sprinkle remaining cheese on top. Bake uncovered 5 min. to melt. Remove from oven; let sit for 15 min. before serving.
EASY BEEF PASTA	6 cloves garlic, minced 28 ounce can crushed tomatoes 2 cups minced veggies (onion, celery, carrot) 1 cup. mushrooms, sliced 1 cup beef broth 2 tablespoons red wine vinegar 1½ teaspoons Italian seasoning ¼ teaspoon red chili flakes optional: ½ cup half and half Salt and pepper, to taste 12 ounce pasta Parmesan cheese for serving	Place beef in slow cooker; season generously with salt & pepper. Add onion, garlic, carrots, mushrooms, tomatoes, beef broth, vinegar, red chili flakes, and Italian seasoning. Cook low for 6-8 hours, until meat is fork-tender. Season with salt and pepper. When ready to serve, turn off heat and stir in cream (if using). Prepare noodles according to package directions, drain, toss in olive oil, and divide among bowls.
SLOPPY JOES	1 tablespoon butter 1 teaspoon olive oil ½ green bell pepper, minced ½ large yellow onion, minced 3 cloves garlic, minced 1 tablespoon tomato paste ⅔ cup ketchup ⅓ cup water 1 tablespoon brown sugar 1 teaspoon prepared yellow mustard ¾ teaspoon chili powder ½ teaspoon Worcestershire sauce Salt and pepper to taste	Heat oil; brown the ground beef, season with salt and pepper. Add onion, bell pepper and garlic; saute about 3 minutes. Combine remaining ingredients and simmer for 20 minutes. Serve on your favorite buns.

let's play hot potato

NAKED POTATOES

Did you know? One medium potato has similar calories and fewer carbohydrates than a cup of brown rice or whole-wheat pasta. They're full of iron and vitamin C, high in fiber, loaded with complex carbs, and nearly fat-free!

What they lack in good looks, potatoes more than make up for in versatility. Think of all the ways you've seen spuds prepared: baked, fried, mashed, boiled, shredded, cheesy au gratin, scalloped, down-home hashbrowns, French fries, and everything in between. Read on for some potato advice and a dozen ways to serve them.

POTATO TIPS

- Potatoes are a fabulous shelf-cooking staple: they last 3-4 weeks in the pantry and 2-3 months in the refrigerator.
- When buying, look for clean, smooth, firm-textured potatoes with no cuts, bruises or discoloration.
- Store potatoes in a cool, well-ventilated place, out of the light. (This will avoid sprouting.)
- If you do refrigerate your potatoes, you can reduce discoloration by letting them warm gradually on the counter to room temperature before cooking.
- Extend your spuds' shelf life with perforated plastic bags or paper bags.
- If your potatoes have any greening, cut away the green portions of the skin before cooking and eating.
- Pinkish or brownish discoloration is a reaction with oxygen and is harmless to eat. The color usually disappears with cooking.
- If you encounter any sprouts, cut them away before cooking or eating the potato.
- When you're ready to prepare your potatoes, gently scrub them with a vegetable brush under cool running water. Skip that step if you're peeling.
- If you want to prep your potatoes an hour or two early, you can preserve their color by storing them in cold water with a little lemon juice.
- For recipes with sliced or chopped potatoes, unless you're making a potato casserole or latkes, you'll usually want to rinse away the starch (especially fries!).
- When boiling potatoes to mash them, cook the potatoes first, then peel them.
- When roasting, cut up your potatoes in consistent sizes to ensure even cooking.

12 WAYS TO PREPARE POTATOES

With those basics out of the way, it's time to venture out into some really fun stuff! In case you want to spread your culinary wings, here are a dozen luscious recipes to get you going!

	TOP IT/MIX IT WITH	HOW TO COOK IT
TWICE-BAKED POTATOES	4 large baked russet potatoes ½ cup sour cream ¼ cup butter ¼ cup finely chopped chives thinly sliced green onion salt and pepper to taste Toppings as desired: shredded cheese, crumbled cooked bacon, chopped chives, sliced green onion	Slice potatoes lengthwise and scoop flesh into a bowl. Stir in sour cream, butter, and chives or onion; mix until fluffy. Spoon mixture into potato halves, piling it high. Sprinkle with cheese and bacon crumbles if desired. Bake on pan at 450 F. for 15–20 minutes, until cheese is melted and slightly browned.
POTATO SOUP	4 cups diced potatoes 2 cups diced carrots 1 cup diced celery ½ cup diced onion ¾ cup melted butter 2 teaspoons salt 1½ teaspoons sugar 1 can evaporated milk Shredded cheese for topping	In a large saucepan or stock pot, combine potatoes, carrots, celery, and onion; cover with water and boil until tender. Drain, reserving water. In a medium saucepan, mix butter, salt, flour, and sugar; whisk in evaporated milk and enough potato water to make 4 cups. Pour milk mixture into pot of veggies and heat through. Garnish with shredded cheese.
MOM'S BEST POTATO SALAD	5 medium potatoes, peeled & cubed 6 large chopped hard-boiled eggs ½ cup thinly sliced green onions ¼ cup chopped sweet pickles 1 teaspoon mustard 1 teaspoon celery seed 1 cup mayonnaise Salt and pepper to taste 1–2 sliced hard-boiled eggs for garnish	Cook potatoes in boiling water until tender. Drain and chill. Stir in chopped eggs, green onions, and pickles; toss well. Stir in mustard, celery seed, and mayo; mix well and season with salt and pepper. Garnish with sliced eggs. Chill until ready to serve.
SLOW-COOKER CHEESY POTATO SOUP	2 cups chopped onion 2 cups diced celery 6 cups chicken broth 2 teaspoons salt ½ teaspoon pepper 10 potatoes, cooked, peeled and diced 1½ cups butter 1½ cups flour 2 quarts half-and-half 8 ounces cheddar cheese Shredded cheese for topping if desired	In a stock pot, combine onion, celery, chicken broth, salt, and pepper; cook until veggies are tender. Stir in potatoes. In a large saucepan, combine butter, flour, half-and-half, and cheddar cheese. Cook, stirring constantly, until thickened; do not boil. Stir sauce into potato mixture and pour into slow-cooker. Cook on low 4–6 hours. If desired, top each serving with shredded cheese.

	TOP IT/MIX IT WITH	HOW TO COOK IT
POTATO SKINS	8 russet potatoes, baked & cooled Olive oil Sea salt Freshly ground black pepper 8 ounces shredded cheddar cheese 1 pound cooked and crumbled bacon Toppings: sour cream, chopped chives	Cut potatoes in half lengthwise & scoop out flesh, leaving a ¼-inch border attached to skin. Brush both sides of skins with oil; season with salt and pepper. Turn broiler to high; broil 5–7 minutes per side, flipping once, until skins are crisp & remaining flesh is golden. Top skins with cheese & bacon; broil about 2 minutes until cheese is melted. Top with sour cream, chives, & black pepper.
CHEESY POTATOES	7 medium potatoes, peeled & cubed 1 can cream of potato soup 1 cup French onion dip ¾ cup milk ⅔ cup sour cream ¼ teaspoon salt ¼ teaspoon pepper 16 ounces cubed Velveeta cheese, Minced fresh parsley for topping	Boil potatoes 8–12 minutes, or until tender; drain and cool slightly. In a large bowl, mix soup, dip, milk, sour cream, salt, and pepper; gently fold in cheese and potatoes. Put mixture in a greased 9x13 baking dish. Cover. Bake at 350°F for 30 minutes; uncover and bake 15 additional minutes. Stir before serving and sprinkle with parsley.
CRUNCHY NO-MAYO POTATO SALAD	3 pounds unpeeled baby red potatoes ½ teaspoon salt 2 green onions (minced whites, sliced greens) 1 cup finely diced celery ½ cup diced red onion 1 medium grated carrot Dressing: ¼ cup red wine vinegar 2 tablespoons honey 2 tablespoons Dijon mustard 2 teaspoons minced fresh thyme 1 teaspoon salt ½ teaspoon coarsely ground pepper ½ cup virgin olive oil	Put potatoes and ½ teaspoon salt in a large saucepan; add water to cover. Bring to a boil, reduce heat, and cook, uncovered, 10–12 minutes, or until tender. Drain and cool. Cut cooled potatoes into 1-inch cubes. Set aside. In a large bowl, combine minced onion whites, celery, red onion, and carrot. In a separate bowl, whisk dressing ingredients. To assemble salad, combine potatoes with onion mixture. Drizzle dressing over salad and toss to coat. Top with green onion slices.
FRENCH FRIES	3 large russet potatoes 3 tablespoons oil (or more, as needed) sea salt Optional seasonings: Garlic powder Paprika Rosemary Italian seasoning Seasoned salt Old Bay seasoning	Peel potatoes and cut into long fry sticks; rinse under cool running water and shake off water. Spread potatoes 2 layers deep in a deep pot and pour oil to cover potatoes by 1 inch. Heat over medium heat (oil will start bubbling) and cook for 20–25 minutes, or until fries are very tender. Increase heat to medium-high and cook until fries are crisp and golden, about 10 minutes longer. Remove from pan with slotted spoon, drain on paper towels, and sprinkle with salt.

	TOP IT/MIX IT WITH	HOW TO COOK IT
SWEET POTATO CASSEROLE	Sweet potatoes: 3 cups mashed sweet potatoes* 1 cup sugar ½ teaspoon salt 1 teaspoon vanilla 2 well-beaten eggs ½ cup melted butter topping: 1 cup packed brown sugar ⅓ cup flour 1 cup chopped pecans ⅓ stick melted butter **for mashed potatoes: Cover potatoes with water; bring to boil, reduce heat & simmer 30–35 minutes. Drain & cover with ice water; let sit 1 hour. Cool, peel & mash.*	In large mixing bowl, combine sweet potatoes, sugar, salt, vanilla, eggs, & butter; beat on medium speed for 4 minutes. Pour into greased baking dish; bake at 350°F for 30 minutes. While sweet potatoes are baking, combine brown sugar, flour, nuts, and butter in a mixing bowl; leave out at room temperature. When the sweet potatoes have baked 30 minutes, remove from oven and sprinkle with topping mixture; return to the oven for 10 minutes. Topping should be slightly browned. Let sit for at least 30 minutes before serving.
SCALLOPED POTATOES	4 tablespoons butter (divided) ⅓ cup finely chopped onion 3 tablespoons flour 1 teaspoon salt ¼ teaspoon pepper 2 ½ cups milk 6 thinly sliced potatoes (peeled or unpeeled—your choice)	In saucepan over medium heat, melt 3 tablespoons butter; cook onion in butter for 2 minutes, stirring occasionally, until tender. Stir in flour, salt & pepper. Cook, stirring constantly, until smooth & bubbly; remove from heat. Stir in milk. Heat to boiling, stirring constantly. Boil & stir 1 minute. Spread potato slices in greased casserole dish; pour sauce over potatoes. Cut remaining 1 tablespoon butter into small pieces; sprinkle over potatoes. Bake covered at 350°F for 30 minutes. Uncover; bake 1 hour or until potatoes are tender. Let stand 5–10 minutes before serving.
RANCH POTATOES	8–10 medium potatoes, peeled and cubed 1 can cream of mushroom soup 1¼ cups milk 1 envelope ranch dressing mix 1½ cups shredded cheddar cheese (divided) Salt and pepper to taste 6 slices cooked and crumbled bacon	Put potatoes in a saucepan; cover with water. Bring to a boil; reduce heat & cook about 10–12 minutes until tender; drain. Put drained potatoes in a greased 9x13 baking dish. In a bowl, mix soup, milk, dressing mix, 1 cup cheese. Add Salt & pepper to taste; pour over potatoes. Sprinkle remaining cheese & crumbled bacon on top. Bake, uncovered, at 350°F for 25–30 minutes and potatoes are tender and cheese is bubbling.
AU GRATIN POTATOES	8 baked and diced potatoes 1 medium diced onion salt and pepper to taste 1 cube butter 2 cans cream of chicken soup 4 cups shredded cheddar cheese 2 cups sour cream Salt and pepper to taste	Combine potatoes, onion, and salt and pepper. Set aside. In a saucepan, combine butter, soup, and cheese; cook over low heat until butter and cheese are melted. Stir in sour cream. Pour over potato mixture; pour into greased baking dish. Bake covered at 325°F until heated through, about 20–25 minutes.

3 BASIC POTATO RECIPES

Some of the simple recipes are always the best.
Let's look at how to make three basics:

PERFECT CREAMY MASHED POTATOES

1. Use the right kind of potato. For mashing, Russets are best—you'll get light, fluffy mashed potatoes. Don't use red potatoes—they hold their shape so well that you'll get lumps.

2. Get the potatoes ready: wash them well, cut out dark spots, peel them, unless you want rustic mashed potatoes, and cut them into cubes a few inches in size. The cubes should all be about the same size so they cook uniformly—the bigger the chunks, the longer they take to boil.

3. Put the potatoes in a large saucepan and put enough cold water in the pan to cover the potatoes with 2 inches of water. If desired, salt the water (just be aware that the potatoes will absorb the salt). Bring the water to a boil, reduce to a lively simmer, and cook for 10–20 minutes. You'll know they're done when you stick a fork into a cube and it starts to fall apart; you don't want them too soft or mushy. Do not put a lid on the pan; the potatoes will get gluey.

4. While the potatoes are cooking, get your liquid ready. You can use milk, or cream (make rich and creamy mashed potatoes) or chicken stock (makes potatoes that are lower in fat but less creamy). Heat the liquid just until it's warm.

5. Drain the potatoes then put them back in the pan on the stove. Add room-temperature butter and start mashing, using a ricer (for creamiest and fluffiest), potato masher, two forks, or the back of a wooden spoon. Gradually add the warm liquid, stirring until the potatoes bind together. Never add the liquid all at once, or you might add too much and get a mushy mess.

6. Taste the potatoes and adjust the seasonings; add more butter, salt, and/or pepper if needed. Make sure to serve them while they're warm.

Freeze it!

Mashed potatoes are pretty much perfect for "double and freeze" or even "triple and freeze." For tips, check out the chart on page 113.

PERFECT ROASTED POTATOES

1. The best potatoes for roasting, bar none, are Yukon golds—they're not too starchy, not too waxy, have thin skins, and are consistent in size. You can use others but trust me. Yukons are best.

2. Wash the potatoes, cut them in half, and arrange them cut-side down on a rimmed baking sheet, spacing them evenly apart. Pour enough water over the cookie sheet to cover it with a thin layer of water (about 1½ to 2 cups).

3. Cover the baking sheet with a double layer of tin foil and crimp it tightly around the edges so it will hold in the steam.

4. Bake the potatoes at 425 °F for 25–30 minutes, or until you can easily pierce them with a fork. (Do your piercing through the foil in case you have to bake them a little more.) Let the potatoes cool for 5 minutes, peel up a corner of the foil with tongs, and drain off the water. (Protect your hands; that water will be HOT.)

5. Remove the foil and pour ¼ C. olive oil over the potatoes; season them generously with salt and pepper. Once the potatoes have cooled enough to handle, toss them with your hands to evenly coat them with oil. Arrange them on the baking sheet again, cut side down.

6. Crank the oven up to 500 °F and roast the uncovered potatoes for 20–25 minutes. The potatoes should be crisp and deep brown and the oil should be sizzling. Remove from the sheet with a spatula.

THE PERFECT BAKED POTATO

1. Prick the potatoes all over with a fork and rub the skin with butter (not oil—you'll thank me later); season generously with coarse salt and coarse-ground pepper. Do not wrap the potato in foil; it steams the potatoes. Not what you're after in a baked potato.

2. Place the potatoes on a baking sheet in the middle of the oven and roast at 350 °F until the skin is crisp and they are very soft when squeezed, 60–80 minutes, depending on the size of the spud. (Some will tell you to put the potato directly on the oven rack. I promise you won't want to clean the mess off the floor of the oven.)

3. Brush the salt and pepper off the outside of the potatoes or you'll never be able to eat the skin (which, after all, is the most nutritious part!). Cut each potato open and season with salt, pepper, and butter. (Those are the basics, of course; you can go wild and add sour cream, shredded cheese, sliced green onion, crumbled cooked bacon, chives, and just about anything else your heart desires.)

this is a piece of cake

NAKED CAKE MIX

You know it well: that box of cake mix sitting on the pantry shelf, all but daring you to do something memorable with it. You know, besides just a plain old cake.

Well, do I have some tricks for you! If you do decide you want to bake a cake, start with a plain old cake mix (no fancy add-in ingredients) and make it lots more scrumptious by adding some simple things to the mix:

CAKE MIX-IN IDEAS

- **INSTANT PUDDING MIX**
  Use chocolate pudding mix for chocolate cakes, butterscotch or vanilla pudding mix for light-colored cakes, lemon pudding for lemon cakes. You won't believe how moist your cake is!
- **SNACK-PACK PUDDING**
  Don't have any pudding mix? No problem! Stir a container of snack-pack pudding into the cake batter.
- **SODA POP**
  You read that right—mix in a can of soda. Use dark soda for chocolate, Sprite or 7Up for light-colored cakes.
- **VANILLA EXTRACT**
  Add one to two tablespoons vanilla extract to the batter.
- **EGGS**
  The mix probably calls for two or three. Forget it—add four large eggs.
- **EGG YOLKS**
  Use the number of eggs called for on the mix but add two extra egg yolks.
- **WHOLE MILK**
  Instead of using water, use whole milk. This has to be whole milk—no fat-free, reduced-fat, soy, or almond milk.
- **BUTTERMILK**
  Replace the water with buttermilk, but add a little more; you need a bit more liquid to make up for the thickness of the buttermilk.
- **SOUR CREAM**
  Substitute sour cream for the water in a cake mix. Make sure you mix it two to three minutes longer to get it all incorporated.
- **HOT WATER**
  If you stick with water, use HOT water. It helps the flavors in the mix "bloom."
- **MAYONNAISE OR MIRACLE WHIP**
  Stir 2 tablespoons mayo or Miracle Whip into the batter.
- **SOFTENED/MELTED BUTTER**
  Skip the oil the mix calls for and use butter instead. The different is dramatic.
- **LEMON JUICE**
  Add some lemon juice to yellow cake mix to boost the flavor.
- **ADD-INS**
  There are all kinds of things you can stir into your cake batter to make it taste better! Try chocolate chips, chopped nuts, mashed bananas, butterscotch chips, Andes mint pieces, raisins, dried cranberries, dried apricots . . . you get the drift.

12 CREATIVE WAYS TO USE A CAKE MIX

You won't believe the number of fun things you can do with cake mix—and I'm giving you a dozen great ideas to get you started! So, face down that cake mix and whip up something awesome! Unless otherwise indicated, all recipes below use one boxed cake.

DESSERT	TOP IT/MIX IT WITH	HOW TO PREPARE IT
CAKE MIX COOKIES	½ cup vegetable oil 2 eggs Mix-ins of your choice, such as chocolate chips, M&Ms, chopped nuts, raisins, mini marshmallows	Use any flavor cake mix. Combine the cake mix, oil, eggs, and mix-ins; stir well to blend all ingredients. Refrigerate for 20 minutes. Scoop onto greased or parchment-lined cookie sheet; bake at 350 °F for 9–11 minutes.
PEANUT BUTTER AND JELLY ROLLS	2 eggs ⅓ cup canola oil ½ cup peanut butter (creamy or crunchy) ½ cup jelly 1 cup peanut butter chips	Use white cake mix. Combine cake mix, eggs, oil, and peanut butter; set aside ½ C. mixture. Press remaining mixture into greased 8-inch square pan. Spread with jelly. Mix remaining ½ C. cake mixture with peanut butter chips until crumbly; spread over jelly. Bake at 350 °F for 20–25 min.
CAKE POPS	¾ cup prepared frosting 5 cups chocolate or white chocolate chips ½ stick Crisco shortening Toppings (such as sprinkles or chopped nuts) Sucker sticks	Use chocolate or white cake mix. Bake cake mix in a 9x13 pan as directed, using pudding, extra eggs, whole milk, or butter to make it moist. Cool completely. Crumble into a large bowl and use an electric mixer to turn it into fine crumbs. Beat in frosting until well blended. Cover and freeze for 30 min. Form into 1½-inch balls, put on waxed-paper-covered pan, and freeze for an hour. Melt chips and Crisco until smooth; dip balls, letting excess run off. Top with desired topping. Chill 10 min to harden the coating; insert sucker sticks.
FUDGY DOUBLE-CHOCOLATE COOKIES	½ cup softened butter 1 egg 1 packet instant coffee dissolved in 2 tablespoons water 1 tablespoon vegetable oil ½ teaspoon vanilla 1½ cups chocolate chips 1½ cups white chocolate chips 1½ cups chopped nuts (optional)	Use chocolate cake mix. Beat butter until smooth; stir in egg, coffee, oil, and vanilla until well blended. Add cake mix in batches to blend well. Stir in chips and nuts, if desired. Roll into balls; bake on ungreased baking sheet at 350 °F for 7–10 min, or until tops of cookies start to crack. Let cool.

DESSERT	TOP IT/MIX IT WITH	HOW TO PREPARE IT
RED VELVET PUPPY CHOW	½ cup powdered sugar ¾ cup white chocolate chips ¼ cup chocolate chips (milk or semisweet) 2 ounces softened cream cheese 1½ tablespoons milk 5 cups Rice Chex cereal Add-ins as desired, pink or red M&Ms, heart sprinkles	Use red velvet cake mix. In a large bowl with lid or large zip-top bag, combine cake mix & powdered sugar. Set aside. Melt chips & stir until smooth; stir in cream cheese & milk. Pour over Rice Chex. Dump cereal into bowl or bag with cake mix & powdered sugar; shake vigorously until all cereal is coated. Dump onto a cookie sheet & let cool. Mix in any desired mix-ins. (If you use cream cheese & milk, store in fridge.)
CINNAMON WAFFLES	1 teaspoon cinnamon 1 teaspoon vanilla extract	Use vanilla, yellow, or spice cake mix. Mix cake mix according to package directions; stir in cinnamon and vanilla. Bake in waffle maker for 2–3 minutes. Can top with glaze if desired.
CHOCOLATE ALMOND BISCOTTI	1 cup flour ½ cup melted butter 2 large eggs ½ cup chocolate syrup 1 teaspoon vanilla ½ teaspoon almond extract ½ cup chopped almonds ½ cup miniature chocolate chips White chocolate chips for drizzle	Use chocolate cake mix. Beat all ingredients but almonds & chocolate chips until well-blended. Stir in almonds & chocolate chips. Divide dough in half; shape each into a 12x12 log. Bake on ungreased cookie sheet at 350 °F for 30–35 min; should be firm. Cool on rack for 20 min. After cooled, cut into ½-inch-thick diagonal slices; bake on ungreased cookie sheets at 350 °F for 10–15 min, or until firm. Drizzle with melted white chocolate chips if desired.
WHITE CHOCOLATE CHIP CARAMEL CORN	6–8 cups popped popcorn ½ cup melted butter ½ cup cake mix ¼ cup packed brown sugar ¼ cup granulated sugar ¼ cup light corn syrup 1½ teaspoons vanilla extract ½ cup (or more!) white chocolate chips ½ cup (or more!) peanuts Optional add-ins: Reese's Pieces, toffee bits, peanut butter chips, milk or semisweet chocolate chips, butterscotch chips, sprinkles	Use white, vanilla, or yellow cake mix. In a medium saucepan, melt butter; stir in cake mix, sugars, & corn syrup; stirring constantly, cook over medium heat for 3–4 min. DO NOT BOIL. Remove from heat, let cool 30 seconds, stir in vanilla. Pour mixture over popcorn, coat evenly. Spread evenly on a Silpat or parchment-lined cookie sheet; bake at 250 °F for 18–24 min (if it starts to brown, take out immediately). Sprinkle with add-ins and let cool; break into chunks.

DESSERT	TOP IT/MIX IT WITH	HOW TO COOK IT
CHOCOLATE CRINKLE COOKIES	⅓ cup vegetable oil 2 eggs 1 teaspoon vanilla Powdered sugar	Use Devil's food cake mix. Mix all ingredients except powdered sugar; refrigerate dough for 15–30 min. Form chilled dough into balls; roll in powdered sugar. Bake on ungreased cookie sheet at 350 °F for 9–11 min.
MUG CAKE	6 tablespoons chocolate cake mix 1 tablespoon water 2 tablespoons unsweetened applesauce 1 tablespoon semi-sweet chocolate	Use chocolate cake mix. Combine ingredients in a microwave-safe mug. Sprinkle as many chocolate chips as you want on top. Microwave for 1 minute on full power. Allow the cake to cool for a few minutes before you eat it.
RICE KRISPIES TREATS	3 tablespoons butter ½ tablespoons vanilla 10-ounce bag miniature marshmallows ⅓ cup cake mix 6 cups Rice Krispies cereal rainbow sprinkles (optional)	Use vanilla or strawberry cake mix. Melt butter over low heat; stir in vanilla. Add marshmallows & stir until completely melted. Stir in 1 T. cake mix at a time until well blended. Pour in cereal & stir to coat evenly. Add sprinkles if desired and stir to distribute evenly. Pour in greased dish; press with hands to create even layer. Let cool for 30 minutes before cutting.
BANANA SPICE MUFFINS	¾ cup milk or almond milk 1 cup vanilla Greek yogurt ½ cup egg whites 2 tablespoons olive oil 2 mashed bananas 1½ cups granola	Use spice cake mix. Combine cake mix, milk, yogurt, egg whites, and olive oil; blend well. Stir in bananas. Spoon batter into prepared muffin tins. Top with granola. Bake at 350 F for 18 minutes.
FUDGY BROWNIES	⅓ cup milk ½ cup melted butter 6 ounce semisweet chocolate chips 1 cup chopped nuts (optional) *Top with caramel sauce or ice cream	Use Devil's food cake mix. Combine cake mix, milk, and butter; stir until dough forms. Stir in chocolate chips and nuts (if desired). Bake in a greased 9x13 pan at 350 °F for 24 minutes. Let cool.
CAKE MIX QUICK BREAD	1 small box vanilla instant pudding mix 1 cup water ½ cup vegetable oil 3 eggs Mix-ins as desired, such as sprinkles, chopped nuts, chocolate chips, or raisins Frosting if desired	Use yellow cake mix. Mix batter ingredients for 2 minutes with electric mixer; stir in mix-ins as desired. Bake in 2 greased loaf pans at 350 °F for 45–50 minutes, or until toothpick inserted in center comes out clean. Cool and remove from pans. Can frost if desired.

from my family to yours

FAVORITE FAMILY RECIPES

APPETIZERS & SIDES

FRUIT DIP

You know when people beg for a recipe, but you're almost embarrassed to show how easy it is? This fruit dip is one of those. I never kept marshmallow creme on hand—until now. This easy-to-make recipe will be the big hit at your next party!

INGREDIENTS

7 ounces marshmallow creme
5 ounces cream cheese
1 teaspoon lemon juice
½ teaspoon vanilla extract

DIRECTIONS

Microwave marshmallow creme, cream cheese, and lemon juice together for one minute.

Add in vanilla; mix well. Serve with sliced or skewered fruit.

Freeze it!

This fruit dip can be prepared ahead and frozen in a freezer-safe container. Thaw in the refrigerator.

JOAN'S CHEESE BALL

My mom's best friend Joan was my second mother growing up. Every Christmas, Joan gifted neighbors her famous cheese ball, and we'd fight over it to the point mom may have hidden it from us. To this day, it's my favorite cheese ball. It's delicious and super easy to make.

INGREDIENTS

- 3 ounces cream cheese, softened
- 2 cups shredded, sharp cheddar cheese, softened
- 2 tablespoons lemon juice
- 1/8 teaspoon ground pepper
- 1/4 teaspoon garlic powder
- 1 1/2 teaspoons chili powder
- 1 1/2 teaspoons paprika
- 1/4 cup finely chopped walnuts (or pecans), optional

DIRECTIONS

Mix cheeses, lemon juice, pepper, and garlic powder with an electric mixer, until just combined. Form into a ball with hands.

Combine chili powder and paprika in a bowl; roll cheese ball in the mixture. Roll cheese ball in nuts (optional).

Store in cling wrap and refrigerate until serving. Serve with crackers or vegetables.

BLACK BEAN DIP

Years ago I was throwing an epic Halloween party. I wanted one more appetizer that looked dark and brooding, but was quick and easy, plus, I needed to have all the ingredients. I made this bean dip recipe, and it was the absolute HIT of the party!

INGREDIENTS

1 (15-ounce) can black beans, rinsed & drained
1 cup fresh cilantro + extra for garnish
½ cup salsa
½ cup plain fat-free yogurt, or sour cream
1 teaspoon ground cumin
¼ teaspoon salt

DIRECTIONS

Combine all ingredients in blender or food processor; blend until desired consistency (can be either smooth or chunky).

Spoon into a serving bowl and garnish with cilantro. Makes 8 ¼-cup servings.

Serve with crackers or chips, can be served room temperature, or slightly warmed.

"THE BEAN DIP"

One of my besties, Lindsey has this awesome bean dip that I ask her to bring whenever we have gatherings involving food. One day, I shared her recipe on Instagram and it went crazy. Now it's referred to as "The Bean Dip." Check out Lindsey's other delicious recipes @healthyhappyhome.

INGREDIENTS

2 cans refried beans
1 cube cream cheese
1 can diced green chiles
3 tablespoons taco seasoning (to taste)
1-2 cups shredded cheddar cheese
Salt and pepper to taste

DIRECTIONS

Preheat oven to 350°F. Mix all ingredients with an electric hand mixer until well blended.

Pour mixture into a baking dish and bake until hot and bubbly. (Check at 20 minutes.)

EASIEST SALSA EVER

Years ago I was at my friend Tiffany's house, and I ate some mind-blowing homemade salsa. I begged her for the recipe and was surprised to see many of the ingredients were canned! Over the years I've adapted Tiff's Salsa, and it's a constant go-to recipe!

INGREDIENTS

1 can whole tomatoes (or fresh)
4 (10-ounce) cans tomatoes, undrained (drain if using fresh tomatoes)
1 jalapeño, seeded
½ onion
1 clove garlic
1 bunch cilantro
½ teaspoon salt
½ teaspoon sugar
½ teaspoon cumin
Juice of 1 lime
1 teaspoon red pepper flakes (optional)

DIRECTIONS

Place all ingredients in blender or food processor. Blender makes it a smoother salsa, food processor makes it more thick and chopped. If you want more heat, leave some seeds in the jalapeño. Red pepper flakes, if used, result in deeper flavor but don't add heat.

Pulse until you get the consistency and chunkiness you want. Note: If you like your salsa chunkier, I prefer to add my onion at the very end after blending everything else, and only pulse it slightly so the onion stays more of a diced consistency, rather than blended.

Store in the refrigerator for a few days or freeze for later. When freezing in a mason jar, leave enough space in jar or container to allow for expansion.

Follow Tiffany at @ImpressivelyEasyCooking

ALLISON'S PICO

My Aunt Allison is the coolest. She and I have always had a special bond, and when we get together, we could chat for hours. When I was in college she had me up for dinner, and made this pico "salsa" of sorts, that I have been obsessed with ever since. It's SO versatile!

INGREDIENTS

1 can black beans, rinsed & drained (may use kidney or other beans)
1 bunch fresh cilantro, chopped
1 can white shoe peg corn (can use regular corn)
1 can diced tomatoes (or 2 cups fresh tomatoes, diced)
Red onion, diced (optional)
Lime juice (optional)
1–2 teaspoons red pepper flakes (optional)

DIRECTIONS

Mix all ingredients. If using lime juice or red pepper flakes, stir in shortly before serving. Refrigerate for at least 3 hours so the flavors can mix.

Serve with tortilla chips and enjoy!

It's also a gorgeous garnish to put on top of chicken, fish, burritos, tacos, or just about anything!

Optional add-ins or substitutions (all "to taste"): finely diced red onion, Italian or other oil-based salad dressing, avocado, cotija cheese or queso fresco, diced jalapeno (seeded), diced bell pepper, green onion (finely chopped).

CRANBERRY SALSA

When my sister-in-law Lindsay sent me this recipe years ago, I thought, "cranberry, jalapeno, and cilantro? There's no way that's good." Now, friends and family members ask me to make this salsa A LOT throughout the Christmas season. There are NEVER leftovers. (P.S. It tastes best with Wheat Thins.)

INGREDIENTS

12 ounces fresh cranberries
1-2 jalapenos, seeded
½ bunch green onions
¼ cup cilantro
½ cup sugar
½ teaspoon cumin
1 tablespoon lemon juice
2 8-ounce packages cream cheese, softened

DIRECTIONS

Add cranberries, seeded jalapenos, green onions, and cilantro to a food processor. Pulse until it reaches the desired consistency.

Move to a mixing bowl, and add sugar, cumin, and lemon juice. Stir until well mixed. Spread over softened cream cheese that has been spread on a serving dish, and serve with crackers or chips.

NOTE: If you have time, put the cranberry salsa portion in the refrigerator to allow it to come together. Spread it over softened cream cheese when you're ready to serve.

PUMPKIN CREAM CHEESE DIP

You now know my love affair with cream cheese, right? Ready to take it to the next level? Toss in some pumpkin and you've got yourself your new favorite fall treat! You're welcome.

INGREDIENTS

- 2 cups (1 15-ounce can) pumpkin puree
- ½ cup brown sugar, loosely packed
- 2 tablespoons maple syrup
- 1 teaspoon ground cinnamon
- ⅛ teaspoon ground nutmeg
- 1 tablespoon lemon juice
- ⅛ teaspoon salt (or just a sprinkle)
- 8 ounces cream cheese, softened
- 1 cup pecans, chopped
- 4 slices bacon, cooked until crispy and crumbled
- 2 green onions, chopped

DIRECTIONS

In a large bowl, mix together the 2 cups of pumpkin puree, ½ cup of brown sugar, 2 tablespoons of maple syrup, 1 teaspoon of cinnamon, ⅛ teaspoon of nutmeg, 1 tablespoon of lemon juice, and a sprinkle of salt. Remove ½ cup of the pumpkin mixture and reserve for a separate use.

Add the 8 ounces of softened cream cheese. Using a hand mixer or stand mixer, blend until mostly smooth and any cream cheese lumps are very small. Stir in the chopped pecans, crumbled bacon, and green onions. Refrigerate until ready to serve. Serve with vegetables, crackers, apples and pears.

GREEN BEANS & BACON

We serve these delicious green beans as a side, especially on Holidays and nice Sunday dinners, and it's inevitably one dish that is licked completely clean. My tip: use real bacon bits in a pinch to save the time, mess, and smell that comes with cooking bacon!

INGREDIENTS

2 ½ pounds green beans
Kosher salt to taste
½ pound bacon, roughly chopped
1 small yellow onion, finely chopped
3 cloves garlic, minced
1 teaspoon red pepper flakes
½ cup toasted pecans, chopped
Juice of ½ lemon
Freshly ground pepper

DIRECTIONS

Place green beans and salt in a large pot of boiling water; cook about 5 minutes, until bright green in color and crisp-tender. Drain. Shock beans in bowl of ice water to stop the cooking. Drain and pat dry.

In a large, heavy sauté pan, cook bacon about 5 minutes, until crisp. Or, heat real bacon bits in 1 tablespoon oil in a pan for a minute or two. Drain bacon on a paper towel. Spoon off excess bacon grease, leaving 2 tablespoons in pan.

Sauté onions in bacon grease until soft and tender, about 5 minutes. Sprinkle in garlic and red pepper flakes; sauté about 1 minute, or until fragrant. Stir in green beans and pecans; cook until just heated through, about 5–6 minutes. Stir bacon into pan; toss with lemon juice. Season with salt and pepper. Serves 6–8.

GRANDMA'S GREEN BEAN CASSEROLE

As a youth, I always hid my half-eaten Thanksgiving green bean casserole. I never understood the potential of this side dish until my sister-in-law Shelby's grandma's magical recipe! Now it's the one I go back to for third helpings. I promise you've never had one as good as this!

INGREDIENTS

2 tablespoons butter
1 ½ tablespoons all-purpose flour
1 ½ teaspoon salt
1 teaspoon sugar
½ cup diced onion
1 cup sour cream
3 (14.5 oz.) cans (or 43.5 oz. fresh) French-style green beans, drained & rinsed
2 cups shredded cheddar cheese
½ cup crumbled buttery round crackers
1 tablespoon butter, melted
Fried onions

DIRECTIONS

Preheat oven to 350°F. Melt butter in a large skillet over medium heat. Stir in flour until smooth; cook for one minute.

Stir in the salt, sugar, onion, and sour cream. Add green beans and stir to coat. Add cheese. Stir to incorporate throughout the mixture. Transfer the mixture to a 2 1/2 qt. casserole dish.

In a small bowl, toss together cracker crumbs and remaining butter; sprinkle over cheese. Sprinkle with fried onions.

Bake for 30 minutes or until the top is golden and cheese is bubbly.

SARAH'S GREEN RICE

Bubba's brother Nate, and his wife Sarah, are great cooks. While Nate is famous for his pies, I have to say that Sarah's Green Rice recipe is an all-time favorite of mine! The mild chili flavor, the warm, cheesy goodness, makes it a perfect side for just about any meal.

INGREDIENTS

2 tablespoons vegetable oil
1 cup uncooked long-grain white rice
2 ¼ cups white onion, finely chopped
1 can green chilies, diced
6 green onions, thinly sliced
1 clove garlic, minced
¼ teaspoon salt
¼ teaspoon cumin
1 ¾ cup chicken broth
1 ½ cups Monterey Jack cheese, shredded and divided
⅓ cup cilantro, coarsely chopped

DIRECTIONS

Preheat oven to 375°F and heat oil in large skillet over medium heat; stir in rice and cook, stirring constantly, for 2 minutes or until rice turns opaque. Add white onion; cook and stir 1 minute. Stir in chilies, green onions, garlic, salt, and cumin. Stir in broth.

Bring to a boil over high heat then reduce heat to low; cover and simmer 15 minutes, or until rice is almost tender. Remove skillet from heat. Add 1 cup cheese and chopped cilantro. Stir in lightly to mix.

Pour mixture into a greased 8 x 8 baking dish. Top with remaining ½ cup cheese. Bake uncovered for 15 minutes, until cheese is melted and starting to turn golden brown. Garnish with cilantro if desired. Serves 4–6.

BERRY PRETZEL JELL-O SALAD

When I moved to Utah, I quickly learned: Utah LOVES Jell-o, and salad (that isn't actually salad). When I got married, I was asked to bring a jello salad side to a family dinner. I found this recipe, adapted it over the years, and now it's a favorite, especially at Thanksgiving.

INGREDIENTS

- 1 (6-ounce) package raspberry Jell-O
- 2 cups boiling water
- 2 cups pretzels
- ½ cup butter
- ¼ cup sugar
- 1 (8-ounce) package cream cheese, softened
- 1 cup sugar
- 1 (8-ounce) frozen Cool Whip, thawed
- 1 (12-ounce) bag frozen raspberries, thawed in fridge
- 1 (12-ounce) bag frozen strawberries, thawed in fridge

DIRECTIONS

Preheat oven to 350°F. Combine Jell-O and boiling water; set aside to cool to room temperature. Use rolling pin to crush pretzels in a resealable plastic bag. In a saucepan, melt butter; add ¼ cup sugar and pretzels. Mix well. Lightly press into a 9 x 13 baking dish; bake 10 minutes and cool to room temperature.

While pretzel mixture cools, beat cream cheese and 1 cup sugar on medium speed until well combined. Using a spatula, fold in Cool Whip; mix until well combined. Spread cream cheese mixture over cooled pretzels; spread all the way to the edges to form a seal so Jell-O can't leak through to pretzels. Refrigerate 30 minutes.

Spread raspberries and strawberries evenly over cream cheese mixture. Pour Jell-O mixture over raspberries and strawberries and refrigerate until Jell-O is set. Makes 12 servings.

STRAWBERRY SPINACH SALAD

Wanna know a secret? I don't really like salads. Well, I guess they're okay (except for all the lettuce). The exception is this recipe... it's one of the only salads you'll ever see me make. You might as well call it Jordan's Salad because I love it so much.

INGREDIENTS

Fresh baby spinach
Fresh strawberries, sliced in half
Mozzarella cheese

SUGAR TOASTED ALMONDS
½ cup sliced raw almonds
1 tablespoon butter
2-3 tablespoons white sugar

DIRECTIONS

Strawberry spinach salad: Eyeball all the salad ingredients according to your desired taste! It's a salad, don't stress! Top with almonds, and serve dressing on the side.

Sugar toasted almonds: Melt butter over medium-low heat. Add almonds and sugar. Saute until sugar has melted and everything has incorporated, but watch carefully so they don't burn! Cool on parchment paper, then add to salad.

POPPYSEED DRESSING

One of my favorite salad dressings to go with the strawberry spinach salad and other sweet salads! You are going to love this! You can even save this in the fridge so you can use it for a few weeks for your family!

INGREDIENTS

¾ cup white sugar
½ cup honey
1 teaspoon paprika
1 teaspoon mustard
1 teaspoon onion, finely grated
½ cup lemon juice
1 cup vegetable oil
1 teaspoon poppy seeds

DIRECTIONS

Mix all ingredients, except oil and poppy seeds, in a blender. Gradually add oil and poppy seeds and continue blending.

Serve with salad. Refrigerate remaining dressing for later use. Keeps 3 weeks.

EASY CHEESY SCALLOPED POTATOES

When I think of scalloped potatoes, I think of my little brother, Nate. He'd try to throw them away when my parents weren't looking, but he had to eat them anyway. For us scalloped potato lovers, this delicious, crowd-pleasing recipe is so easy and it's sure to be a hit!

INGREDIENTS

1 large white onion, chopped
2 cloves garlic, minced
¼ cup butter
¼ cup all-purpose flour
½ teaspoon salt
¼ teaspoon black pepper
2½ cups milk
1½cups cheddar cheese
8 cups yukon gold potatoes, thinly sliced

DIRECTIONS

Preheat the oven to 350°F and grease a 9x13 dish. Cook onion and garlic in a saucepan until tender. Stir in flour, salt, and pepper. Add milk and stir over medium heat until thickened and just starting to simmer. Remove from heat, and mix in cheese until melted. Set aside.

Place half the potatoes in the dish. Top with half the cheese sauce. Repeat layers. Cover tightly with foil and bake for 45 minutes. Uncover and bake for an additional 45 minutes or until the potatoes are tender. Let stand uncovered for 10 minutes before serving.

SHELBY'S FAMOUS CREAMED CORN

The first time I tried creamed corn was when my sister-in-law, Shelby, made it for Thanksgiving a few years ago. I kid you not, I've literally had dreams about it since. It's just that good. Now at every family function, we always ask her to bring this delicious, easy recipe.

INGREDIENTS

40 ounces corn (canned or frozen)
8 ounces cream
8 ounces whole milk
1 teaspoon salt
2 tablespoons sugar
⅛ teaspoon cayenne pepper
2 tablespoons melted butter
2 tablespoons flour
Parmesan cheese, to taste

DIRECTIONS

Combine first six ingredients in a medium pot. Bring to a boil over medium-high heat. Simmer 5 minutes.

Melt butter in a small saucepan and whisk in flour. Simmer until blended; slowly add to corn. Mix well and remove from heat once slightly thickened. Optional: Place cooked corn in a casserole pan, sprinkle with Parmesan cheese, and place under broiler until browned.

SWEET POTATO CASSEROLE

We rarely ate out when Bubba and I were getting out of debt. We finally splurged on a fancy meal with the most amazing steak, but the food we went gaga over was the sweet potato side! We have such great memories of it, and we've made this recipe many times.

INGREDIENTS

CRUST:

1 cup brown sugar
1/3 cup flour
1 cup chopped pecans
1/2 cup butter, melted

SWEET POTATO MIXTURE:

3 1/2 cups mashed sweet potatoes (okay to use canned, drained)
1 cup sugar
1/2 teaspoon salt
1 teaspoon vanilla
2 eggs, well beaten
1/4 cup melted butter

DIRECTIONS

Preheat oven to 350°F. Grease a 2-quart baking dish. In a small mixing bowl, prepare topping by combining all crust ingredients. Set aside.

In a large mixing bowl, combine sweet potatoes, sugar, salt, vanilla, eggs, and melted butter. Mix thoroughly. Pour into greased 2-quart baking dish.

Sprinkle topping evenly on top of sweet potatoes.

Bake for 30 minutes. Allow to set at least 30 minutes before serving. Try your best not to pass out, or eat the whole pan.

COTTAGE CHEESE FRUIT SALAD

As a Utah transplant, if there's one thing I've learned, it's that is Utah loves its "creative salads." This is a recipe I've grown to love. Use up that frozen cottage cheese and Cool Whip! Tip: If your kids don't like cottage cheese, blend it up to hide it.

INGREDIENTS

- 2-3 cups fruit
- 16 ounces cottage cheese
- 3 ounces sugar-free Jell-o (strawberry or raspberry)
- 8 ounces Cool Whip (or homemade whipped cream)

DIRECTIONS

Drain, dice, and slice fruit to the desired size. Combine fruit, Jell-o, and cottage cheese (blend the cottage cheese before adding for a more smooth consistency).

Mix well. Fold in Cool Whip and chill!

BREAKFAST

CABIN CASSEROLE

Is it just me, or does food taste better at a cabin? It's something in the air, I'm telling you! Whenever we go to our family cabin, I make what we call Cabin Casserole for breakfast. It is the most delicious, easiest, most crowd-pleasing breakfast casserole on the planet.

INGREDIENTS

1 (16-ounce) package pork breakfast sausage
12 eggs (I add 13-15 to make it more egg-y if the eggs aren't very big)
1½ cups milk
2 teaspoons dijon mustard
¼ teaspoon black pepper
1 (20-ounce) bag frozen hash browns
1½ cups cheddar cheese, shredded & divided

DIRECTIONS

Spray 9 x 13 baking dish with cooking spray.

In a skillet, cook sausage over medium heat 5–7 minutes, or until no longer pink. Drain.

In a large bowl, beat eggs, milk, mustard, and pepper; whisk until well mixed. Stir in hash browns, 1 cup cheese, and cooked sausage. Pour into baking dish, cover, and refrigerate at least 8 hours but no longer than 12 hours.

Preheat oven to 350°F. Remove dish from refrigerator, remove cover, and top with remaining ½ cup cheese. Bake 45–55 minutes, or until center is just set. Cool 10 minutes before serving.

NANA SYRUP

Nana syrup is one of Bubba's mom's best gifts to mankind. I've been obsessed with it ever since I first met Bubba's family and tasted it. It's also known as Arizona Syrup (where she lives)... and while it's worth the 10-hour drive to get some; luckily you can make your own.

INGREDIENTS

1 stick butter

½ cup buttermilk (or milk)*

1 cup sugar

1 teaspoon vanilla

½ teaspoon baking soda

*If you don't have buttermilk on hand, combine 1 tablespoon vinegar + ½ cup whole milk and let it sit for 5 minutes.

DIRECTIONS

In a large saucepan (yes, large! It foams and expands so give yourself extra room!), melt butter over medium heat. Add buttermilk, and sugar. Bring to a boil, stirring occasionally, then remove from heat.

Stir in vanilla and baking soda. Watch out, it will foam and expand! Stir gently. Serve warm, and try not to lick your plate!

Serve on anything from waffles, to pancakes, and anything else that you can justify putting syrup on.

KEITH'S CONFERENCE CREPES

Twice per year, our church has a special international broadcast called General Conference. We stay in our PJ's, snuggle up, and watch inspirational talks from speakers from all over the globe. One of our traditions is to make crepes. This recipe is from my brother-in-law, Keith, and they're delicious.

INGREDIENTS

2 eggs, beaten
1½ cups milk
1 cup flour
1 tablespoon oil
2 tablespoons sugar

DIRECTIONS

Mix all ingredients in blender.

Lightly spray a skillet pan with nonstick cooking spray. Pour ⅛ cup batter into pan; swish to thinly coat the pan.

Brown both sides. Serve warm with butter, powdered sugar, fruit, peanut butter, Nutella, or whatever toppings you like...and of course, Nana syrup!

MINI "CHEAT" QUICHES

Years ago I helped throw a baby shower for a best friend. I found this recipe and instantly fell in love with how quick, easy, and fool-proof these are! I like to make a triple batch and eat them all week. I call them "cheat" quiches because they're cute, delicious & easy!

INGREDIENTS

6 slices bacon (or ½–1 cup real bacon bits)
1 onion, chopped (or 2–4 tablespoons dried minced onion)
5 eggs, beaten
½ cup buttermilk baking mix (I use Bisquick)
1–2 tablespoons green onion, chopped (can use parsley if preferred)
1–2 cup cheddar cheese, shredded

DIRECTIONS

Preheat the oven to 350°F. Grease 2 mini muffin pans. If using slices of bacon, fry bacon until crisp. Drain and crumble or dice; set aside.

Combine all ingredients. Spoon batter into greased muffin pans, filling cups to the top.

Bake for 10 minutes, or until the tops are slightly browned. Allow quiches to cool before removing from the pan with a small knife or spatula.

NOTE: Try one or more of the following combos—if you like it in an omelet, you'll like it in these: spinach, artichokes, and mozzarella or Swiss cheese; crab, onion, and Swiss cheese; mushrooms and spinach; or ham, diced peppers, and Swiss cheese. Experiment with different combos and have fun with it!

FRENCH TOAST STICKS

I adapted these fan favorites for a Rachael Ray segment (along with a month's worth of make-ahead breakfasts). We make a huge batch and freeze, then broil or toast them to reheat. They're crunchy because they're made with cereal, which makes Bubba extra happy!

INGREDIENTS

4 eggs
⅓ cup half-and-half
1 tablespoon vanilla extract
½ cup sugar
1 teaspoon cinnamon
1 ½ cups bread crumbs
1 ½ cups sweetened cereal, crushed to fine crumbs
2 tablespoons salted butter, melted
12 slices bread, cut into 3 strips

DIRECTIONS

Crack the eggs into a shallow dish, like a pie plate. Add the half-and-half, vanilla, ¼ cup sugar and ½ teaspoon cinnamon. Whisk lightly until combined; set aside. In a separate shallow dish, stir together the breadcrumbs, crushed cereal and remaining ¼ cup sugar, and ½ teaspoon cinnamon. Use a fork to stir in the melted butter.

Dunk the bread strips in the egg mixture, turning to coat. Then lay them in the dish with the crumb mixture, turning them over, sprinkling, and pressing so the crumbs totally cover the surface.

Place on a lined baking sheet to either bake or flash freeze for later. To bake, preheat the oven to 425°F. Bake until golden brown around the edges, about 10-12 minutes (15-18 minutes if baking from frozen).

BREAKFAST EGG MUFFINS

I discovered this recipe a few years ago, and I love it. I even made them on a Rachael Ray Show appearance as a good make-ahead breakfast for the week. They were a hit! Experiment with different mix-ins and flavors. They store and reheat well, and my kids love 'em!

INGREDIENTS

- 1 pound breakfast sausage (or any cooked meat)
- 1 whole onion, diced
- 15 large eggs
- 1 dash salt
- ¼ teaspoon black pepper
- 1 whole bell pepper, diced
- 1 cup cheese, grated

DIRECTIONS

Preheat oven to 350°F. Spray muffin tin with cooking spray. Cook sausage over medium-high heat until almost done. Add onion; cook over low heat until sausage is cooked and onion is translucent. Remove from heat; set aside to cool.

Mix together eggs, salt, and pepper; whisk until combined. Mix in cheese and bell pepper. Add cooled sausage. Spoon into muffin cups. For mini muffins bake for 10-12 minutes until puffy and just set. For regular muffins, bake for 20-22 minutes.

MINI GERMAN PANCAKES

Bubba's dad served a church mission in Denmark. As a result, his family has deep Danish ties, and they love eating Ebelskivers for special holidays. My kids love them, but they're a lot of work. Win-win? We make Ebelskivers at Christmas and enjoy these easy mini German pancakes all the time.

INGREDIENTS

- 6 large eggs
- 1 cup milk
- ½ teaspoon vanilla extract
- 1 cup (5 ounces) all-purpose flour (white or wheat)
- ¼ teaspoon salt

DIRECTIONS

Preheat the oven to 400°F. Heat a mini muffin pan in the oven for 10 minutes while you're making the batter.

Combine the eggs, milk and vanilla in a blender and blend on low speed until smooth, about 10-20 seconds. Add the flour and salt and blend until just combined.

Remove the hot pan from the oven and spray each cup thoroughly with cooking spray. Carefully pour batter into cups, filling to about half full. Bake immediately for 8-10 minutes or until lightly browned.

Dump the pancakes out onto a clean kitchen towel while still warm, and keep covered until you're ready to serve. Top with desired toppings.

BISCUITS AND "GRAGY"

Bubba's Grandpa Beck was known for making the most delicious gravy. One day when Bubba was a toddler, he looked up while eating and said, "Good gragy, Beck!" And we've called gravy "gragy" ever since. Here is his secret recipe, perfect for those slower weekend mornings.

INGREDIENTS

- Grandma Mary's Southern Biscuits (see pg. 232)
- 12 ounces ground sausage
- ½ cup butter
- ½ cup flour, sifted
- 4 cups whole milk
- 1 teaspoon salt
- Pepper
- Dash of cayenne pepper

DIRECTIONS

Make Grandma's Mary's Southern Biscuits (pg. 232). While the biscuits are baking, brown sausage in a large skillet over medium heat. Remove sausage to a bowl; set aside. Leave 3 tablespoons grease in the pan for flavor; discard the rest.

Melt butter in the skillet over medium-high heat. Add flour; whisk until smooth. Cook for 1-2 minutes or until bubbly and slightly browned. Add salt, pepper, and cayenne. Whisk in the milk, one cup at a time, allowing the gravy to thicken. Turn heat to low.

Add a little extra milk at a time if the gravy feels too thick. Add cooked sausage to the gravy and heat through. Add salt and pepper to taste. Serve warm.

BREADS & ROLLS

GRANDMA MARY'S SOUTHERN BISCUITS

My Grandma Mary grew up in the deep South. Though cancer took her far too early, she left me with many fond memories of her cooking. My mom taught me to make these biscuits, just as her mom, my Grandma Mary, taught her. We love to slather these with butter and honey!

INGREDIENTS

3 cups self-rising flour
(or 3 cups all-purpose flour + 4 ½ teaspoons baking powder, ¾ tsp salt)
¼ cup vegetable oil
1 ¼ cups buttermilk, well shaken
Butter

DIRECTIONS

Place flour in a large bowl. Make a well in the middle of the flour. Pour vegetable oil into the well. Gradually pour in the buttermilk and mix with a fork or fingers. Don't over-mix. Knead with hands a little in the bowl to thoroughly combine.

Dust the counter with flour. Roll biscuit dough out with a rolling pin; it should be thick. Cut biscuits into circles with a glass and place them on a cookie sheet; they will rise, so space them well. Let biscuits sit on cookie sheet while oven preheats to 400°F. Put a little dab of butter on each biscuit and bake for 10 minutes. Makes 6 or 7 biscuits.

Tip: To reheat biscuits, cut in half and place on a cookie sheet cut-side up. Broil on low (watch closely) just until the inside of the bistcuit is golden. Don't heat the biscuit in the microwave or it will become soggy.

FOCACCIA BREADSTICKS

If it's got carbs, I want it in my mouth. With just a few minutes and just a few ingredients, you have some bomb.com (oh yes I did) breadsticks that would go with just about any meal! Tip: Make a double batch and freeze some for a quick side on a busy night!

INGREDIENTS

1 tablespoon yeast
1 ½ cups warm water
2 tablespoons sugar
½ teaspoon salt
3 cups flour
½ cup butter, melted, divided
Garlic salt, Parmesan cheese, onion salt

DIRECTIONS

Dissolve yeast in warm water. Stir in sugar, salt, and flour. Mix and knead for 3 minutes. Let rest for 10 minutes.

Spread ¼ cup melted butter on jelly-roll pan. Spread dough over melted butter. Spread remaining ¼ cup melted butter on top of dough.

Cut with pizza cutter once lengthwise, then across 4 times to make 10 breadsticks. Sprinkle with garlic salt, Parmesan cheese, and onion salt.

Let rise 10 minutes. Bake at 375°F for 20 minutes.

EASIEST BREAD RECIPE

If there is anything I'm NOT, it's a baker. So for me to call this recipe "easy" is saying something! This recipe originally came from my friend Liz, the Food Nanny. She is amazing and so is her bread! I've adapted it over the years, but it still holds the award for the best, and easiest, bread.

INGREDIENTS

2 ½ cups milk
¼ cup butter
⅓ cup honey
2 ½ teaspoons active dry yeast
1 egg, beaten
2 teaspooons salt
5–7 cups all-purpose flour

DIRECTIONS

Combine milk, butter, and honey; heat in microwave for 45 seconds. Stir; heat for another 45 seconds. Cool to warm but not hot (as warm as a warm bath).

Pour the lukewarm milk mixture into a large bowl or heavy-duty mixer. Add yeast and let it proof for 5 minutes until bubbly. Add egg, salt, and enough flour to make a moderately stiff dough.

Knead for about 6 minutes by hand or in a stand mixer. Form dough into 2 loaves and place in generously greased bread pans. (Use shortening, not nonstick cooking spray.) Cover with a dishtowel and let rise until double.

Bake at 350°F for 30–35 minutes on the middle rack until browned on top. Top with melted butter if you want to be extra fancy, or substitute wheat flour for a healthier option.

BEST EVER FRENCH BREAD

Years ago when my blog was brand new, I tried making French Bread. My first attempts led to some ugly looking loaves! I snapped some unflattering photos, posted it to the blog, and these were repinned thousands of times. Pretty or not, these loaves are going to rock your world!

INGREDIENTS

2½ cups warm water
2 tablespoons yeast
3 tablesoons sugar
2 tablespoons white vinegar
1 tablesoon salt
⅓ cups vegetable or canola oil
6-7 cups flour (a little more if needed)
Cornmeal
1 egg, beaten

Freeze it!

Freeze your room-temperature bread in an airtight freezer bag. Store in the freezer for up to 2 months. Thaw on the counter.

DIRECTIONS

In large bowl, combine water, yeast, sugar, and vinegar; let sit until it bubbles (3–5 minutes). Stir in salt, oil, and flour. If dough is too soft/sticky, add more flour, ½ cup at a time, until dough is soft but firm enough to shape into loaves. Knead for about 5 minutes. Put dough in cold oven with small pot of boiling water (keeps dough moist while it rises). Watch the dough; punch it down 3–5 times, whenever it gets to the top of the mixing bowl.

When dough rises to top again, place dough on greased counter top. Divide into 2 (for large loaves) or 3 (for small loaves) pieces. Spray baking sheet with cooking spray then sprinkle thin layer of cornmeal. Roll dough pieces into elongated French bread shapes. Using sharp knife, slash tops of loaves diagonally 3–5 times. Brush tops with beaten egg. Let rise 30 minutes or until doubled. Bake at 375°F for 30 minutes or until golden brown.

20-MINUTE CORNBREAD

This family favorite is an easy recipe I picked for a college class, and I struck gold! This cornbread is quick and yummy, and it's the perfect side for soup, chili, and more. Tip: I like to double this recipe to make two pans since it reheats well for leftovers!

INGREDIENTS

1 cup flour
¾ cup cornmeal
2 tablespoons sugar
2 ½ tablespoons baking powder
¾ teaspoon salt
1 tablespoon butter
2 eggs, beaten
1 cup milk or buttermilk
¼ cup oil or melted butter

ADD-INS AS DESIRED:
Cheese (shredded), green chilies, creamed corn, corn kernels, bacon (cooked and crumbled)

DIRECTIONS

Preheat oven to 400°F. In a medium bowl, mix flour, cornmeal, sugar, baking powder, and salt. Set aside. Put butter in a 9-inch baking pan; place in oven for a few minutes until it melts. Swirl the pan around so the melted butter coats the bottom of the pan.

In a small bowl, combine eggs, milk, and oil. Add egg mixture all at once to the flour mixture and stir just until moistened. Stir in any add-ins. Do not over mix, ingredients should just be moistened. Mixing too much causes crumbly cornbread.

Pour batter into pan right away; don't let the batter sit. Bake for 15 minutes or until toothpick inserted in the center comes out clean. Cut into wedges; serve warm with honey.

GRANDMA'S BANANA BREAD

Ready for another Grandma Mary recipe? This is her banana bread. Only, for this one, the memories I have are of my mom making this bread. We would all cheer a little when we saw nasty bananas on the counter because it inevitably meant banana bread was coming!

INGREDIENTS

½ cup butter (1 stick)
2 cups sugar
2 eggs
1 cup milk
1 teaspoon vanilla
1 teaspoon baking soda
2 teaspoons baking powder
3 cups flour
3 ripe bananas, mashed
1 cup nuts, chopped (optional)

DIRECTIONS

Preheat oven to 350°F. In a large bowl, cream butter. Stir in sugar, eggs, milk, vanilla. Mix well. Add dry ingredients and mix well. Mix in bananas and nuts (if you want them). Divide batter into 2 full-sized, well-greased bread pans.

Bake 45 minutes to 1 hour, or until the middle is no longer gooey.

NOTE: If you have nasty bananas but aren't ready to use them yet, peel them, stick them in a ziplock bag, and toss in the freezer. When you're ready to use them, let them thaw before making the banana bread. If the top of the loaves starts to brown too quickly, either move the rack to a lower position in the oven or cover the tops of the loaves with a loose piece of foil. I like to sprinkle extra sugar on the piping hot bread as soon as it comes out of the oven. It gives a nice, sweet little surprise! This bread freezes great and also makes great muffins.

LITERALLY THE BEST CINNAMON ROLLS

Holy CINNAMON ROLLS, Batman! You won't believe how easy they are, the bread machine does most of the work! No bread machine? No worries—you can also do these with a mixer! You're welcome. Or I'm sorry. Either way, enjoy.

INGREDIENTS

DOUGH:

1 cup warm milk

2 eggs, room temperature

⅓ cup margarine, melted

4 ½ cups bread flour

1 teaspoon salt

½ cup white sugar

2 1/2 teaspoons bread machine yeast

FILLING:

1 cup brown sugar, packed

2 1/2 tablespoons cinnamon

⅓ cup butter, softened

DIRECTIONS

For Bread Machine: Place dough ingredients in the pan of the bread machine in the order recommended by the manufacturer (my machine specifies wet ingredients first). Select dough cycle; press Start.

No Bread Machine: Put warm milk in a stand mixer and sprinkle yeast in. Let the yeast proof and bubble for 5 minutes. Add eggs, margarine, salt, and sugar, mix with dough hook. Add the flour slowly and allow to soak up the liquid. Beat the dough on medium speed with a dough hook for 5–7 minutes or until dough is elastic/ smooth. Dough may be sticky, and that's okay. If your mixer doesn't have a dough hook, combine ingredients and knead by hand.

Cover dough, place in a warm spot, and let rise until doubled. Don't be tempted to roll out before it has doubled in size!

INGREDIENTS

FROSTING:

1 3-ounce package cream cheese
¼ cup butter, softened
1 ½ cups powdered sugar
½ teaspoon vanilla
⅛ teaspoon salt

Freeze it!

Bake the rolls, frost them, then wrap and freeze them. Warm them up in the microwave later. Or you can wait to frost your rolls after they're warmed.

DIRECTIONS

Meanwhile, in a small bowl, combine brown sugar and cinnamon for the filling. Set aside.

After dough has doubled in size, turn out onto lightly floured surface, cover, and let rest for 10 minutes. Roll dough into a 24x12 rectangle about ¼ inch thick.

Spread dough with softened butter. Sprinkle evenly with sugar/cinnamon mixture. Reserve some mixture to sprinkle on top of rolls once they are rolled up.

Roll up the dough from the LONG side of the rectangle—you'll get more rolls that way! Roll dough tightly and seal it by pinching tightly when you finish rolling; sealing it helps keep the filling from leaking out. Cut into 12–16 rolls, each about 2 inches thick.

Place rolls in lightly greased baking pan; depending on how thick you cut the rolls, you may have to bake them in 2 or 3 separate pans. Sprinkle with reserved cinnamon-sugar mixture. Cover and let rise until doubled, at least 30 minutes.

Bake at 375°F until golden brown, about 15 minutes. Don't over-bake! While rolls are baking, beat frosting ingredients until well mixed. Spread frosting on warm rolls before serving.

NOTE: Alternate filling method: Combine brown sugar, cinnamon, and butter into a paste. Spread onto the dough with your hands or a greased spatula. Some think this method helps prevent the filling from leaking.

Cut the rolls easily and quickly with fishing line or unscented/unflavored dental floss. Not only is it super easy, but it prevents squished rolls.

Pro tip: To speed the rising process, turn your oven on to 200°F for 5 minutes, turn it off, cover the rolls, and put them in the oven. They rise much more quickly in the oven, so monitor them carefully.

CHEESE STUFFED CRESCENTS

This recipe is God's gift to carb-lovers. I mean cheese in a hot, flaky roll... Is there anything better? This recipe is so easy that even the kids can help!

INGREDIENTS

2 cans crescent rolls
8 pieces string cheese
4 tablespoons butter
4 cloves garlic, minced
1 teaspoon Italian seasoning
1 teaspoon fresh parsley, minced
1 teaspoon fresh basil, minced

DIRECTIONS

Preheat oven to 375°F. Line a baking sheet with silicone mat or parchment paper and set aside. In a small bowl, combine melted butter with Italian seasoning, garlic, parsley and basil.

Unroll crescent rolls and separate into triangles. Brush with garlic butter mixture, reserving some to brush on tops of assembled rolls. Place halved string cheese at widest end, and roll up (tucking in the edges to seal).

Brush tops with more garlic butter. Bake for 10-12 minutes, or until lightly browned.

THE BEST HOMEMADE ROLLS

Alisha is the first long-term employee we ever had at The Page Company. She's become a dear friend (aka family member) over the years. These are her famous rolls she was generous enough to share with all of us. You can thank me (her) later!

INGREDIENTS

2 cups warm water
⅔ cup dry milk
2 tablespoons dry yeast
¼ cup sugar
2 teaspoons salt
⅓ cup butter (the real stuff) softened, plus more for coating
1 egg
5 - 5 ½ cups of flour

DIRECTIONS

In a stand mixer or large mixing bowl, combine the dry milk and water; mix until milk dissolves using a whisk attachment. Add the yeast in, let it mix for a few seconds; then, as the mixer is still going, add the rest of the ingredients one by one: sugar, salt, butter, then egg.

Turn off the mixer, and add 2 cups of flour. Still using whisk attachment, mix the flour on low until incorporated, then mix on medium speed for two minutes. At this point, switch out whisk attachment for the dough hook attachment. Add 2 more cups of flour. Follow the same process, mix on low until incorporated, then mix on medium for two minutes.

Add flour ½ cup at time (you may need to knead by hand if dough is too stiff) until you get a soft, smooth, not stiff dough. It shouldn't be too sticky. (Sometimes I need more than 5 ½ cups of flour.) Coat another bowl with about a tablespoon of vegetable oil, then add the dough, turning it around in the oil, so it is covered. Cover with plastic wrap or towel and let rise about 45 minutes, until doubled in size.

Flour counter or board, and coat your dough in the flour. Flatten dough and roll out in a rectangle, about 18 inches long and 9 inches wide (it should be about ¼ inch thick).

Brush the dough with melted butter, and cut the dough in half long ways, so you have two long strips, then cut the opposite direction to have two inch strips. Roll each strip up, and place seam side down on a cookie tray, lined with parchment paper. Place them as close as you want (I usually do about 4 across, and as many rows as I can). My rolls always come out different sizes. Cover with plastic wrap, and let rise 1 to 1 ½ hours. Bake at 375°F for 15-18 minutes, until light brown. Brush with melted butter, YUM!

RUSTIC BREAD

When I had my twins, my friend Melanie brought over a delicious dinner and a loaf of the most amazing bread ever. I tweaked and adapted the recipe, and now I have my favorite bread recipe of all time. It's a massive hit on my Shelf Cooking blog!

INGREDIENTS

3 cups warm water
2 ¼ teaspoons (1 package) active dry yeast
1 tablespoon sugar
6 cups (750 grams) flour
3 teaspoons salt

DIRECTIONS

Mix yeast, sugar, and water in large mixing bowl or stand mixer. Let sit for about 5 minutes until bubbly. Add flour and salt. Mix until combined into a soft dough. (The dough is sticky, but you can add ¼ cup flour at a time if it's too sticky to handle.)

Cover loosely with plastic wrap and a kitchen towel. Let rise for 1-3 hours, if possible! I've run out of time before and let it rise for only 30-60 minutes and it still works, but the longer, the better!

Preheat the oven to 450°F and place a pizza stone or flipped-over cookie sheet in the oven to heat up. Fill a baking dish with 2 inches of water and place it on the bottom rack to create steam for an extra crispy crust.

Sprinkle flour on the counter, turn out the dough, fold it in on itself, divide it in half, and form it into 2 balls. Don't knead or handle the dough more than you need to. Add a little flour if it's too sticky. Cut an X shape on the top of the balls with a sharp knife.

Place loaves on a lightly floured pan, then place on top of the hot pizza stone or cookie sheet. Bake for about 25-30 minutes or until golden brown and cooked through.

NOTE: You can bake the bread right on the hot cookie sheet and it'll be just fine. Just be careful handling the hot pan!

HONEY BUTTER

INGREDIENTS

2 sticks of butter, softened
1 teaspoon vanilla
¼ cup honey, more or less to taste

DIRECTIONS

In a mixing bowl, mix butter for about a minute (use a whisk or paddle attachment; both work great) until butter starts to get light and fluffy.

Add vanilla; mix for a couple seconds until vanilla is mixed in. Add honey. Mix for about 20 minutes on low, until butter is super soft and airy. Spread on your homemade rolls and enjoy!

SOUPS

GO-TO TACO SOUP

What's your "go-to" meal? That one meal that, no matter how late it is, or how busy of a day it's been, or how tired and hungry everyone is...you always have the ingredients on-hand to whip up this quick meal that pleases everyone? Go-To Taco Soup is ours!

INGREDIENTS

1 pound ground beef
1 onion, chopped
1–2 tablespoons taco seasoning
3–6 cups water, divided
1 can corn, undrained (can use frozen)
1 can black beans, rinsed & drained
1 can kidney beans, rinsed & drained
1 can diced tomatoes, undrained
Tomato paste to taste (start with 1 tablespoon and add to taste)
Cilantro to taste (optional)
Chili powder to taste (optional)

TOPPINGS:
Red onion (diced), Cheese (shredded), Cilantro (chopped), Green onion (sliced), Tortilla chips, Lime juice, Sour cream, etc!

DIRECTIONS

On Stovetop: In large stock pot, brown ground beef with onion. Drain Grease. Add taco seasoning, 2 cups water, corn, black beans, kidney beans, tomatoes, and tomato paste. Add cilantro (if desired). Stir and simmer for a few minutes. If soup is watery, add tomato paste and taco seasoning. If soup is too thick, add more water. Add chili powder (if desired) for a little kick. Simmer on low up to 3 hours, or until ready to serve. Top individual bowls of soup with desired toppings.

Slow Cooker: Brown ground beef and onion on the stove; add taco seasoning to taste, then put in slow cooker. Add all canned ingredients. Add water until it reaches the desired consistency. (Do not add cilantro until the end.) Cook on low 4–8 hours. Top individual bowls of soup with desired toppings.

LINDSAY'S TOMATO BISQUE

One of the things I love about cold winters is the excuse to make soup all the live-long day! This tomato bisque is so easy, and something I crave with a nice, melty grilled cheese. Bubba's sister, Lindsay, introduced me to this and I will forever be indebted to her for it!

INGREDIENTS

1 onion, sliced thin
1 tablespoon butter
2 (15-ounce) cans diced tomatoes
1 bay leaf
1½ teaspoon brown sugar
4 teaspoons fresh basil, chopped, divided
2 whole cloves
Salt to taste
½ teaspoon black pepper
1 pint cream
1 cup milk

DIRECTIONS

Sauté onion in butter until onion is soft. Add tomatoes, bay leaf, brown sugar, 2 teaspoons basil, cloves, salt, and pepper. Simmer on low for 15-20 minutes (or however long you have).

Remove bay leaf and cloves; puree soup in a blender or with a hand blender. Strain, then add cream and milk; heat slowly over medium heat.

Garnish with remaining basil and other seasonings as desired. This is delicious served in with my rustic bread (page 242). Tip: Make the rustic bread into smaller loaves and hollow out a loaf to make your own bread bowls!

TUXEDO SOUP

Before we had kids, I worked with at-risk youth. Kelly, my boss, became a dear friend of mine. She shared this recipe with me and every time I make it, I think of her! It's a great "dump whatever you have lying around" soup that always ends up tasting great.

INGREDIENTS

- 3 cans chicken broth
- 1 can green beans, undrained
- 1 can Italian-style stewed tomatoes undrained (dice them first if you want smaller tomato pieces)
- 10 ounces chicken breast, chopped (canned chicken or leftover rotisserie chicken works great)
- 1–3 tablespoons lemon pepper (to taste)
- 1 teaspoon lemon juice
- Pepper to taste
- 2 cups bowtie pasta, uncooked
- ½ cup sour cream

DIRECTIONS

In a large pot on the stove, combine all ingredients except pasta and sour cream.

Bring to a boil; add pasta. Simmer until pasta is al dente. Stir in sour cream.

NOTE: You can use wheat pasta. You can use 6 cups water and 6 chicken bouillon cubes instead of broth. Instead of lemon pepper, you can use lemon and herb seasoning.

You can also get creative with the canned veggies! I've added: 1 can French-cut green beans, 1 can peas, peeled/chopped zucchini, carrots, feel free to experiment!

LOADED BAKED POTATO SOUP

When we were newlyweds, budgeting and working our tails off to get out of debt, we ate a lot of potatoes because they are inexpensive, filling, and easy! This soup has been a favorite all these years later. Eating affordably does NOT mean you have to sacrifice flavor!

INGREDIENTS

6 cups potatoes, diced, peeled/unpeeled (or use leftover baked potatoes)
1 small onion, diced
Water
2 tablespoons chicken bouillon seasoning or chicken broth base
½ cup butter
½ cup flour
6 cups milk
2 cans corn, drained
seasonings to taste (salt, pepper, onion powder, Ranch dressing mix)
1 cup sour cream
Real bacon bits to taste (or bacon, browned and crumbled)
Shredded cheddar cheese
Parsley or chives for garnish

DIRECTIONS

In large pan, add potatoes and onions and add enough water to just cover them. Stir in bouillon. Bring to a boil and cook until potatoes are tender. (If using baked potatoes, boil onions first until softened, then add baked potatoes to the water just for 1–2 minutes to heat and soften.)

Meanwhile, in medium stock pot, melt butter over medium heat. Whisk in flour until smooth and thick. Gradually stir in milk 1 cup at a time, whisking constantly until thickened. Stir in corn and potato/onion mixture. Bring to boil, then reduce heat to simmer. Add salt, pepper, and additional seasonings to taste. (I add a little onion powder and about 2 tablespoons Ranch dressing mix.)

When ready to serve, stir in sour cream and bacon. Top each bowl with cheddar cheese and pinch of parsley or chives for a pretty garnish.

COBE & NAT'S CHILI

Living in Utah, you really come to love winter comfort foods. This delicious chili recipe from Bubba's brother Cobe and sister-in-law Natalie is a total winner! It's a family-favorite staple, especially at our cabin on a snowy winter day.

INGREDIENTS

1 pound ground beef, browned & drained
1 small onion, chopped
3 cans kidney beans, rinsed & drained
3 cans diced tomatoes (do not drain)
1 can tomato sauce
1 can tomato soup
1 can corn, drained
½ cup ketchup
1 ½ teaspoons salt
¼ teaspoon garlic powder
2 teaspoons cumin
1 ½–2 teaspoons chili powder
½ teaspoon pepper
Shredded cheese for topping (optional)

DIRECTIONS

Combine all ingredients in a large soup pot. Simmer on low at least until heated through; simmer longer to enhance the flavor.

If desired, top each serving with shredded cheese. This is delicious served with my 20-minute cornbread (see page 236).

Freeze it!

Allow chili to cool, then freeze by placing in an airtight container or freezer bag. Thaw overnight or on the stove.

INSTANT POT ZUPPA TOSCANA

My entire life I have had a deep, unbreakable love for Olive Garden soup, salad, and breadsticks. My favorite soup has always been the Zupa Toscana, so imagine my delight when I found an easy recipe that rivals the original...that is made in the Instant Pot or stove!

INGREDIENTS

- 2 tablespoons olive oil
- 1 medium onion, diced
- 1 pound mild Italian sausage
- 4 cloves garlic, minced
- 4 large Russet potatoes, unpeeled & thinly sliced (feels like a lot of potatoes but they cook/break down!)
- 1 teaspoon Italian seasoning
- 6 cups chicken broth
- 2 cups fresh kale or spinach, or arugula, diced
- 1 cup heavy cream or half-and-half (or more to taste if you want it creamier)
- ½ teaspoon red pepper flakes

DIRECTIONS

Using saute setting on Instant Pot, heat olive oil. Add onions; cook until transparent. Add Italian crumbled sausage; cook until brown. Add garlic; cook 1 min., until fragrant. Drain excess grease; return to pot. Stir in potato slices, Italian seasoning, chicken broth. Lock lid into place. Set to Sealed.

Cook at high pressure for 6 min. using Manual setting. Allow natural pressure release for 10 min., followed by quick release. When pressure valve drops, remove lid; stir kale into pot (the heat will wilt it). Pour in cream or half-and-half and red pepper flakes, stirring. Makes 6 servings.

On the stove: Cook onions, sausage, garlic, potato, and chicken broth as instructed in a pot on the stove. Simmer for 10 minutes, or until potatoes are soft. Remove from heat and follow remaining instructions. Serve with my Focaccia Breadsticks (p. 233) and salad.

CHEESEBURGER SOUP

Truth: I'm not much of a cheeseburger gal. I'll eat one occasionally, but I never crave them. Cheeseburger soup, however? Totally different story! This creamy, hearty goodness hits the spot every time, and it's made from ingredients you have on-hand!

INGREDIENTS

4 tablespoons butter, divided
½ pound ground beef
¾ cup onion, finely chopped
¾ cup carrot, finely chopped
¾ cup celery, finely chopped
1 teaspoon dried basil
1 teaspoon parsley flakes
3 cups chicken broth
4 cups cubed potatoes
¼ cup flour
1½ cups milk
2 cups cubed cheddar cheese
¼ cup sour cream

DIRECTIONS

In a large soup pot, melt 1 tablespoon butter over medium heat; stir in beef and vegetables. Cook until beef is browned. Stir in basil and parsley. Add broth and potatoes. Bring to a boil, then reduce heat and simmer 10–12 minutes, until potatoes are tender.

In a small pan, melt remaining 3 tablespoons butter; stir in flour until smooth. Add milk, stirring until smooth and thickened. Gradually add milk mixture to the soup, stirring constantly. Bring to a boil, reduce heat to simmer, and stir in cheese.

When cheese is melted, add sour cream and heat through; do not boil. Top with chives, diced tomatoes, and bacon bits to take it up a notch if you'd like! Makes 8 servings.

SIX-MILLION-DOLLAR CLAM CHOWDER

When Grandma Mary died, my aunt Allison went through Grandma's recipes and made a cookbook for all the family for Christmas. It is a cookbook I treasure, especially the recipes that were photocopied with Grandma's own handwriting on them. This one is a family favorite!

INGREDIENTS

- 2 cans minced clams
- 1 cup onions, chopped (more if desired)
- 1 cup celery, finely chopped (more if desired)
- 2–3 cups potatoes, chopped (more if desired)
- ¾ cups butter
- ¾ cup flour
- 1 quart half-and-half
- 1 teaspoon thyme
- 1½ teaspoons salt (more if desired)
- Pepper to taste
- ½ teaspoon sugar (if desired)

DIRECTIONS

Drain juice from clams into medium saucepan. Add onions, celery, and potatoes; add enough water to barely cover the vegetables. Add salt to the water. Cover; simmer over medium heat until potatoes are tender, about 10-12 minutes.

In a separate pan, melt butter; whisk in flour until smooth. Add half-and-half; whisk until smooth and thick. (It takes a while; be patient and let it get really thick.)

Add the half-and-half mixture to the vegetable mixture. Stir in clams and heat through. Watch the chowder closely, as it scorches easily. Season with salt, pepper, thyme, and sugar (if desired—grandma's special touch).

Serve with my French bread, rustic bread, or my Focaccia Breadsticks (pg. 233).

BUTTERNUT SQUASH SOUP

Truth be told, I've never been a huge butternut squash fan...until this recipe waltzed into my life. Now I can't get enough of it. While I discovered this recipe years ago, it is on constant repeat for any justifiable season (and reason) at my house.

INGREDIENTS

6 cups butternut squash (about 2 squash)
Olive oil or melted butter (enough to coat squash)
6 tablespoons onion, chopped
4 tablespoons butter
3 cups water
4 cubes chicken bouillon
8 ounces cream cheese
½ teaspoon dried marjoram
¼ teaspoon cayenne pepper
1 teaspoon oregano
Black pepper, to taste

DIRECTIONS

Cut squash in half lengthwise and scoop out seeds and inside guts.

Cook squash in oven: Coat entire squash in olive oil or melted butter. Place skin side on cooking sheet. Roast in oven at 375°F for 45 minutes until soft and fork-tender.

Cook squash in microwave: Place cut-side down on plate. Microwave 8-10 minutes until soft. Continue microwaving in 1-minute increments until soft. Check by using tip of sharp knife, which will cut skin easily.

While squash cooks, saute onion in butter until soft. Scoop out cooked squash and put in blender along with cooked onion and other ingredients. Blend until smooth. Return to saucepan and heat through, don't allow to boil. (Add more seasonings to taste, but keep in mind the flavors intensify the longer it sits.)

PASTA E FAGIOLI

I'm an 85 year old woman at heart. I love the early-bird special at Olive Garden for soup, salad, and breadsticks. My kids love this yummy soup. I love it because it's a good way to sneak in veggies, beans, and other things I have on hand!

INGREDIENTS

2 tablespoons virgin olive oil, divided
1 pound ground spicy Italian sausage (or ground beef)
3 cloves garlic, minced
1 onion, diced
3 carrots, peeled and diced
2 stalks celery, diced
1 zucchini, diced
3 cups water
1 ½ teaspoons chicken bouillon
1 (16 ounce) can tomato sauce
1 (15 ounce) can diced tomatoes
1 teaspoon dried basil and oregano
¾ teaspoon dried thyme
1 cup ditalini pasta (or elbow macaroni)
1 (15 ounce) can red kidney beans
1 (15 ounce) can Great Northern beans

DIRECTIONS

Cook pasta according to instructions. In a large pot over medium heat, heat 1 tablespoon olive oil. Add Italian sausage; crumble and cook until browned, about 5 minutes. Drain excess fat; set aside.

Add remaining olive oil to the pot. Cook garlic, onion, carrots, celery,and zucchini for about 4 minutes, stirring occasionally. Stir in water and bouillon, tomato sauce, diced tomatoes, sausage, and spices. Boil; reduce heat and simmer, covered, until vegetables are tender, about 15 minutes. If needed, add one cup of water to stretch the soup while cooking. Drain and rinse cans of beans, and stir into the soup with noodles; heat through. Serve immediately while hot.

Top with shredded Parmesan cheese and parsley if desired.

SAUCES

GRANDPA BECK'S SPAGHETTI SAUCE

Grandpa Beckstead was famous for a few things: being in a professional barbershop quartet, his smile and laugh, and his spaghetti! Grandpa Beck passed away years ago, and we named our 3rd child after him. We hope his spaghetti warms your home!

INGREDIENTS

1 pound ground beef or Italian sausage 1 small onion, minced
2 teaspoons garlic, minced (to taste)
1 package spaghetti sauce mix (McCormick was Grandpa's favorite!)
2 cans diced tomatoes
1 can tomato paste
Spices to taste (see notes)
1 jar Ragu, any flavor
1 cup water, if needed
1 can mushrooms
Grated mozzarella cheese
Grated Romano or Parmesan cheese

DIRECTIONS

In a large pot, cook ground beef and onions until beef is browned and onions are transparent. Add garlic and stir until fragrant, 1-2 minutes.

Stir in spaghetti sauce mix, tomatoes, tomato paste, and spices to taste. Add Ragu sauce, and water to get the consistency you like. Add mushrooms (dice them first if you don't like large pieces in your sauce).

Simmer for 15–20 minutes to let the flavors develop, and the sauce thicken. Add a handful of mozzarella to the sauce, let it melt down and mix in. Serve over pasta topped with Romano or Parmesan cheese.

NOTE: Add one or more of the following spices to taste: Italian seasoning, onion powder, garlic powder, basil, oregano, salt, and pepper. Add water if the sauce is too thick.

ALFREDO SAUCE

If I was on a deserted island and could only take 3 things with me, It would be chapstick, a sparkly cold cup, and this Alfredo sauce! It's just that good. The best part is it only takes a few ingredients, and a few minutes. Toss it in a casserole, pasta dish, or on top of just about anything!

INGREDIENTS

½ cup butter or margarine
½ cup heavy whipping cream
1 clove garlic, minced (or 1 tablespoon garlic power if preferred)
1 teaspoon Italian seasoning (optional)
¾ cup grated Parmesan cheese
½ teaspoon salt
Dash of pepper

DIRECTIONS

Warm butter and cream in a pot over medium heat. Stir frequently until butter is melted, and mixture starts to bubble.

Reduce heat to low, add garlic, Italian seasoning (if desired), and simmer for 6 minutes, stirring frequently, until slightly thickened.

Remove from heat and stir in cheese, salt, and pepper.

CHEESE SAUCE

Truth: I've got picky eaters. Further truth: throw this cheese sauce on just about anything to make it your kids' new favorite meal! I prefer to use this sauce to make homemade mac & cheese! It's shelf-cooking friendly, as it only uses a few ingredients you already have!

INGREDIENTS

2 tablespoons butter
2 tablespoons all-purpose flour
1 cup milk
1½ cups shredded cheddar cheese
1 pinch salt & pepper, to taste

DIRECTIONS

Melt butter in a pan over medium heat. Whisk flour into melted butter, until smooth.

Whisk in milk, cook and stir about 3 minutes or until mixture starts to thicken. Add cheese and stir until melted, about 2 minutes more. Add salt & pepper to taste.

Serve over pasta for a homemade mac & cheese, or serve over broccoli or cauliflower.

TERIYAKI MARINADE

INGREDIENTS

1 cup soy sauce
1 cup water
¾ cup brown sugar
¼ cup Worcestershire sauce
3 tablespoons distilled white vinegar
3 tablespoons vegetable oil
⅓ cup dried onion flakes
2 teaspoons garlic powder, or 2 cloves minced garlic
1 teaspoon fresh ginger, grated
1 tablespoon cornstarch (for thickening, if needed)

DIRECTIONS

In a medium bowl, whisk the soy sauce, water, brown sugar, Worcestershire sauce, vinegar, oil, onions, garlic powder, and ginger. Stir together until sugar dissolves. Add corn starch if it feels too runny.

Marinate chicken, beef, or pork (it's delicious on everything!) in the sauce for at least 1 hour, up to 24 hours. Toss the sauce once done marinating. Grill, bake, or cook your meat however you like, and enjoy the juicy tenderness!

NOTE: I like to reserve some of the sauce in the fridge before marinating, and pour it over the meat while cooking. Reserved sauce is also delicious over rice.

TOMATO CREAM SAUCE

INGREDIENTS

2 tablespoons olive oil
1 onion, diced
2 cloves garlic, minced (or 2 teaspoons garlic powder)
1 (14.5 ounce) can Italian-style diced tomatoes, undrained
1 tablespoon dried basil leaves, or diced fresh basil teaspoon
½ teaspoon white sugar
½ teaspoon dried oregano
¼ teaspoon salt
¼ teaspoon ground black pepper
½ to 1 cup heavy cream or half & half (to taste)
½ tablespoon butter

DIRECTIONS

In a medium saucepan, sauté onion and garlic in olive oil over medium heat, until onions are tender. Add tomatoes, basil, sugar, oregano, salt and pepper. Bring to boil, reduce heat to medium and simmer for 5 minutes or until some of the liquid evaporates and the sauce thickens.

Remove from heat; stir in cream to taste (½ C if you prefer less cream, 1 C if you're like me and will take all the cream you can get!) and butter. Stir until butter is melted. Reduce heat and blend sauce with a hand blender until you get the creamy consistency you want. Simmer 5 more minutes. Serve over pasta.

SWEET AND SOUR SAUCE

INGREDIENTS

¼ cup white sugar
½ cup brown sugar
⅓ cup white vinegar
⅔ cup water (or pineapple juice if you have it! Tastes amazing)
¼ cup soy sauce
¼ cup ketchup
2 tablespoons cornstarch

DIRECTIONS

In a medium saucepan, combine all ingredients except cornstarch. Bring to a boil over medium-high heat. Reduce heat to medium, but keep a slight boil. Remove ½ cup of sauce, put in a small bowl off to the side. Stir cornstarch into small bowl of sauce until well combined.

Slowly stir cornstarch mixture into the saucepan, continuously stirring until the sauce has thickened to your desired consistency. Serve over meatballs, with tempura, or over rice with chicken or shrimp.

VINAIGRETTE

INGREDIENTS

3 tablespoons oil
1 tablespoon vinegar
Salt
Pepper
Additional seasonings

DIRECTIONS

Mix all ingredients together. Let stand for 10 minutes if you're adding in extra seasonings. Mix again, then add to salad.

Store any unused dressing in the refrigerator for up to 6 days.

BASIL PESTO SAUCE

INGREDIENTS

1 large bunch fresh basil leaves (about 3 cups), OR 2 cups basil + 1 cup spinach
1 ½ cups walnuts (or pine nuts)
4 cloves garlic, peeled
¼ cup grated Parmesan cheese
1 cup extra virgin olive oil
Salt and pepper, to taste

DIRECTIONS

In a blender or food processor, blend basil leaves, nuts, garlic, and cheese. Slowly drizzle in olive oil while still blending.

Stir in salt and pepper. Serve over pasta, or bake on chicken or fish.

PEANUT SAUCE

INGREDIENTS

½ cup peanut butter
2 tablespoons low sodium soy sauce
1 tablespoon rice vinegar
¼ cup honey
1 tablespoon lime juice
3 garlic cloves
1 tablespoon fresh ginger
Dash of salt
Dash of cayenne
2-4 tablespoons warm water

DIRECTIONS

Combine all ingredients except water. Add water slowly until desired consistency, depending on whether you want a sauce (about 2 tablespoons water) or dressing (4 tablespoons water).

Lime juice and ginger are optional... they definitely give it more of a zing!

HOMEMADE BBQ SAUCE

INGREDIENTS

1½ cups brown sugar
1½ cups ketchup
½ cup red wine vinegar (or white vinegar)
½ cup water
¼ cup Worcestershire sauce
2 tablespoons dry mustard
2 cloves garlic, minced
2 teaspoons paprika
2 teaspoons salt
1½ teaspoons black pepper
½ - 1 teaspoon ground cayenne pepper (to taste)

DIRECTIONS

In a blender, combine all ingredients. Blend until smooth. Pour into a saucepan, and bring to a boil. Reduce heat and simmer for 5 minutes to let the flavors blend. Serve with your favorite BBQ and enjoy!

NOTE: This will fill a 32 ounce ketchup bottle exactly. Cut back on the brown sugar to make it less sweet, or add more Worcestershire for more "steak sauce" flavor.

RED ENCHILADA SAUCE

INGREDIENTS

¼ cup vegetable oil
2 tablespoons flour
3 tablespoons chili powder
1 (8 ounces) can tomato sauce
1 ½ cups chicken broth (or water)
½ teaspoon ground cumin
½ teaspoon garlic powder, or 1 clove minced garlic
½ teaspoon onion salt
salt to taste

DIRECTIONS

Heat oil in a skillet over medium-high heat. Stir in flour and chili powder, reduce heat to medium, and cook 2-3 minutes until lightly browned, stirring constantly to prevent burning.

Gradually, stir remaining ingredients into the flour and chili powder until smooth, and continue cooking over medium heat approximately 10 minutes, or until thickened slightly. Season to taste with salt.

Double the recipe if you have a large pan, or want to double and freeze one pan! (Highly recommended)

GREEN ENCHILADA SAUCE

INGREDIENTS

1 tablespoon olive oil
1 small white onion, peeled and diced
1 jalapeño, cored (seeds removed) and diced
4 cloves garlic, peeled and minced
1 cup chicken or vegetable stock
4 (4-ounce) cans diced green chiles
1½ teaspoons ground cumin
½ teaspoon chili powder (optional)
1 teaspoon fine sea salt
½ teaspoon freshly-ground black pepper

DIRECTIONS

Heat oil in a sauté pan over medium-high heat. Add onion and jalapeño and sauté for 5 minutes, stirring occasionally, until the onion is softened and translucent. Add garlic and cook for 1-2 more minutes, stirring occasionally, until fragrant.

Transfer the onion mixture to a blender or food processor. Add stock, green chiles, cumin, chili powder, salt and pepper. Then puree until completely smooth.

Taste and season with additional salt, pepper and/or cumin if needed. Serve immediately, or refrigerate for up to 4 days, or freeze for up to 3 months.

BALSAMIC GLAZE

INGREDIENTS

16 ounces balsamic vinegar
½ cup sugar

DIRECTIONS

Add vinegar and sugar to a saucepan and bring to a boil. Lightly boil (don't burn it!) until it's reduced by half, stirring occasionally.

Allow to cool, then store in an airtight container in the refrigerator for up to 2 weeks.

Great on pizzas, chicken, salads, etc!

BASIC WHITE SAUCE

INGREDIENTS

1 cup milk
2 tablespoons butter
2 tablespoons all-purpose flour
¼ teaspoon salt
⅛ teaspoon pepper

DIRECTIONS

In a small saucepan over low heat, melt butter over low heat. Stir in flour, salt, and pepper. Cook over medium heat, stirring constantly, until mixture is smooth and bubbly; remove from heat.

Slowly stir in milk. Heat to boiling, stirring constantly; boil and stir 1 minute.

NOTE: You can add optional ingredients like mushrooms, bacon, green onions, steamed or roasted vegetables, and/or cooked chicken.

TARTAR SAUCE

INGREDIENTS

1 cup mayonnaise
½ cup minced dill pickle
1 teaspoon dried dill
2 tablespoons lemon juice
2 tablespoons minced onion
Salt & black pepper, to taste

DIRECTIONS

Mix ingredients in a small bowl. Chill in the refrigerator for 2-3 hours prior to serving.

Serve over fish, oysters, clams, or your favorite seafood.

BASIC GRAVY

INGREDIENTS

3 tablespoons butter
3 tablespoons cornstarch
1 tablespoon water
1 cup meat pan drippings
2 cups chicken broth (or beef stock)
Salt & pepper, to taste

DIRECTIONS

In a small saucepan, melt butter over medium heat. In a small bowl, combine cornstarch and water to make a slurry. Whisk slurry into the butter in the pan. Add pan drippings and broth/stock.

Bring mixture to a boil, then reduce heat and simmer gently until slightly thickened. Season with salt and pepper. Simmer for 8-10 minutes, stirring occasionally to prevent burning.

Serve with mashed potatoes and chicken, turkey, or beef.

MAIN DISHES

GARLIC BROWN SUGAR CHICKEN

One of my best friends in the world is a total foodie. The first time we had her over, I was intimidated, so I tweaked a family-friendly chicken recipe and it was a hit. If it's good for the foodie, it's good for everybody. My picky kids even like it! Win-win!

INGREDIENTS

4 large boneless, skinless chicken breasts
4 garlic cloves, minced (or 3 tablespoons minced garlic from a jar)
4 tablespoons brown sugar
1 tablespoon olive oil
Additional herbs and spices as desired (I use rosemary, a little thyme, and salt and pepper to taste)

DIRECTIONS

Preheat oven to 425°F. Spray a 9x13 baking pan with cooking spray.

In a small sauté pan, sauté garlic in oil on medium heat until tender. Remove from heat, stir in brown sugar. Add additional herbs and spices as desired.

Season chicken with salt and pepper to taste. Place chicken in baking pan and cover with garlic mixture; poke chicken a few times with a fork so the sauce gets inside it.

Bake uncovered 15–30 minutes, depending on the thickness of the chicken, until juices run clear.

SLOW-COOKER CREAM CHEESE CHICKEN

Knock-knock. Who's there? Your new favorite dinner! Take all of God's greatest creations, throw them in a pot, and you get this crowd-pleaser (it's also one of my dad's favorites). I freeze sour cream and cream cheese, so this dish is shelf-cooking perfection. Tip: Serve over pasta or rice.

INGREDIENTS

4 boneless, skinless chicken breasts (fresh or frozen), or thighs
⅛ cup butter, cubed
1 (10.75 oz) can cream of chicken soup
1 can (10.75 oz) worth of milk
1 (0.7 oz) package Italian-style dressing mix
1 (8 oz) package cream cheese
1 cup sour cream

Freeze it!

Place in separate, small containers so it cools more quickly. Place in airtight freezer containers to store for up to 1 month. Thaw in the fridge overnight before reheating.

DIRECTIONS

Put chicken and butter in a greased slow cooker. In a small bowl, combine chicken soup, milk (just fill the empty soup can with milk then pour it in the bowl), and Italian dressing mix. Stir until well combined. Pour over chicken.

Cook on low 5-6 hours for fresh chicken, 6-8 hours if frozen, or until chicken is done and breaks easily with a fork. Shred chicken in the slow cooker. Cube the cream cheese, then add cream cheese cubes and sour cream to slow cooker. Stir until combined.

Continue cooking on low 30-60 min. or until cream cheese is melted and everything is incorporated. Season with salt & pepper to taste, and serve over egg noodles or nice.

CHEESY BACON CHICKEN

This recipe was an accidental viral sensation. One time, I found this recipe, tweaked it a bit, and it ended up being the most delicious, indulgent chicken ever. Then it went crazy on Pinterest. To date, it's one of the most popular chicken recipes we've ever published.

INGREDIENTS

4 boneless, skinless chicken breasts
5 ounces Worcestershire sauce
4–8 slices bacon (depending on taste)
2 tablespoons butter (optional)
½ onion, sliced
8 ounces fresh mushrooms, sliced
8 ounces monterrey jack, provolone, swiss, or mozzarella cheese

DIPPING SAUCE:
Mayonnaise
Dijon mustard

DIRECTIONS

Place chicken in bag and cover generously with Worcestershire sauce. (Pound chicken thin if needed) Refrigerate overnight, or at least 1 hour.

Cook bacon, drain, and set aside. Cook onions and mushrooms in bacon grease or 2 tablespoons butter until soft. Set aside in a bowl. Pre-heat oven to 400°F. Remove chicken from bag; discard marinade. Place chicken in pan, and cook for 6 minutes on each side (cover pan with lid/foil to keep chicken from drying out).

Add extra Worcestershire sauce to keep moist (as needed). When chicken is done, place it on new baking sheet lined with foil. Top with bacon, onion, and mushrooms (optional), then top with cheese. Broil on low until cheese is melted and bubbly; watch closely so it doesn't burn! To make dipping sauce, mix mayonnaise and dijon mustard to taste.

DELICIOUS CHICKEN

It all started with leftover graham crackers I needed to use from a camping trip. I was skeptical about this recipe, but the sweetness of the graham crackers, the saltiness of the seasoning, and the savoriness of the chicken are so good. I often make this unique crowd-pleaser for guests!

INGREDIENTS

8 tablespoons butter, divided
3–4 cups potatoes, peeled (if preferred) and thinly sliced
1 can corn or 16-ounce bag frozen corn
3–4 large boneless, skinless chicken breasts, cut into chunks or strips
Seasonings as desired

CRUMB MIXTURE:
1–½ cups graham cracker crumbs
1 teaspoon salt
1 teaspoon basil
Pinch of rosemary

DIRECTIONS

Preheat oven to 375°F. Put 4 tablespoons butter in a 9x13 dish; place in the oven as it's preheating so the butter melts (don't let it burn!). Take pan out, then line bottom of pan with potatoes; top potatoes with corn. Season to taste with at least 1 teaspoon each of salt, pepper, basil, and other seasonings (as desired).

In a separate bowl, combine cracker crumbs and seasonings (as desired). Dip chicken pieces into 4 tablespoons melted butter, then coat completely in crumb mixture. Place chicken on top of corn and potatoes.

Sprinkle extra crumb mixture on top, cover and bake 60 minutes or until chicken is done and potatoes are tender. Once tender, uncover and bake 10 additional minutes to brown the chicken. Garnish as desired.

NOTE: Baking time depends on thickness of chicken.

PARMESAN-DIJON CHICKEN

The first time I made this recipe, I was skeptical. But let me tell you, the Dijon mustard in this recipe is a surprising flavor profile (or so I've heard people say on Chopped). It's a hit with my picky family! Bonus -- it's perfect for using up that bottle of Dijon in your fridge.

INGREDIENTS

- ¾ cup dry bread crumbs
- ¼ cup grated Parmesan cheese
- ¼ cup butter or margarine, melted
- 2 tablespoons Dijon mustard (more if desired)
- 6 boneless, skinless chicken breast halves

DIRECTIONS

Preheat oven to 375°F.

Mix bread crumbs and cheese in large resealable plastic bag. In a shallow dish, mix butter and mustard. Dip chicken one piece at a time into butter mixture, then shake in bag to coat with crumb mixture. Place in greased 9 x 13 pan.

Bake uncovered for 20–25 minutes, turning once, until juice of chicken is no longer pink when centers of thickest pieces are cut.

GRANDMA'S CHICKEN POT PIE

Surprise! Another Grandma Mary recipe! I'm embarrassed to admit it took me years to make this because chicken pot pie felt so intimidating. Now I've completely changed my mind. This comfort food makes everybody feel good. I take it to others because it's easy to freeze, plus my kids absolutely love it.

INGREDIENTS

1⅔ cups frozen mixed vegetables, thawed
1 cups cooked chicken, cut into chunks
1 (10.5-ounce) can cream of chicken soup
1 cups baking mix (Bisquick)
½ cup milk
1 egg
Seasonings to taste (rosemary, garlic, poultry seasoning, salt, ground pepper)

DIRECTIONS

Preheat oven to 400°F.

Combine veggies, chicken, and soup; pour into a 9-inch greased pie plate.

Stir baking mix, milk, and egg until well blended. Pour over top of chicken/vegetable mixture.

Bake 30 minutes or until golden brown.

SLOW-COOKER CHICKEN CURRY

I absolutely love curry. LOVE it. I didn't often make curry because I worried it wouldn't taste good or would be complicated, but I love this recipe -- and so do my kids. I make it hearty with plenty of potatoes and carrots, and I add a touch of cream for decadence.

INGREDIENTS

- 1 tablespoon butter
- 1 onion, chopped (can use dried onions)
- 1 (10.5-ounce) can cream of mushroom soup
- 1 (10.5-ounce) can cream of chicken soup
- 1 (14-ounce) can coconut milk
- 1 packet dry onion soup mix
- 3 tablespoons curry powder (or to taste)
- ½ teaspoon black pepper
- 2 teaspoons cayenne pepper (or to taste)
- 3 large boneless, skinless chicken breast halves, trimmed, cut into chunks
- 1 cup green peas
- 2 cups sliced fresh mushrooms (or 1 small can)
- Peanuts to taste (if desired)

DIRECTIONS

In a skillet over medium heat, melt butter; add onion and cook until browned, 5–10 minutes. Set aside.

In a large bowl, combine soups, coconut milk, dry soup mix, curry powder, pepper, and cayenne pepper until well mixed.

Place chicken into the bottom of slow-cooker. Pour mixture over chicken. Stir in onion, peas, and mushrooms.

Cook on high for 1 ½ hours. Turn heat to low and cook an additional 1 ½–2 hours.

Serve over rice.

CHICKEN TACO SPAGHETTI

What do you get when you combine the three most random ingredients? The yummiest spaghetti recipe you never expected! The first time I tried it, I was skeptical, but my whole family loves it. One of my life sayings is, "Ain't nobody mad about tacos." This truth also applies to taco spaghetti!

INGREDIENTS

16 ounces spaghetti
2 cups chopped, cooked chicken
1½ cups salsa
1½ cups sour cream
2 (10-ounce) cans cream of chicken soup
2 tablespoons taco seasoning
3 cups cheese

DIRECTIONS

Preheat oven to 350°F. Cover 9x13 baking dish with cooking spray.

Cook pasta according to directions, drain well.

Place pasta back in pot. Add chicken, salsa, sour cream, soup, taco seasoning, and 1 cup cheese. Stir well to combine. (Using tongs helps!)

Top with remaining 2 cups cheese. Cover with aluminum foil sprayed with cooking spray, so the cheese doesn't stick.

Bake about 25 minutes or until heated through and bubbly.

CAFÉ RIO PORK

If you've been to Cafe Rio, you know its famous sweet pork. And while nothing can replace the magic of Cafe Rio deliciousness fresh from the restaurant, this is a very close second. If you're not a pork lover, that's okay! You can always use chicken instead! It's so good.

INGREDIENTS

3 to 4 pound pork sirloin roast
1 cup salsa
1 cup brown sugar
2 cloves garlic, minced
2 teaspoons cumin
1 cup chicken broth
1 onion, minced

DIRECTIONS

Place the roast in a slow-cooker.

In a large bowl, combine all other ingredients. Pour over roast.

Cook on low for 12 hours.

NOTE: You can swap out chicken for pork to make Cafe Rio sweet chicken!

Freeze it!

Shredded pork freezes beautifully. Pack it in a freezer-safe container and store for up to 3 months. Thaw in the fridge overnight and reheat in the microwave or on the stove.

SMOTHERED BAKED TILAPIA

I. Love. Seafood. I'm always worried it won't taste as good at home as it would from a restaurant, but this recipe is an exception to that rule! I make this tilapia when I want to impress other seafood fans coming for dinner. It is so easy and really good.

INGREDIENTS

½ cup Parmesan cheese
¼ cup mayonnaise or cream cheese
3 tablespoons lemon juice
2 tablespoons dried basil
1 teaspoon onion powder
4-6 tilapia fillets, thawed

DIRECTIONS

Preheat oven to broil and line a baking pan or sheet with aluminum foil. In a bowl, mix together all ingredients, except tilapia. Arrange fillets in a single layer on the pan and broil for 3 minutes on each side.

Remove from the oven and smother the top side of the fillets generously with Parmesan mixture. Broil 2-3 more minutes or until the mixture is lightly browned and the fish flakes easily with a fork.

ROTINI BAKE

Rotini Bake is like baked ziti's low-maintenance cousin. It's cheesy baked pasta that my family loves, and it's so dang simple. This is one of those no-fuss meals you'll love plain, but you can also dress things up by adding roasted vegetables or meats (we like Italian sausage).

INGREDIENTS

12 ounces uncooked curly rotini or small tube pasta
1 pound ground beef
1 (26-ounce) jar spaghetti sauce
2 eggs, slightly beaten
1 (16-ounce) carton cottage cheese
3 cups grated mozzarella cheese, divided
1 cup grated Parmesan cheese
Salt and pepper, to taste

DIRECTIONS

Preheat oven to 350°F. Cook noodles al dente according to package directions; drain. While noodles cook, brown and drain ground beef in a frying pan. Stir spaghetti sauce into cooked beef. Add salt and pepper to taste.

In a large bowl, combine eggs, cottage cheese, 1 ½ cups mozzarella cheese, and Parmesan cheese. Gently fold cooked pasta into cheese mixture.

Spread a third of the beef mixture over the bottom of a greased 9 x 13 pan. Spread half the noodle mixture over the beef. Repeat layers, ending with beef. Cover and bake 40 minutes.

Uncover, sprinkle remaining mozzarella cheese over top, and return to oven. Bake an additional 5–10 minutes, or until cheese is melted. Makes 6–8 servings.

SLOW-COOKER MAC & CHEESE

If there's one thing to know about me, it's that I have the heart of a five-year-old and love to eat like a toddler. Give me a corn dog, mac and cheese, or chicken nuggets, and I'm happy. I'm particular about mac and cheese, and I've tried many recipes. This. Is. Delicious!

INGREDIENTS

8 ounces elbow macaroni, cooked
1 (12-ounce) can evaporated milk
1 ½ cups whole milk
¼ cup butter, melted
1 teaspoon salt
Dash of pepper
2 large eggs, beaten
2 (10-ounce) bricks grated sharp cheddar cheese (about 5 cups), divided
Dash of paprika

DIRECTIONS

Spray a 4-quart slow-cooker with cooking spray. In the slow-cooker, combine macaroni, evaporated milk, milk, butter, salt, pepper, eggs, and all but ½ cups cheese. Sprinkle ½ cups cheese over the top of the macaroni mixture and sprinkle with paprika.

Cover and cook on low for 3 ¼ hours. Do not over cook or the mac and cheese will get clumpy!

Stir and serve hot.

TAMALE CASSEROLE

Tamale casserole is another crowd pleaser at our house. It's the yummy, savory corn appeal of tamales but way easier — plus, it uses ingredients you're likely to already have on hand. Serve it with chips and rice, or even over salad.

INGREDIENTS

½ pound lean ground beef
½ onion, chopped
1 cup spaghetti sauce
1 cup corn, frozen or canned, drained
1 can kidney beans, drained
1 can black beans, drained
½ teaspoon salt
3 teaspoons taco seasoning
¾ cup cold water
1 cup grated cheddar cheese

TOPPING:
¾ cup water
½ teaspoon salt
⅓ cup yellow cornmeal
1 tablespoon butter
Sour cream

DIRECTIONS

Preheat oven to 375°F. In a medium pan over medium heat, brown ground beef. Add onions, stir, and cook until onions are soft. Stir in spaghetti sauce, corn, beans, salt, and taco seasoning. Add water and stir. Reduce heat and simmer about 15 minutes.

Add the cheese; stir until melted. Pour into a greased 8 x 8 baking dish, or pan that can go in the oven.

Topping: In a small saucepan, combine water, salt, and cornmeal. Stir. Bring to a boil, stirring constantly, and cook until thick. (Watch carefully, so it doesn't burn.) Remove from heat and stir in butter.

Spread cornmeal mixture evenly on top of casserole. Bake uncovered for 30 minutes. Serve immediately topped with dollops of sour cream.

BAKED ITALIAN SANDWICH

This is a favorite childhood recipe that mom transferred to me when I was a newlywed. And while I was too initially too intimidated to cook for others, I could always nail this awesome recipe. The truth is, you really can't mess it up. It's just that good.

INGREDIENTS

4 tablespoons butter
2 eggs
½ cup milk
Italian bread crumbs
Parmesan cheese (shredded or grated)
1 loaf French bread
Sliced cheese (Provolone or Mozzarella)
Sliced ham
Spaghetti or marinara sauce, for dipping

DIRECTIONS

Preheat oven to 425°F. Put butter in large casserole dish. Put in oven while it's preheating so butter melts. Remove once butter covers entire bottom of dish. Slice bread. Mix bread crumbs and Parmesan cheese in a dish. (Just eyeball it! You can make more if you run out.) Beat 2 eggs and milk in separate dish.

Assemble sandwich: Dip one side of a piece of bread in milk mixture, then coat in crumb mixture. Set in buttered pan. Add slice of cheese, 2-3 slices of ham, and another slice of cheese. Top with another bread that's been dipped in milk and crumb mixtures. Repeat until pan is full.

Bake sandwiches: Bake for 5-8 minutes, flip, and bake another 5-8 minutes. Don't over bake! To get a crispy finish on the bread, broil for 1-2 minutes. Keep a close eye on them! They burn fast. To serve, warm a little spaghetti or marinara sauce in microwave to dip sandwiches in.

FRY BREAD TACOS

These fry bread tacos are a favorite when we have company over for dinner. It's as easy as a taco bar but way more fun — and it's perfect for using up leftover chili. I like to double the fry bread recipe so we have extras for dessert!

INGREDIENTS

2 ½ cups all-purpose flour
2 teaspoons baking powder
½ teaspoon rapid-rise (active dry) yeast
½ teaspoon salt
1 cup warm milk (110°F)
1 tablespoon butter, melted
Shortening or vegetable oil for frying

TOPPING:
1 pound cooked ground beef
1 tablespoon virgin olive oil
½ onion, diced
Taco seasoning, salt & pepper, to taste
1 can refried beans
1 can black beans, drained
1 can red kidney beans, drained
1 can diced tomatoes + chilis, drained
Olives, lettuce, tomato, cheese, sour cream

DIRECTIONS

Make fry bread: In mixing bowl, whisk flour, baking powder, yeast & salt. Whisk melted butter into warm milk; add mixture to dry ingredients. Stir just until mixture forms slightly sticky ball. Do not over work dough. Cover with plastic wrap; rest dough 5-10 min. Heat 1-inch oil in large cast iron skillet to 350-360°F over medium-high heat. Divide dough into 8 sections. Flour hands; pat dough into 6" circles. Gently add to hot oil; cook until golden brown. Flip; cook other side. Remove; drain on paper towels. Serve warm with toppings. Serve leftover fry bread as a dessert with butter, honey & powdered sugar.

Add toppings: In skillet over medium-high heat, combine cooked, heated ground beef & onions; cook until onions are tender. Stir in taco seasoning & refried beans. Add beans, canned tomatoes & chilis. Cover; simmer 10-15 min. Add water if mixture is too thick. Spoon mixture over fry bread; top with optional taco toppings. Tip: Replace ground beef with leftover chili.

HONEY GARLIC SHRIMP

Seafood is my favorite food; and this simple, no-fail recipe always turns out well. It's a really delicious meal to throw together and serve over rice. Make this when you want something quick and easy (but a little fancy, too)!

INGREDIENTS

¼ cup honey
¼ cup soy sauce
1 tablespoon fresh minced garlic
1 teaspoon cornstarch
1 pound medium uncooked shrimp, peeled, deveined (tails on or off)
1 tablespoon virgin olive oil
Optional: chopped green onion, salted peanuts, and sesame seeds for garnish

DIRECTIONS

Combine honey, soy sauce, and garlic in a small bowl. Marinate shrimp in half of the mixture, refrigerate for 15 minutes. Cover and refrigerate remaining marinade.

Heat olive oil in a large skillet over medium-high heat. Remove shrimp from the marinade and add to the pan; cook one side until pink (about 45 seconds). Flip shrimp. Pour in remaining marinade and add cornstarch to thicken the sauce; cook until shrimp is cooked through and sauce is thickened, about one minute.

Serve shrimp with sauce and a garnish of green onion, salted peanuts, and sesame seeds. Serve over basmati or brown rice, noodles, or steamed vegetables.

FRENCH DIP SANDWICHES

My absolute favorite meal at Kneader's (a popular local restaurant) is their French dip sandwich. My slow cooker version is just as delicious, broiled and bubbly, but for a fraction of the price. Plus, it's the perfect meal when roasts go on sale!

INGREDIENTS

3-4 pounds rump roast or chuck roast, excess fat trimmed
2 tablespoons virgin olive oil
3 cups low-sodium beef broth
2 teaspoons Worcestershire sauce
4 tablespoons butter
2 sweet yellow onions, thinly sliced
3 cloves of garlic, minced
1 bay leaf
Salt and pepper, to taste
6 - 8 rolls split in half (or 2 6" hoagie rolls cut in half)
8-12 slices cheese (provolone, pepper jack, or swiss)

DIRECTIONS

Heat oil in a large pan over medium-high heat. Season roast with salt and pepper. Add the meat to the pan; sear on all sides until browned. Transfer meat to a slow cooker. Add remaining ingredients (except rolls, cheese, and butter); cook on low 8 hours or high 4 hours or until beef is tender. Once roast is tender, remove from the juices and let rest for 15 minutes. Shred or slice beef.

For the au jus, place a fine mesh strainer over a large bowl; pour the slow cooker juices through the strainer. Transfer the sliced meat back into the slow cooker. Add a bit of au jus to moisten the meat. Season to taste with salt and pepper. Reserve the remaining au jus for dipping. For more au jus, thin with beef broth. Split, butter, and toast rolls under the broiler. Cover with cheese; melt under the broiler. Add meat. Serve sandwiches with au jus on the side for dipping.

EPIC MEATLOAF

I love meatloaf, but not everyone is a huge fan (like Bubba). Good news: this is one of those really good meatloaf recipes everyone craves—even Bubba! Plus, it's my team member Jenny's great grandmother's tried-and-true recipe, so you'll taste her love with every bite!

INGREDIENTS

MEATLOAF:
1 egg
¾ cup milk
1 pound lean ground beef
1 cup shredded cheese
½ cup quick oats
½ cup chopped onions
1 teaspoon salt

SAUCE:
⅔ cup ketchup
½ cup packed brown sugar
1 ½ teaspoons mustard

DIRECTIONS

Preheat oven to 350°F. Finely chop onions. In a large mixing bowl, beat the egg and milk with a whisk. Slowly fold in meat, cheese, oats, onions, and salt. Mix thoroughly with your hands.

Divide mixture into 8 equal portions and form 8 mini loaves, then place in a greased glass 9×13 dish or pan where they don't touch. Put in the oven and bake for 20 minutes. While your meatloaves cook for the first half, prep the sauce by mixing the ketchup, brown sugar, and mustard in a bowl.

After the loaves have been cooking for 20 minutes, remove from oven and top with the ketchup mixture. Put back in the oven and cook for an additional 25 minutes or until heated to 160°F. Let cool for 5 minutes, then serve and enjoy!

DESSERTS

3-INGREDIENT CHOCOLATE CHERRY CAKE

I grew up in the tiny Oregon town called The Dalles, the cherry capital of the world. When I was 12, a youth leader taught us how to make this cake. Years later, I made it to impress Bubba before we dated (spoiler alert: it worked). The secret is in the frosting!

INGREDIENTS

CAKE:
2 eggs
1 (21-ounce) can cherry pie filling
1 package chocolate cake mix

FROSTING:
1 cup sugar
5 tablespoons butter or margarine
1 heaping cup chocolate chips
⅓ cup milk

DIRECTIONS

To make cake: Preheat oven to 350°F. In a medium bowl, beat eggs; add pie filling and stir to combine. Add cake mix; mix well.

Pour batter into greased 9 x 13 pan. Bake 35 minutes. Cool before frosting.

To make frosting: In a medium saucepan, combine sugar, butter, and milk. Bring to a boil, stirring frequently, until sugar dissolves. (To check whether the sugar has dissolved, stick your finger in the mixture and rub it; if it's still gritty, it hasn't dissolved.)

Remove from heat. Add chocolate chips; stir until melted. When the frosting starts to thicken, spread it on the cooled cake. (Don't wait too long, or the chips will solidify!) Top with optional whipped cream, cherries, or shaved chocolate, if desired.

CHOCOLATE CREAM CHEESE BROWNIES

Truth? If there's cream cheese in it, sign me up. Plus, brownies are one of Bubba's favorite desserts. I first made these for a Christmas party as newlyweds, and they disappeared before I even got one! This beautiful dessert is also a great way to use frozen, thawed cream cheese.

INGREDIENTS

1 box brownie mix, prepared (with all required ingredients)
1 teaspoon vanilla extract
¼ teaspoon almond extract
½ cup chopped nuts
4 tablespoons butter, softened
2 (3-ounce) packages cream cheese, softened
½ cup sugar
2 eggs
2 tablespoons flour

DIRECTIONS

Preheat oven to 325°F. Prepare brownie batter with all required ingredients plus vanilla, almond extract and nuts, if desired. Don't over mix. Pour half of batter into greased 9x13 pan.

Filling: In mixing bowl, beat butter, cream cheese, and sugar until light and fluffy. Add eggs, flour, and 1 teaspoon vanilla; mix well. Spoon over batter in pan.

Spoon remaining chocolate batter over cream cheese mixture. Using a knife, cut through batter to create a marbled effect. Don't overdo it—if you do, the batters will blend together and it won't look marbled.

Bake for 35-40 minutes or until a toothpick inserted near the center comes out clean. Cool on a wire rack before cutting into bars. Store in the refrigerator. Makes about 2 dozen.

EASIEST EVER OREO TRUFFLES

Oh my gosh. The first time I had these mind-blowing Oreo truffles (made by my friend Bree's sister) was at a college party. This 3-ingredient recipe has been blowing minds ever since! It's fun to try different cookie flavors and different coatings, like candies and chopped nuts. Get creative!

INGREDIENTS

1 package Oreo cookies
1 package cream cheese
12 ounces chocolate melting wafers
White chocolate, sprinkles, or chopped nuts to garnish (if desired)

DIRECTIONS

Put Oreos in blender or food processor; pulverize. Add entire block of cream cheese; pulverize again until it forms a dough. You shouldn't see any white; if necessary, mix/knead with hands. Shape dough into walnut-size balls. Chill in refrigerator for 1 hour.

In a microwave-safe bowl, melt chocolate in the microwave for 1 minute. Stir. Microwave for 30 seconds; stir. Repeat just until chocolate is melted; if you cook it too long, it will seize and will not melt.

Dip balls in chocolate; lay on waxed paper to harden in the fridge.

If desired, garnish with white chocolate drizzle, sprinkles, or chopped nuts.

DEATH-BY-CHOCOLATE BUNDT CAKE

Betcha five bucks this is the best bundt cake you'll ever have (and probably the easiest, too). The sneaky ingredient is sour cream, and the cake mix base makes it easy peasy! You can even use frozen, thawed sour cream.

INGREDIENTS

¼ cup sour cream
4 eggs
½ cup water
½ cup oil
1 (15.25-ounce) box chocolate cake mix
1 (3.9-ounce) small box instant chocolate pudding mix
2 cups semisweet chocolate chips
Powdered sugar

DIRECTIONS

Preheat oven to 350°F. In a large bowl, beat sour cream, eggs, water, and oil until thoroughly mixed. Stir in cake mix and pudding mix; when thoroughly combined, stir in chocolate chips and mix well.

Pour into greased, floured bundt cake pan. Bake for 45-55 minutes or until a knife inserted into the cake comes out clean.

While still hot, invert cake onto a serving platter. When cake has cooled, sift powdered sugar over the top of the cake. Note: Instead of dusting with powdered sugar, this cake can also be topped with glaze or frosting if desired.

BEST HOMEMADE CARAMEL

This caramel is Bubba's mom's famous family recipe. It was originally a caramel corn recipe, but once I started making it, I realized it was too good for just popcorn. Since sharing on our blog, this popular recipe has made hundreds of thousands of apples around the world happy.

INGREDIENTS

½ cup butter (1 stick)
2 cups brown sugar
1 cup light corn syrup
1 can sweetened condensed milk

DIRECTIONS

In a large saucepan, melt butter over medium heat. Whisk in sugar, syrup, and milk. Continue to whisk over medium to medium-low heat until sugar dissolves and the mixture comes to a boil.

Keep mixture lightly boiling, whisking continually, over medium to medium-low heat until it almost reaches a soft-ball stage or your desired thickness for you.

Pour over 2–4 batches of popped corn, use for caramel apples, use for dipped pretzel rods, or use as a dip.

NOTE: Soft-ball stage is when you can drop a bit of caramel into a glass of water and roll it into a very soft ball with your fingers without it dissolving in water. You can also use a candy thermometer. It's up to you, but you'll probably want the caramel a bit closer to soft-ball stage if you're using it as a dip or on apples or pretzels and a bit softer if you're pouring it over popcorn.

CHOCOLATE CHIP COOKIES

Though I prefer chocolate chip cookie dough, Bubba's favorite dessert of all time has always been (and probably will always be) freshly-baked, homemade chocolate chip cookies. I've tried many recipes over the years, but this is my forever go-to.

INGREDIENTS

1 cup butter
1 cup packed brown sugar
½ cup granulated sugar
¾ teaspoon baking soda
½ teaspoon salt
2 eggs
1 teaspoon vanilla
2 ½ cups all-purpose flour
1 (12-ounce) bag semisweet chocolate chips
1 ½ cups walnuts or pecans, chopped (optional)

DIRECTIONS

Preheat oven to 375°F. In a large mixing bowl, beat butter with an electric mixer on medium to high speed for 30 seconds. Add brown sugar, granulated sugar, baking soda and salt. Beat until mixture is combined, scraping sides of bowl. Beat in eggs and vanilla until combined.

Beat in as much of the flower as you can with the mixer, then stir in remaining flour. Stir in chocolate chips, and if desired, nuts.

Drop dough by rounded teaspons 2 inches apart un ungreased cookie sheet. Bake for 8 to 9 minutes or until edges are light brown. Transfer to a wire rack; cool.

HEB'S YOGURT TRIFLE

One of my best college friends Heather ("Heb") made this dessert, and it was beautiful, light, and delicious. Use a clear glass bowl to display the layers, and get creative with cake mixes and yogurt flavors! It's a perfect dessert for baby and bridal showers or spring or summer parties.

INGREDIENTS

1 cake mix
2 small cartons (5.3 oz each) yogurt
1 small box instant pudding mix
2 cups cold milk
1 small carton frozen Cool Whip, thawed
Fruit, sliced or chopped

DIRECTIONS

Make cake mix as directed on box, omitting oil and replacing it with 2 cartons of yogurt. Bake as directed. Let cool. When completely cooled, use a fork to break the cake up.

Make pudding according to package directions using 2 cups milk. In a glass bowl or dish with tall sides, layer half the cake pieces. Top with layers of half the pudding, half the Cool Whip, and half the fruit. Repeat layers, ending with fruit. Refrigerate until you serve the dessert; keep leftovers in the fridge.

NOTE: You can use any flavor cake mix—vanilla, lemon, strawberry, etc... Use yogurt and pudding mix flavors that go with the cake mix you choose. Get creative: try vanilla cake, peach yogurt, and peaches; lemon cake, blueberry yogurt, and blueberries; and so on. For a chocolate dessert, use chocolate cake mix, plain yogurt, chocolate pudding mix, and raspberries or cherries.

DONUT BITES

We had just moved into a new neighborhood and wanted to make friends, so we hosted a dessert party one Sunday afternoon. I made these donut bites and they disappeared in a flash. (While it's probably not true, I think these donuts are magical because we made lots of friends that day.)

INGREDIENTS

1 can biscuits
4-6 cups vegetable oil for frying
2-3 tablespoons sugar
1 teaspoon cinnamon, optional

DIRECTIONS

Cut your biscuits into quarters and heat oil in a pot on the stove. Check your oil and make sure it's hot enough. (Test one donut bite to make sure the oil isn't too hot before throwing a bunch in.)

Cook for 40-50 seconds on one side, then flip and cook for another 40-50 seconds on the other side. Set donut holes on a paper towel to cool off.

Coat in sugar or cinnamon-sugar mixture. Optional: Dip in some kind of delicious chocolatey sauce.

ACKNOWLEDGMENTS

You know, it's interesting. Several years ago, when it was just me working by myself (with an occasional part-time contractor) in the back of my mind, I always thought how neat it would be to write a cookbook. But not just any cookbook... a kitchen bible of sorts. A book that would give people the confidence to cook how grandma used to. Never in my wildest dreams would I have thought this would be possible. Alternatively, never in my wildest dreams did I expect this 12 month project to take over 3 years of blood, sweat, tears, and triumphs. And, really, I never could have done it by myself. I would like to thank the masterminds who have made all of this happen.

First and foremost, thank you to my husband Bubba for being the world's best co-pilot, dance partner, and child wrangler. Thank you for supporting me in all my crazy endeavors, even though they usually add to our chronic sleep deprivation. And to my adorable and tolerant kids, thank you for dancing with me in the kitchen, cooking alongside me, and for (mostly) not complaining about testing recipes and eating leftovers (especially the bad ones).

I want to thank my mom, Tami, and my late Grandma Mary for teaching me how to cook from the heart, and to make magic out of random ingredients. And while I still don't like cooking (truth bomb, I know), I understand, honor, and respect its importance, and I am grateful for the legacy these two great ladies have both left behind.

To the extremely talented Melanie Burk, thank you for taking my vision and turning it into absolute magic... all while pregnant and giving birth to your sixth child, homeschooling, and surviving a pandemic no less. Your balance of patience and commitment is unbelievable. Without you, this book wouldn't have happened. You have gone above and beyond more times than I can count, and for that I will always be indebted. Thank you, thank you, thank you!

To Kathy Jenkins, thank you for your tireless research and for giving voice to my disorganized thoughts, and Jenn Burgess for coming in the clutch and editing like your life depended on it. Couldn't have done this without you both!

To Carisa Smith, Jamie Van Eaton, Dave Brown, and Jenny McDaniels, thank you for late-night writing sessions, fact-checking, recipe testing, and for making my Shelf Cooking vision come to life on the blog, in this cookbook, and in homes around the world.

A huge thank you to the entire Page Company team: Alisha, Angie, Ashlynn, Brandi, Brittany, Emily, Josi, and Rachel (and anyone else who has joined since writing this!). Though my name is on the cover, you, my dream team, are the reason this book was able to happen. Your hard work behind the scenes means I can do what I feel I've been placed on this Earth to do: to create, and to connect with families.

And last but certainly not least, I want to thank you, my Freebs Nation. It's funny, but as I sit here and write this, I don't think about millions of people around the world. I literally picture one woman sitting across from me with a cheeseball between us, chatting about life. I thank you personally for being here. I can say, build, or create whatever I want, but none of it means anything unless you're here. You continue to show up day after day to support me and my team, and you have made the Page Company something much bigger than I ever could. I feel like I know you personally. I pray for you, I think about you every day, and I want you to know that this book is for you.

XOXO, Jordan

INDEX

LISTED BY INGREDIENT

for extra guidance see page 325

C

D

E

H

I

J

K

L

M

P

V

W

Y

HOW TO USE THE INDEX

Not sure how to use this index? This section is for you!

USING THE INDEX- START WITH AN INGREDIENT

1. Have something in your fridge or cupboard that you need to use up? Look for the item in the index to see what recipes you can make.

2. Have an ingredient that you need to substitute? Something that you need to freeze properly? Then look for that item in the index to see tips, info, and substitutions!

LOOKING FOR INFORMATION?

1. We got you! Start on page 2 & 3 to see the different sections we have in this book. This will help you find the information or section you are looking for.

2. If you are looking for a specific recipe, we've made a recipe index below to help you find that section even faster! Happy Cooking!

RECIPE SECTION INDEX

ABOUT JORDAN PAGE

After going through tough financial times, Jordan Page—popular blogger, YouTuber, and public speaker—got out of debt in record time and now shows people that it's possible to live a millionaire lifestyle BECAUSE of a conservative budget...not in spite of it. Her award-winning money management, organization, productivity, and family-systems principles have reshaped the lives of hundreds of thousands of families all over the globe.

Jordan's proven Shelf Cooking method has created an entirely new approach to mealtime. *Shelf Cooking 101* unlocks the ultimate secrets to saving money on most families' biggest budget buster—FOOD.

Jordan has been featured on *Rachael Ray*, the *Today* show, *Inside Edition*, *TLC*, *Good Morning America*, and more. Jordan is an entrepreneur, inventor, mother of eight kids, Utah transplant, and kitchen dancing enthusiast.

www.shelfcooking.com
www.funcheaporfree.com
www.thepagecompany.com